# PARACLETE
## THE
# Advocate

## LONNIE D. MILLS

# PARACLETE THE ADVOCATE

iUniverse books may be ordered through booksellers or by contacting:

iUniverse
1663 Liberty Drive
Bloomington, IN 47403
www.iuniverse.com
1-800-Authors (1-800-288-4677)

ISBN: 978-1-5320-3889-1 (sc)
ISBN: 978-1-5320-3888-4 (e)

Library of Congress Control Number: 2017918914

Print information available on the last page.

iUniverse rev. date: 02/20/2017

# CONTENTS

Introduction................................................................................. xi

Chapter 1:  Christians Dependency on the Holy Spirit
            (The Paraclete) ................................................. 1
Chapter 2:  The Five Fold Ministry...................................... 29
Chapter 3:  Two Choices Eternal Salvation or
            Eternal Damnation..............................................35
Chapter 4:  Obeying God's Laws by Keeping His Precepts ........... 40
Chapter 5:  Spiritual Wellbeing............................................ 44
Chapter 6:  Blessed are Those Who Walk in the Holy Spirit ........ 50
Chapter 7:  Jesus Exposes the Hypocrisy of the Religious
            Organizations................................................... 56
Chapter 8:  Apostacy in the Christian Churches........................... 65
Chapter 9:  The Old Covenant Revealing Sin as was Given
            to Moses........................................................ 70
Chapter 10: Israelites Given the Law..................................... 92
Chapter 11: Inauguration of a New Sacrificial Lamb.................... 95
Chapter 12: Seek Help from None Other than God...................... 98
Chapter 13: The Shekhinah Dwells in the Heart of Believers
            Producing "Fruits of the Spirit" ...........................101
Chapter 14: God's Revelations and Allowances are for His
            Purpose..........................................................115
Chapter 15: The Egog Disposition of the Apostle Peter.................119
Chapter 16: Apostle Peter Becomes a Testament of
            Holiness and Love ............................................131

Chapter 17: Mosaic Laws Including Dietary Laws...........................135

Chapter 18: Abraham's Unique Relationship With God in Faith
of the Holy Spirit Faith that Led to Friendship...........140

Chapter 19: Things of God are Revealed When His Spirit
Dwells in our Heart .......................................................144

Chapter 20: Peter's Affirmation of Jesus's
Messiahship Blessed, Then He is Rebuked..................145

Chapter 21: Faith is the Key to the Gates of Heaven.....................149

Chapter 22: The Use of Anointing Oils Symbolically ....................151

Chapter 23: Modern Medicine has Biblical Roots ..........................156

Chapter 24: Sustenance Received from God by the Holy Spirit .....160

Chapter 25: The Perfect Sacrifice, Jesus, The Lamb of God ..........162

Chapter 26: Faith in a God we Cannot See (Only His Works)........170

Chapter 27: War Between Nations is Normally Caused by Sinful
People Absent of the Paraclete .....................................173

Chapter 28: Put Aside Unbelief: Have Faith in
the Light Which is Jesus Christ ....................................181

Chapter 29: Growing in Faith and Knowledge................................184

Chapter 30: Hall of Fame for People of Faith .................................188

Chapter 31: Christians Martyred.....................................................196

Chapter 32: Martin Luther's Intolerance for the Sale of
Indulgences................................................................. 202

Chapter 33: Reformers Opposed the 14th-16th
Centuries European Churches......................................205

Chapter 34: Judas Iscariot's Betrayal Fulfilled
the Prophesy of Jeremiah ............................................210

Chapter 35: Religious Leader's Greed Prevented "Watching and
Spiritual Intercession" ................................................213

Chapter 36: Only God can Provide Righteousness .........................215

Chapter 37: Men Try to Explain Creation and Legalities
other than the "Word" of the Omnipotent God ........ 224

Chapter 38: It is Difficult to Deceive a Christian
that is Imbued in God's "Word" ................................. 234

Chapter 39: We Shall All Stand Before the
Judgement Seat of God.................................................241

Chapter 40: Each Should Give Unto the Lord According to
their Abilities and Talents .......................................... 244

Chapter 41: Focus on Following Jesus ................................. 248

Chapter 42: The Righteous Shall be Separated
from the Wicked ........................................................254

Chapter 43: The Desires of the Flesh are Antithetical to the
Walk in the "Spirit" ..................................................258

Chapter 44: Whosoever Believes In Their Heart Will
Be Filled With Living Water ..................................... 264

Chapter 45: The Savior's Salvation is Accessible to Anyone Who
Comes to Him in Faith Seeking Mercy ..................... 269

Chapter 46: Focus on Carnality Causes the Loss of Godly Birth
Right and Blessings ...................................................273

Chapter 47: Be Warned of Written or Spoken Personal
Presuppositions of Biblical Text (Eisigesis) ...................278

Chapter 48: The Mind of Christ in Us ...............................285

Chapter 49: Unimaginable Sacrifice and Suffering for the
Salvation of Mankind ............................................... 289

Chapter 50: Call on the Lord Jesus Regardless
the Circumstances......................................................291

Chapter 51: Generational Apostatizing ............................. 298

About the Author.................................................................305

# INTRODUCTION

THE TERM PARACLETE IN THE Christian religion refers to the Holy Spirit or Holy Ghost. Christians believe in the doctrine of a Triune God, the Father (God), The Son (Jesus) and the Holy Spirit or Holy Ghost. Paraclete is transliterated from a Greek word meaning called beside or alongside to help. The apostle John uses the term "advocate" in his first epistle speaking of the Holy Spirit as someone who will come to your defense against the accusations of Satan. *(I John 2:11 KJV MY little children, these things write I unto you, that ye sin not. And if any man sin, we have an advocate with the Father, Jesus Christ the righteous :)* The Holy Spirit as our "Paraclete" (in the New Testament) is the indwelling of God Himself inside his believers at all times. In the Old Testament of the Holy Bible, in contrast to the New Testament, the Holy Spirit would enter and leave certain individuals based on their faith and sin inclination. Before Jesus ascended to Heaven to sit at the right hand of the Father, He spoke to the disciples teaching and encouraging them that the Paraclete would be with them always. *(Matthew 28:20 KJV teaching them to observe all that I have commanded you. And behold, I am with you always, to the end of the age.")*

The most common symbol of the Paraclete (Holy Spirit) is the dove, a bird that is normally white in color. The dove often is used to symbolize love and peace. In the book of Genesis chapter eight after the world flooded, Noah first sent out a raven that went back and forth over the earth until the flood waters were dried up from the land (Genesis 8:7). Next Noah sent a dove out to see if the land was dry but the dove found no dry land to perch on. After seven days had passed, he sent the dove out again. This time the dove returned with a leaf that it had plucked from an olive tree signifying to Noah that the water was abated from the earth. After seven more days had passed, he sent the dove out again but it never returned (Genesis 8: 8-12). The modern representation of a peace offering had its beginning with the dove carrying an olive branch in its beak. In the New Testament when Jesus was baptized in the Jordan River, the heavens opened up to Him and the Spirit of God descended and lit upon Him like a dove. The three synoptic Gospels of Matthew, Mark, and Luke record this event and is also recorded in the Gospel of John (Mt 3:16; Mk 1:10; Lk 3:22; Jn 1:32). All three members of the Trinity, God the Father, Jesus the Son of God, and the Holy Spirit are referred to in the Gospel of Matthew 3:16-17 KJV *And Jesus, when he was baptized, went up straightway out of the water: and, lo, the heavens were opened unto him, and he saw the Spirit of God descending like a dove, and lighting upon him: And lo a voice from heaven, saying, This is my beloved Son, in whom I am well pleased.* There are many symbols of the Paraclete (Holy Spirit) in both the Old and New Testaments of the Holy Bible. I will not go into detail concerning the ones I have listed here. I found many while researching this subject and have only listed the ones that I think theologians find most relevant. Listing placement has nothing to do with relevancy: <u>WATER</u> (Ezekiel 47:1-12, Zechariah 14:8, Luke 3:16, I Corinthians 2:13), WIND/BREATH (Genesis 2:7, Ezekiel 37:9, John3:8, John 20:22, Acts2:2, II Timothy3:16), FIRE (Matthew 3:11), OIL (Psalms 23:5), and CLOUD (Exodus 16:10). I have found that theologians on this subject of the Holy Spirit symbols vary in the number of such symbols. Some theologians and authors suggest twenty or more symbols of the Paraclete. All are symbols of the Holy Spirit, whether in the Old or New Testament, comfort and aid us in the understanding and glorification of Jesus Christ.

From Wikipedia, the free encyclopedia: The Christendom doctrine of the Trinity (Latin: Trinitas, lit. 'Triad', from trinus, "threefold") [1] holds that God is three consubstantial persons [2] or hypostases [3]—the Father, the Son (Jesus Christ), and the Holy Spirit—as "one God in three Divine Persons"

(Footnotes: 1 Oxford Dictionarie 2. The Family Bible Encyclopedia,

1972 p. 3790. 3 See discussions in Wikisource-logo.svg Herbermann, Charles, ed. (1913). "Person". Catholic Encyclopedia. New York: Robert Appleton Company).

The actual word "trinity" is neither in the Holy Bible nor Strong's Concordance of the Bible. Christians rely on the Holy Bible to receive understanding and instructions from God. What cannot be gleaned from the scriptures is the teaching specifically of a Triune God. The Holy Spirit cannot be understood as an actual being but rather is the Divine power of God. There are passages in the Old and New Testaments that definitely make references to a triune God. In the Gospel of Matthew, Jesus spoke to His disciples (11) about a mission program that is known as "The Great Commission": Matthew 28: 19 KJV *"Therefore go and make disciples of all nations, baptizing them in the name of the Father and of the Son and of the Holy Spirit."*

In the King James Version of the Holy Bible, Holy Ghost is used ninety times. Holy Ghost and Holy Spirit have the same meaning. Christian doctrine teaches that God is three distinct persons or hypostases. The three distinct persons are God the Father, Jesus the son, and the Holy Spirit. This Trinitarian doctrine was declared to be Christian during the fourth century. Newer translations of the Holy Bible use the term "Holy Spirit". Not all Christian denominations adhere to this doctrine of a Triune God. The Nontrinitarians Christians are comparatively small in number when compared with the number of Trinitarian Christians.

In the Greek New Testament, the word is most prominent in the Johannine writings. It appears in the Gospel of John where it may be translated into English as "counselor", "helper", encourager, advocate, or "comforter"

The early church identified the Paraclete as the Holy Spirit. In first-century Jewish and Christian understanding, the presence of the Holy Spirit is to claim rebirth of prophecy.

The Paraclete or Holy Spirit is not a human being but rather it is a spirit sent by God that lives within believers. After Jesus was resurrected from the dead, He remained on earth for forty days before His ascension to be at the right hand of the Father, God. He said to them that He would not leave them to be disheartened by His departure. The word of encouragement that Jesus spoke to them was that He would ask the Father to send them a gift, a "comforter, the Paraclete or Holy Spirit that would remain with the Christian believers forever. *(John 14:25-26 KJV 25 These things have I spoken unto you, being yet present with you. 26 But the Comforter, which is the Holy Ghost, whom the Father will send in my name, he shall teach you all things, and bring all things to your remembrance, whatsoever I have said unto you.).*

I haven't earned a degree from a theological college as the criteria for writing this book; I am just a Christian layperson. My source of direction that I took while writing this book is solely based on leaning not on my own understanding, but reading the Word, and praying for understanding from the Holy Spirit (The Paraclete) to guide me. I am making this statement because the Bible says that God is no respecter of any particular individual. God does not show favoritism to any individual regardless of their status. He does not favor based on nationality or material wealth *(Acts 10:34-35 KJV 34 Then Peter opened his mouth, and said, of a truth I perceive that God is no respecter of persons: 35 But in every nation he that feareth him, and worketh righteousness, is accepted with him).* The Apostle Paul's letter to the Romans emphasizes this point that is taught in both the Old and New *Testaments (Romans 2:11 KJV For there is no respect of persons with God).* He will come to all who seeks Him. Praise the Lord! I have known for a long time before and after my second water baptism that I am completely void of any knowledge or life that is not afforded to me by God, Amen. Some of the content may not be immediately apprehended and understood concerning the intent of my message by many that have studied scripture intensely and are set in their beliefs. Many devout Christians may not accept the comparisons that I use because of non-canonical references. Although I use many Biblical verses, I am not trying to write another version of the Bible. There are plenty versions out there that can be obtained by new technology and literature containing commentary by gifted and blessed doctorate theologians. My wife, Lois L. Mills, has assisted me with editing and her knowledge from studying and reading the Bible for many years is greatly appreciated. Writing this book places great anxiety on me because I feel that there is so much to be learned from the Word that God left in the Sixty Six documents or books called the Holy Bible in which thirty-nine are called the Old Testament and twenty-seven which are called the New Testament of which they are approximately four hundred years apart. The four hundred year span between the Testaments are called the "Intertestamental period. This period began after the last Old Testament Bible prophet Malachi purportedly around 450 before Christ (B.C.). This period ended purportedly around 4 B.C. and the New Testament of the Bible begins with the first book the Gospel of Matthew (Hebrew –"the gift of Yahweh"). There were non-canonical books written during this time. But this does not mean that nothing was being written about the history of the Jewish people. Some writings in addition to the Old and New Testaments are included in some denominational Bibles such as the Catholic Bible. I have read some of this intertestamental material. Some Christian Bible students use these intertestamental writings for a historical perspective of the Jewish people during this period.

(Versions of Biblical translations used: English Standard Version –ESV, Amplified Bible- *AMP COPYRIGHT © 1954, 1958, 1962, 1964, 1965, 1987 by The Luckman Foundation*, New International Version- 1984 © & 2010 © – *NIV*, King James Version- *KJV*, AND New King James Version- *NKJV.*

OLD TESTAMENT of the Holy Bible – abbrv. OT NEW TESTAMENT of the Holy Bible – abbrv. NT

PARACLETE, HOLY GHOST, HOLY SPIRIT, FAITH, GRACE and SIN in the HOLY BIBLE

*ACTS: 1-8 KJV 8 But ye shall receive power, after that the Holy Ghost (PARACLETE) is come upon you: and ye shall be witnesses unto me both in Jerusalem, and in all Judaea, and in Samaria, and unto the uttermost part of the earth.*

The individual seeking the salvation of God must have faith and must be a witness for Jesus. Power to witness is by the means of the Holy Spirit.

EPH 2:8 *For by grace you have been saved through faith. And this is not your own doing; it is the gift of God.*

Faith- the Hebrew word translated as faith is pronounced Emunah. It must be emphasized that having faith and the belief that the God of the Holy Bible is paramount to receive the gift of His eternal salvation offered to us. It is impossible for the faithless to please Him and receive this gift. Faith is generally defined as having complete trust in someone or something. Christians have faith and belief that God exists without ever seeing Him. It is by spiritual apprehension and the word of God in the Holy Bible. God actually defines "faith" in the Holy Bible found in the 11th chapter of Hebrews verses 1-3: *"Now faith is the substance of things hoped for, the evidence of things not seen. For by it the elders obtained a good report. Through faith we understand that the worlds were framed by the word of God, so that things which are seen were not made of things which do appear".* Scientists defined in ref.com: *are people who use research and experiments to learn more about the natural world. Scientists use scientific methods to derive knowledge systematically, performing repeatable experiments to ensure that their conclusions are valid and accurate.* The Holy Bible does not try to scientifically or by any other method try to prove the existence of God. There are things that are not seen but are accepted as existing such as gravity, air or oxygen, ultraviolet light, etc. The writings of the Apostle John in the NT of the Holy Bible, which includes the Gospel of John, 3 epistles of John (letters), and the book of Revelation, are called *Johannine corpus".* Scholars' debate over the authorship of these writings but the author doesn't claim to be a biblical scholar but accepts that these writings in the Bible were penned by the Apostle John. In the New Testament of the Holy Bible there is one concept used in the synoptic gospels, Johannine writings (Apostle John), the book of Acts, and the Epistles, is the one concept pisteuein/Pistos to define faith. It is revealed by God by his Son, Jesus, that the way to receive salvation for eternal life, we must trust and believe. We must believe that God is active today by the means of the Holy Spirit and the Church of Jesus (God). We must believe that God provided propitiation and expiation for the atonement of our sins. Christians know that none are without sin. Followers of Jesus know that sin was inherited from Adam as he passively allowed his wife, Eve, to handle the deception by Satan in the Garden of Eden. This deception allowed sin, death, and the inducement of all kinds' departures from the will of God. God is Holy and he wanted Adam and Eve to be Holy. The Apostle Paul statement from the book of Romans 3:10 KJV: *"As it is written, There is none righteous, no, not one:"* when Paul made this statement, "it is written", he was speaking of what was written in the Old Testament (Septuagint also known as lxx –this was the first effort to translate the old Hebrew Bible into Greek. Seventy or seventy-two Jewish scholars performed this translation in Egypt in the third and second B.C. because by the second and first B.C. most Israelites spoke Greek as their primary language or pre-Christian Hebrew Bible because the New Testament bible part of the Bible was not yet written. The apostle Paul uses six Old Testament citations in the book of Romans 3:10-18 as follows: Romans 3:10-12 is a quote from Psalm 14:1-3. Romans 3:13 is a quote from Psalms 5:9; 140:3. Romans 3:14 is a quote from Psalm 10:7. Romans 3:15-17 is a quote Isaiah 59:7, 8. Romans 3:18 is a quote from Psalm 36:1.

Quotation marks were not used by New Testament writers and the quotations were not necessarily verbatim. The apostle Paul used these quotations to emphatically convey that Jews that practiced the Mosaic Laws were no less sinless in comparison to the gentiles who did not. The point is that no one should consider selves sinless because of their own works. Only by the work of the shed blood of Jesus on the cross at Calvary atones for our sins.

In the OT God or Yahweh only allowed the Levite priests to enter into the inner sanctuary of the temple, called "The *Holy of Holies,* once a year. The priests acted as middlemen to make atonement and sacrifices for God's chosen people, the Israelites. In the New Testament God, allowed the sacrificial work of Jesus, His only begotten Son, to die on the cross and be resurrected to restore the relationship with Him that was lost by Adam in the Garden of Eden. This doctrine of atonement allows each us to approach and have a relationship with God in his Son's name (Jesus) without going through a middleman. The sacrificing of his son Jesus for the atonement of our sinfulness is a tremendous gift that cannot be obtained by works. He is not compensating us for something we did. That is why it is called a gift or a special favor by God for those with faith and belief. We can approach God for repentance of sins and He is willing to offer forgiveness and that sin is remembered no more. Propitiation and expiation sound somewhat intimidating because they are used mostly in Christian theology and not commonly used in everyday conversation. These two words can be both oppositional and complementary to each other. Dictionaries define expiation, in a biblical way, with taking away guilt through the payment of a penalty or the offering of atonement. Propitiation, on the other hand, brings about a change in God's attitude, so that He moves from being at enmity with us to be for us. Through the process of propitiation, we are restored to fellowship and favor with Him. (Definitions are partially from: What Do Expiation and Propitiation Mean? FROM R.C. Sproul Mar 25, 2016) Holman Illustrated Bible dictionary 2003: expiation falls under the concept of propitiation. In scripture, it cannot exist without propitiation. Other terms used for propitiation are appeasement and placation.

We all have an internal war going on between us and the deceitful one (Satan). Any Bible study reading plan should start with prayer so that the Holy Spirit will give you spiritual insight into the meaning of some most difficult text in the bible. The Bible, starting with the Old Testament first book of Genesis through the New Testament last book of Revelation is about the coming of God to the earth as a man (Jesus) to make a sacrifice for us as atonement for our sins. No one can come to the Father but through Jesus Christ. The knowledge of God's Word will enhance your faith. You must have faith to believe that God will do what He says He will do. There are good ministers who have received "Favor" but there are bad ones who claim "Favor". Holy Scripture tells us that there will be false prophets and an anti-Christ coming to the world in the end times. All indications today point to the facts that end –times are rapidly approaching.

Some years ago, I remember hearing and reading about how deforestation was affecting global climate. In the 1970s South America was the leader of the deforestation of the Amazon rainforest for human habitation and agriculture. The web has a site titled Tropical

Rainforest facts that gives information about the deforestation in South America. It was said that forestation, especially trees, absorb greenhouse gases that would otherwise enter the atmosphere and increase global warming. My understanding concerning greenhouse gases is that the main component of these gases is carbon dioxide. The greenhouse effect, as I understood it when I first came across the term, simply explained is that the earth receives light and ultraviolet energy from the sun. The earth discharges some of this energy back to the atmosphere. Greenhouse gases present in the atmosphere do not allow all of this energy or infrared radiation to escape the atmosphere based on concentrations present. The energy that does not escape is dispersed back to the earth. This causes the global temperature to rise causing more severe weather, rising sea levels, etc. over a period of time according to scientists who study climate change.

Sources that emit greenhouse gases expelled to the atmosphere are coal (used in electricity generation, steel production, cement manufacturing and liquid fuel), chlorofluorocarbons (used in refrigerants like R-12 and R-21 currently replaced by hydrofluorocarbons with less greenhouse gas emissions), oil and natural gas (fossil fuels), chemical plants, agriculture (deforestation), methane and ammonia (from farm animal waste), etc. Global climate change caused by humans is a highly debatable subject especially along political party lines in America where there are adherents and detractors.

The Bible does not say anything about climate change but chaotic changes described in the Olivet Discourse in the bible (Synoptic Gospels of Matthew 24, Mark 13, and Luke 21) have some similarities to climate change. A week before His death, as Jesus and disciples were leaving the temple in Jerusalem, He told them that all of the temple buildings would be destroyed. Later, as Jesus was sitting on the Mount of Olives, they came to Him and asked Him privately what signs to look for His return and the end of the age. Jesus had previously informed His disciples of His impending persecution and death (See Matthew 16:21-28). These biblical scriptures of the Olivet Discourse have been interpreted as the Second Coming of Jesus by some Christians. Jesus does not tell His disciples the exact time of

His return. Jesus admonished His disciples not to be deceived by false prophets about end time events, rather look for chaotic signs such as nations rising against nations, famine and earthquakes. Jesus told His disciples that despite all of the sorrows (birth pains) before the uncertain arrival of end times, those who endure will be saved (see Matthew 24:13-15).

The founding fathers of the American constitution prayed before creating laws. The ruling by the present day Supreme Court of America ruled in favor of allowing prayer before legislative sessions. There still remain fervent debates about how much separation should there be between the church and the state. The paraphrased doctrine of Thomas Jefferson, "separation of church and state" Establishment Clause and Free Exercise Clause of the First Amendment to the Constitution of the United States which reads: "Congress shall make no law respecting an establishment of religion, or prohibiting the free exercise thereof..."

The Bible tells us in Acts 10, that the people of a city in the ancient city of Berea, which is today called Veria, located about 50 miles from Thessalonica, heard the Word from the Apostle Paul, but were diligent enough to study Holy Scripture for themselves for authenticity. (Acts 17:10-12 ESV 10 *The brothers immediately sent Paul and Silas away by night to Berea, and when they arrived they went into the Jewish synagogue. 11 Now these Jews were NOBLER than those in Thessalonica; they received the word with all eagerness, examining the Scriptures daily to see if these things were so. 12 Many of them therefore believed, with not a few Greek women of high standing as well as men.* This is what we need to do. Worshipping God on Sunday and hearing the Word from a man God has chosen is also great, but throughout the week we need to study the Bible to authenticate what we have heard.

Jesus was led into the wilderness by the Holy Spirit immediately after being baptized by John the Baptist to be tempted by Satan (See Matthew 4:1). Each time Satan tried to tempt Him; He quoted Holy Scripture to refute Satan's attacks of temptation. Satan left Jesus after hearing the Word. We need the Word to do warfare with Satan which, in turn, will allow us to engage the "Holy Spirit" for help. Without knowing the Word we become helpless against his attacks. Now with the Word, prayer, and supplication, we have the weapons needed to do battle. There are many that know the Word but are not obedient to the word. A man named Lot in the Old Testament had faith and was obedient to God. Disobedience to God caused his wife to become a pillar of salt as the immoral cities of Sodom and Gomorrah were destroyed by God. (Genesis 19:23-26 *English Standard Version (ESV) 23 The sun had risen on the earth when Lot came to Zoar. 24 Then the LORD rained on Sodom and Gomorrah sulfur and fire from the LORD out of heaven. 25 And he overthrew those cities, and all the valley, and all the inhabitants of the cities, and what grew on the ground. 26 But Lot's wife, behind him, looked back, and she became a pillar of salt). Study the Word, Be obedient and don't look back.* To understand the meaning we have to look at the root word. The Hebrew root aman means firm, something that is supported or secure. The word "emunah" is derived from the root word "aman", meaning firm When the Hebrew word "emunah" is translated as faith, and there is a misconception of its meaning. Faith is usually thought to mean "knowing", but in Hebrew "emunah" is a firm action. To have faith in God is not knowing that God exists or knowing that he will act. It means rather the one with emunah will act with firmness toward God's will. This means he wants God's will because he knows God's will is life and leads him on the correct path.

Habakkuk 2:4 ESV *"Behold, his soul is puffed up; it is not upright within him, but the righteous shall live by his faith. Believers have to have patience and Faith and wait on God for He is working all of the time.* The Apostle Paul used this Old Testament verse in Roman 1:16-17 ESV *16 for I am not ashamed of the gospel, for it is the power of God for salvation to everyone who believes, to the Jew first and also to the Greek. 17 For in it the righteousness of God is revealed from faith for faith, as it is written, "The righteous shall live by faith."* These two verses are the theme of the entire epistle that the Apostle wrote to the Romans while in Corinth.

Sin: Sin is any lack of conformity, active or passive, to the moral law of God. This may be a matter of actions, of thought, or of inner disposition or state. The theological term for the study of sin is "hamartiology" from the Greek "hamartia" for sin, error, or missing the mark. The Apostle Paul used the verb hamartano when he wrote,

"For all have sinned, and come short of the glory of God" (Refer to Romans 3:23 any translation).

The first mention of sin as a noun is a zoomorphism (Gen 4:7 ESV If you do well, will you not be accepted? And if you do not do well, sin is crouching at the door. Its desire is for you, but you must rule over it." With sin crouching at Cain's door, sin is depicted here as an evil demon crouching to pounce on him. One of the first uses of sin as a verb is when Abimelech being prevented from sinning against God in a dream telling him not to touch Abraham's wife Sarah *(Genesis 20:6 KJV And God said unto him in a dream, Yea, I know that thou didst this in the integrity of thy heart; for I also withheld thee from sinning against me: therefore suffered I thee not to touch her).*

People, alone, do have the ability to master this inclination and choose good over evil (conscience) (See Psalm 37:27) and are responsible for sin because each is endowed with free will ("behirah"); yet we are by nature frail, and the tendency of the mind is to do evil: "For the imagination of man's heart is evil from his youth" Therefore God in His mercy allowed people to repent and be forgiven. "Judaism holds that all people sin at various points in their lives, and hold that God tempers justice with mercy. Hebrew has several other words for sin beyond khata, each with its own specific meaning. The word pesha, or "trespass", means a sin done out of rebelliousness. The word *aveira* means "transgression". And the word avone, or "iniquity", means a sin done out of moral failing. The word most commonly translated simply as "sin", khata, literally means "to go astray." Just as Jewish law, halakha provides the proper "way" (or path) to live; sin involves straying from that path. There is basically only one Greek word in the New Testament for "Sin": "hamartano" - In the Greek it means: to "miss the mark." An example is found in Matthew 18:21 (KJV): "Then came Peter to him, and said, Lord, how oft shall my brother sin (hamartano) against me, and I forgive him? Till seven times.

# CHAPTER 1

# Christians Dependency on the Holy Spirit (The Paraclete)

PNEUMATOLOGY IS THE BRANCH OF Christian theology concerned with the Holy Spirit. This book is not intended to be scientific in any aspect as far as a study concerning the study of the Paraclete (Holy Spirit). I am not qualified to even attempt such an adventure in an authoritative manner. I profess that I am a Christian solely dependent upon the Paraclete to even attempt to present in writing my thoughts and belief of a Spiritual being that I have never seen but believe in God's divine Word as presented in the Holy Scriptures by faith, Amen.

I am aware that spiritual growth by the indwelling Holy Spirit provides enhanced revelation of the Word which is also inspired by the Holy Spirit.

I have heard some ministers' say that passages of the Bible that they interpreted many years ago had been changed by new revelation from the Holy Spirit. I have heard some say that during the presentation of a prepared sermon that the Holy Spirit's divine inspiration changed it. This is completely different from taking passage(s) out of a body of surrounding passages to change the original intended meaning. This, in a sense, is actually falsifying what the text actually means. The word that defines this type of distortion is called "contextomy" which simply

1

means to change the meaning of a larger passage by taking out part or parts which takes the real meaning out of context. This is not of the Spirit. Nevertheless, this is not the same type of obfuscation used in an argument to bewilder, confuse, or make unclear something, but is usually done to affirm or amend some other closely related train of thought or passage of scripture.

One example of a verse that is debatably taken out of context is Matthew 18:20 KJV: For where two or three are gathered together in my name, there am I in the midst of them. If we look at the previous verse 16, then it can be understood that Jesus is promising His presence with brothers and sisters involved in the function of disciplinary action in a church environment. One of the out of context thoughts used for this verse is that the church is not needed as long as two or three gathers in the name of Jesus, He hears you. I heard someone say, "I guess if I am stranded on an island by myself, then Jesus can't hear me." Another translation of this verse is that if two or three or gathered in Jesus name, whatever they ask for it will be done. A born-again Christian may petition God while being alone and if what he or she requests of Him is in His will, it will be granted.

When confronted with Biblical scripture that is not clearly apprehended, pray to the Holy Spirit for understanding. Ministers should be precise to ensure that their message is not ambiguous and is presented within the context as intended by the Spirit. Some people rely solely on what they hear from the pastor at the church service and will sometimes repeat what is heard from the pastor without doing their own Biblical research to see if what he is saying is the truth.

The Apostle Paul and His young Minister Timothy, on a second trip to the Jewish synagogue in Berea in Macedonia, observed that the Bereans were more willing to accept the Word of God preached to them as compared to the unbelieving Jews of Thessalonica. They examined the Scripture daily and compared the doctrines presented to them by the apostles to ensure that they were in accordance with the Old Testament Scripture. He called the Bereans nobler because of this. This led many of the Bereans to become believers of Jesus (See Acts 17:10-15).

God surrounds us with His protection if we call on Him faithfully. Why do we need God's protection? Satan has waged a war in this world against God to take possession of His creation. No one on this earth can defend against Satan's wiles depending on their own strategy. Satan is an evil spiritual being and we are fleshly beings unable to overcome him alone. Walking or living by the flesh is in opposition to walking by the Spirit of God. Walking in the spirit means that we have the help of the Holy Spirit to oppose the evil wiles of Satan. When we place our faith in God we receive His protection.

The apostle Paul wrote to the Galatians possibly after his second visit to northern Asia Minor churches, according to some scholars. The purpose of his letter was to rebuke certain tendencies of the Judean Christians to impose laws on Gentile converts to Christianity such as circumcision. The Apostle wanted to make it clear that people are justified by faith in Jesus Christ alone and not by any legalistic rituals imposed by the Old Testament. The Apostle emphasized in his epistle (letter) that the only way to overcome sinful desires is by the power received from "The Holy Spirit" (the Paraclete). (Walk by the Spirit in Galatians 5:16-18)

The underlying meaning of the Book of Job in the Christian Bible that causes even biblical scholars to ponder the tough and perplexing question: "Why does God allow believers, upright, and faithful people to suffer?"

In the first chapter of the Book of Job, readers are made privy to an event that seems unlikely, Satan visiting Heaven and holds a conversation with God (Job 1:6-12). The reader immediately sees why God lets Satan destroy the life of an upright, God-fearing, priestly man like Job. Satan attempted to drive a wedge between God and Job. The reader of book of the Job also is given insight into the fact that Job was not being punished for a sinful act. However, Job, his wife, friends, and his estranged family are not made privy to this test and think that Job had committed some awful sin that displeased God and He brought on this calamitous situation on Job for it. Just as Job was not made privy to the test between God and Satan, believers to this day are perplexed to why bad things happen to upright people and sometimes bad people seem to prosper.

Many scholars consider the Book of Job (pronounced Jobe unlike a place of employment) to be the oldest book of the Bible written by an unknown Hebrew around 1500 B.C. Others believe that the Pentateuch or Torah, the first five books of the Bible written by Moses sometime between 1446 and 1406 B.C., are the oldest books of the Bible. The subject here is not concerning which is the oldest book but rather to discuss the first mention of an "Arbitrator" used in the old book of Job Chapter 9 verse 33(Neither is there any daysman betwixt us, that might lay his hand upon us both". The King James Version of this verse uses the word "Daysman" where other versions of this same verse use "mediator" or "arbitrator". In the book of Job, a man named Job was a very blameless and upright man of God who had become very prosperous. This old text does not make mention of a priest to serve as an arbitrator between God and man so Job served as a priest, so to speak, for his family. Later, it will be pointed out that Satan had access to Heaven to actually hold a conversation with God. During one of Satan's visitations to Heaven, God initiated a proposal to him that He had a servant that regardless of what hardships Satan could place on him short of killing him or laying a finger on him, Job would not turn to evil or turn away from God (Job1:1-22).

Job was unaware of the agreement between God and Satan. Satan destroyed all of Job's livestock, killed his children and left Job with oozing boils from his feet to his head (Boils on the skin are normally or naturally caused by bacterium Staphylococcus aureus infection which causes painful swollen areas on the skin which is caused by the accumulation of pus and dead tissue).

These calamitous events created by Satan seemed to have occurred one after another in a short time frame which, in itself, was highly unnatural. In Job 9:33 mentioned above is where we find Job's belief that God is so mighty and powerful that he needs someone between him and God to justify and explain this calamity that had befallen him. The forensic nature of his request was seeking "Justification" from God by means of a mediator.

The Apostle Paul's epistle to the Romans speaks of "Justification" as an act by God whereby a sinner is found guilty or responsible and is under condemnation but by the belief in Jesus Christ is acquitted. The Old Testament, "Justification "is having faith and belief in God set aside from works. Apostle Paul says that if Abraham, the forefather of the Jews, was justified by works then he would have something to boast about. Abraham, he says, believed God and it was counted to him as being righteous (Romans 4:2-5).

Job is described as a man who was blameless and upright, feared God and eschewed evil (Job 1:10. This verse in the Bible says that Job lived in the land of Uz. Uz is only mentioned in two other verses in the Bible which are Jeremiah 25:20 and Lamentations 4:21. Job 1:1 says that this man, who lived roughly in the area of modern-day southwestern Jordan and southern Israel, feared God and refrained from evil. You see, Job thought he was doing all the right things to please God and did not understand the cause of this horrendous disaster.

Sometimes when God forgives transgressions it is not easily apprehended by the receivers because there is no readily recognizable evidence. Job confessed to God that he was a sinner but he was hard-pressed to understand that he really had been forgiven (Job 7: 21). His situation made him think that he had not been forgiven, not knowing that God thought very highly of him. He did figure out that his dilemma required a mediator between him and God. Job uses the term "Daysman" to define this mediator or arbitrator. This arbiter that Job is requesting in this passage would have to be a divine incarnate being, the second person of the Trinity, God's son Jesus Christ. Jesus is the only mediator between the heavenly Father and man. God had not provided an incarnate being at this time in the OT but Job is seeking Devine intervention. The word daysman in English means "an umpire or arbiter, a mediator."

Satan had not only caused this calamity to happen to Job, He came on to Job's wife's intellect and she proposes to her husband to curse God and die, forget about your integrity, forget about being faithful to God. (Job 2:9). Satan came unto Job's wife s as he had Adam's wife Eve in the Garden of Eden. The difference between Adam and Job is that

Job rebuked this notion tactfully telling her that she spoke as foolish women do. The Bible does not provide much more information about Job's first wife other than words in Job 2:9 and that she and Job had ten children. She didn't speak of Job's halitosis directly in a verse but Job, himself, said that she found his breath repulsive in Job 19:17.

There are works of doubtful authenticity, truth ,and authorship called Biblical Apocrypha. These non-canonical books are found in some Christian Bibles. Some ministers use these texts to supplement the canonical Christian Bible for historical information. Names of individuals not found in the Christian Bible sometimes can be found in Apocrypha books. The historical writings of the first-century Romano-Jewish scholar, historian, and hagiographer, Titus Flavius Josephus born in Jerusalem AD 37 or 38 are used in Bible studies and sermons extensively. The Apocrypha, in the Greek Testament of Job chap. 21-25; 39, indicates that the name of Job's first wife name was Sits or Sitidos. Near the end of the book of Job in the bible where he recovers from his calamitous situation, it is thought that his first wife had died and it was his second wife that birth ten more children (See Job 42:12-15), whose name, according to the Apocrypha, is Dinah, daughter of Jacob and Leah (See Genesis 34:1-4).

Regardless of the suffering placed on Job by Satan, he said I will not blaspheme God and die. Job and his first wife believed that blaspheming God resulted in immediate death. The New Testament of the Bible doesn't speak of immediate death for blasphemy but it does say in that whoever blasphemes the Holy Spirit would not be forgiven (See the Biblical New Testament Gospels of Matthew 12:31, Mark 3:28-30, Luke 12:10, and the book of Hebrews 10:26-29). This blasphemy of the Holy Spirit is to hold onto any sin and never acknowledge or claim the redemptive power of the Holy Spirit until death. To avoid eternal damnation and death, repentance is the solution for the blasphemous person by the Holy Spirit (Paraclete) evoking the individual to sincerely ask for forgiveness. Blasphemy against man is also forgivable.

In the time of calamity, the one suffering should be offered consolation and prayer.

Job had three friends, Eliphaz, Bildad, and Zophar, who heard of his calamitous situation and came to visit him. From a distance, they did not recognize him. They sat for a week crying and weeping with Job without speaking to him after seeing his horrendous condition (Job 2:13). They knew that Job had been a God-fearing man but instead of turning to God for answers and solutions for this horrendous turn of misfortune when they started speaking to him they accused him of committing a punitive sin. Later in chapter 32 of the book of Job, a younger man named Elihu listened to Job and his three older friends until he had heard enough. He rebuked Eliphaz, Bildad, and Zophar for not being able to refute all that Job said, but yet condemned him for sinning. Elihu also rebuked Job for saying almighty God does not listen and that he justified himself rather than leaving this to God.

When we repent, we are confessing guilt and agree to accept God as our Lord and savior. There should be a sense of being remorseful for doing things that displeased God and to seek His forgiveness. We are renouncing and relinquishing our worldly way of life and professing to live according to God's will. Even though we confess guilt, Satan the accuser is forever trying to initiate the prosecution and condemnation of us to eternal damnation. God provided Our Mediator, Comforter, and Savior, by allowing His only begotten son, Jesus Christ, to His shed blood on Calvary as atonement for our sins. This is His gift of grace and not of any anything that we do that we become regenerated so that we can receive eternal life.

If we, by faith, rely on Jesus Christ, we can rely on His promise to protect us from the continuous guiles of Satan, the prince of this world. Jesus gave commands to His disciples, through the Holy Spirit, to be witnesses of the good news (gospel) throughout the world about His crucifixion and that He arose from the dead for the atonement of our sins (Acts 1:1-8)

How could these men even go out into the world and convince Jews or Gentiles that were not there to witness all the teachings, miracles, crucifixion and resurrection of a man named Jesus? They had the Torah with words of the prophets that spoke of the coming of such an individual born of a virgin who would be crucified on a tree and then be raised from the dead for our sins? The witnesses contracted to perform "The Great Commission" were facilitated with the power of the Paraclete to convince those who were not witnesses that this incarnate individual was Jesus of Nazareth. They would have to convince them that this was the savior that was prophesied about in the scripture such as in Isaiah*. He walked the earth forty days after the resurrection.

In the book of Acts 1:8 His last words before His ascension into Heaven to be on the right side of God, was the assurance that they need not worry about how they, themselves, could perform this monumental task, but by the power of the Paraclete coming upon them this would be done. His Word provides us with infallible instructions on how to be in His favor by faith and obedience so that we are able to immure ourselves in His fortress of strength. If you have not yet given yourself over to the Lord, He is waiting patiently for anyone to give themselves to Him. You have to be willing to turn your life over to God and let His will be done. Once this is accomplished, God takes control and He wants you to be still and let Him fight your battles with the unholy ones.

There are many occurrences in both the Old and New Testaments of the Holy Bible that demonstrates how God will provide mercy and grace to those who rely upon Him. In the Old Testament, God's chosen people; the Jews would profess faith in God but would often turn from God. They would fall into worshipping the gods of the non-Jewish people (called Gentiles –all the people that are not Jews) whom they came in contact with. The Jewish people would often walk in the ways of their leaders (kings, queens, and prophets) concerning being obedient or disobedient to God. Some of the Kings of the tribes were very much obedient. One such King was Jehoshaphat that will be focused on because of his example of reliance on God regarding decisions he made although some of his associates were idol worshipers.

The most prominent one was his reliance strictly on God to protect his kingdom of Judah (Juda) from being captured by enemies. Also, King Jehoshaphat, the fourth king of Judah, was considered most capable of all the kings of Judah.

*There are hundreds of prophecies in the Christian Bible

concerning the coming of a Savior or a Messiah (JESUS) to save the Jewish people and thus by the conduit of the Jews save the rest of the World. Finding and commenting on each is another book and research. A few prophesies to peruse in the Holy Bible are in Micah 5:2, Psalms 22, Isaiah 52;13, and Isaiah 53:12 in no particular order.

The original territory called the Holy Land or Promised Land was divided and given to the twelve tribes named after the sons of Jacob. They were Manasseh, Asher, Naphtali, Zebulun, Issachar, Gad, Ephraim, Dan, Benjamin, Reuben, Simeon, and Judah. It may be asked, why is there no tribe named after Joseph, the favorite son of Jacob. (Israel) who is the progenitor of the nation of Israel? Jacob, by adopting his two grandsons, bestowed a double blessing on Joseph's two sons, Manasseh and Ephraim. Levi, the third son of Jacob and his wife Leah, was the ancestor of the priests of the Jewish Temple. These servant-priests of the temple were called Levites. If the Levites had actually received a territory of the Promised Land, there would have been thirteen tribes instead of twelve. The Levites were not given a tribal inheritance in the Promised Land because God was their inheritance. These Levitical priests were placed in forty eight Levitical cities throughout the Promised Land conquered by the twelve Jewish tribes. The tithing of the other generous tribes provided for the needs of the Levites. The third book of the Old Testament, Book of Leviticus, contains instructions for the Levitical priests for worshiping God.

## HOW THE UNITED KINGDOM OF THE ISRAELITES BECAME DIVIDED IMMEDIATELY AFTER THE REIGN OF KING SOLOMON, SON OF KING DAVIS AND BATHSHEBA

This United Kingdom lasted through the reign of Israel's first three kings who were Saul, David, and Solomon in that order. Solomon was the tenth son of King David. Bathsheba (pronounced Bat Sheba), was King David's seventh and greatest wife,* (The story of David and Bathsheba in the Holy Bible in II Samuels 11 and 12).

Bathsheba was married to a soldier in King David's army whose name was Uriah the Hittite. He was away at a battle where King David should have been since kings typically were out in the fields as commanders of their armies. Instead, David was back in Jerusalem taking a stroll on the roof of the king's house. He looked down from the rooftop and saw the beautiful Bathsheba taking a bath to cleanse herself after just completing her menstrual cycle.

Laws were given to the Jewish men and women concerning bodily discharges and the purification processes in the 3rd book of the Old Testament, Leviticus chapter 15. Bleeding from childbirth is also considered to be unclean. The entire 12th chapter of Leviticus is concerning purification after childbirth. According to the Bible in the book of II Samuel 11:4, she had just become ceremonially clean.

According to modern day information from NHS your choices, your health, this would not be a likely time for Bathsheba to get pregnant but she did: "The menstrual cycle is the time from the first day of a woman's period to the day before her next period," says Toni Belfield, a specialist in sexual health information, and a trained fertility awareness teacher. Women are most fertile at the time of ovulation, (when an egg is released from her ovaries) which usually occurs 12-14 days before the next menstrual period begins. This is the time of the month when a woman is most likely to get pregnant.

It is unlikely that a woman will get pregnant just after her period, although it can happen. It is important to remember that sperm can sometimes survive in the body for up to seven days after having sex. This means that it may be possible to get pregnant soon after your period finishes if you ovulate early, especially if you have a naturally short menstrual cycle.

We don't know who seduced who but after seeing her, he inquired about her and sent for her to come to him. Since the Bible states that he inquired about her, surely he knew she was married. It also appears that Bathsheba displayed no opposition to his request. A godly king such as King David knew the Jewish law of adultery expressed in Leviticus 20:10 of the Torah.

Like his father David, Solomon had good and bad qualities. One was allowing his wives, princesses, and concubines, numbered in the hundreds from various kingdoms to worship idols (See I Kings 11:3-8). The Bible contains his Proverbs and songs for he was a very wise king. Solomon's ambitious nature, which provided him great wealth, was problematic because of high taxes and hard labor imposed in building his empire. One of his own officers, Jeroboam (Hebrew - "People will contend"), whom he had placed over the labor force, rebelled against him (See I King 11:28). Since Jeroboam was over the labor force and traveled to the various areas of the United Kingdom, he was aware of the discontent brewing over the hard labor and high taxes especially in the northern territories of Ephraim and Manasseh.

On one of his journeys, a prophet named Ahijah from a town 30 miles north of Jerusalem called Shiloh met him and tore his coat into twelve pieces. He gave Jeroboam ten of the pieces of the coat. Ahijah told Jeroboam that after Solomon's death, God had pledged to allow him to rule over 10 of the 12 tribes (I Kings 11:29 -31). Solomon's son, Rehoboam, was next in line to become king of the 12 United Kingdoms. After Solomon's death, Jeroboam led ten tribes to revolt against the house of David and to secede from the 12 nation Kingdom. The new northern nation of 10 tribes was called Israel or Ephraim.

The first king of this nation was Jeroboam. The southern kingdom took the name Judah and was composed of only two tribes, Judah and Benjamin whose ruler was Rehoboam (Hebrew -"the people have increased'). After the death of Rehoboam's father, King Solomon, and prior to his confirmation as king of the twelve nations, he could have possibly avoided the division of the unified nations if he had listened to the elders. But as previously stated the prophet Ahijah had predicted By the divine knowledge that the nations would divide.

The tribes of the north had presented justifiable complaints about the forced labor and high taxes imposed by King Solomon. The elders advised Rehoboam to compromise with the northern subjects. He, instead, took the advice of his young contemporaries who wanted to increase the tax and labor burdens (I Kings 12:6-8).

At the beginning of King Rehoboam's reign, he sent Adoram (the same person named Adoniram in I King 4:6; 5:14 and Hadoram in II

Chron. 10:18), the official that was in charge of the implementation of the forced labor, to face the hostile and discontented northern subjects and he was stoned to death (I King 12:18). The biblical verse says that king Rehoboam hurried to his chariot and fled to Jerusalem. It is only speculation that the king was out traveling with Adoram perhaps thinking that his ordinances would be acceptable to the people out of respect for his position as king. After the people stoned Adoram to death he realized that his presence did not change the hostile crowd's attitude so he fled for fear of his life in his chariot.

Chariots in biblical days were vehicles generally used for the purpose of war. They were symbols of power to individuals or nations that owned them. Chariots mentioned first in scripture as being used by the Egyptians is first mentioned in Genesis 41:43. Joseph, son of Jacob, who was sold as a slave in Egypt moved up in rank and favor of the Egyptian pharaoh. Joseph was placed in his second state chariot as a mark of distinction as he paraded before the Egyptian people with the pharaoh as a governor or second in command to only him. Of course, the pharaoh was riding in the first state chariot.

Jeroboam became the first king of the ten Northern tribes then called Israel. The Southern Nation ruler was Rehoboam. The first nineteen kings of the Northern Kingdom of Israel were disobedient to God mostly by breaking the very first commandment of the Ten Commandments given by God to Moses on Mount Sinai that is of committing idolatry. The Ten Commandments also called the Decalogue, are listed twice in the Old Testament of the Bible in Exodus 20:1-17 and in Deuteronomy 5:4-21. This disobedience of God's Commandment was committed by the first nineteen kings of the northern kingdom, Israel. This trend of bad kings started with Jeroboam through Hoshea. Out of the first twenty kings of the southern Nation of Judah or Juda, only eight were obedient to God.

Rehoboam, the first king of the Juda, was disobedient. The eight obedient kings of Juda were: Kings Asa, Jehoshaphat, Joash, Amaziah, Azariah (Uzziah), Jotham, Hezekiah, and Josiah. Hezekiah was one of the greatest kings of Juda. When Hezekiah heard that Assyrian Army was about to attack Jerusalem, he ordered the construction of a tunnel to act as an aqueduct to bring water to his people. Hezekiah's Tunnel, also known as Siloam Tunnel and the Tunnel of Shiloh, in Jerusalem was built, according to scholars, in 701 BC. This 1,750-foot long tunnel that stretches from the Gihon Spring to the Pool of Siloam is considered to be an engineering marvel (II Chronicles 32:1-4).

Josiah was considered as one of the best because during his reign there was a religious revival in the nation of Juda (II Kings 23:25)

In the Old Testament of the Holy Scriptures in II Chronicles, the fourth king in the southern part of the Promised Land of Juda or Judah, was a King named Jehoshaphat (Hebrew –for "God judged") This king Jehoshaphat had his faults but the Lord was with him (2 Chronicles 17:3-4). It was mentioned earlier that Jehoshaphat came in contact with idolaters, one (1) of his faults; he was not influenced by them. He followed the commandments of God according to the practices of Israel. One of his worst faults was his connection with idolaters such as with King Ahab the seventh king of the northern nation of Israel. King Ahab (Hebrew-"Father's Brother) practiced idolatry and allowed his Phoenician wife, Jezebel (Hebrew-Izebhel), to dominate him, such as allowing her to introduce the cultish religion of Baal to Israel forsaking the worship of God. Baal was worshiped as a god of fertility. In modern times, the name Jezebel is often used to depict a nefarious female. Synonyms for Jezebel today: harlot, witch, jade, virago, wanton, hussy, and harridan.

Because of the alliance between King Jehoshaphat and King Ahab, Jehoshaphat allowed his son Jehoram or Joram ("Yahweh is exalted") to marry Ahab's daughter (2) Athaliah (Yahweh has announced His exalter nature"). Just to point out here, some historians say that Athaliah was the daughter of King Omri, the sixth king of the divided nation of Israel and the brother of King Ahab. However, Ahab raised her as his daughter. Athaliah had the same influence over Jehoram as Jezebel had over Ahab. She introduced Baal worship to the Kingdom of Judah and eventually became the ruler of Judah for six years. She was the only woman to do so.

Jehoshaphat also allowed Ahab (3) to persuade him to go to war to take back Ramoth-Gilead from Syria which during Moses day was one of the cities used as the refuge for unintentional killers. The thing puzzling about Jehoshaphat is when Ahab told him that he would not wear his kingly garments, but would disguise himself so he would not be recognized as being the King of Israel by the Syrians on the battlefield. Ahab convinced King Jehoshaphat to wear his kingly garments. Could it be that King Jehoshaphat's great faith and dependence on God presented a sense of invulnerability in his mind?

During the battle, the captain of the chariots for the Syrians saw Jehoshaphat and mistook him for Ahab the Israelite king. Jehoshaphat cried out and God heard him and the Syrians then recognized him as not being Ahab. One would think that all of the magnificent things that Jehoshaphat had done for the kingdom of Judah that he would not be duped by such an unintelligent decision proposed by King Ahab (See II Chronicles 18:31-32). King Ahab was mortally wounded by chance when a Syrian archer randomly fired an arrow that pierced Ahab between the scale and breastplate. Jehoshaphat was able to return to his home in Jerusalem and again travel around to bring his people back that had strayed from the Lord. He also traveled throughout Judah again, city by city, and appointed judges that would judge by God's will and not men (See II Chronicles 19:1-8).

There is a song by American gospel singer Yolanda Yvette Adams called "The Battle Is the Lord's" which was her first signature song. This song exemplifies many instances where trust was placed in God to alleviate situations beyond human ability. The event of King Jehoshaphat in II Chronicles 20 is a perfect comparison of the lyrics in Yolanda Adams's song being utilized by this righteous king.

We often exhaust all of the alternatives that we have to try and solve problems when we are in great distress. The very first, never fail solution, should be, with faith, turn the problem(s) over to God. King Jehoshaphat did this exact thing when his kingdom was about to be attacked and ravished by several enemies of Judah. They were the Moabites, Ammonites and some Meunites. Some people came to him and informed him that gigantic armies from this alliance of these three nations were already marching to attack Judah. This alliance of enemies on their way to attack Juda was approximately thirty five miles southeast of the Capital city of Judah, Jerusalem, along the western side of the dead sea.

This army was much larger than that of Judah. Upon hearing this, Jehoshaphat became alarmed and immediately told his subjects to fast and pray to God about this grave situation that appeared to be about to happen. They gave this problem over to the Lord. It was the evilness of these three nations to want to destroy Jehoshaphat and his people and take their possessions. (II Chronicles 20:1-4). It would have seemed humanly natural for Jehoshaphat to immediately inform his army to make haste in preparation to defend Judah. From statistics in scripture concerning Jehoshaphat's military preparedness, he had built fortresses and store cities in Judah for military purposes (II Chronicles 17:12) A census of Jehoshaphat's military taken from biblical scripture of the number of soldiers of valor according to the house of their fathers: Adnah the Chief-300,000 under his command, Jehohanan the captain-260,000, Amasiah the son of Zichri -200,000, Eliada- 200,000 archers, and Jehozabad- 180,000 men (II Chronicles 17:14-18).

With this large body of the military (1.14Million fighting men of valor) waiting for the word of Jehoshaphat to engage in war, he being a Godly King, gave over his life, kingdom and threatening problem to the Lord. The people of Judah were then saved without lifting a sword (II Chronicles 20:21-25). God wants us to bring our problems to Him first without us trying to work it out ourselves. What we normally do is place more faith in what we can do and if that fails then turn to God. God is forever seeking those that wish to turn to Him. (Psalms 14:2 KJV -The LORD looked down from heaven upon the children of men, to see if there were any that did understand, and seek God.)

He will soar to you with extreme speed because God wants to be in communion with His creation. Satan is everywhere roaming to and fro on the earth looking for souls. The Bible says that Satan even roams in Heaven (See Job 1:6-7). Earlier it was discussed in the book of Job that Satan visited Heaven along with the heavenly council before God. Satan was seeking counsel from God concerning permission to test one of God's faithful and turn them away. Satan is depicted as a roaring lion seeking whom it can devour. The application of the lion in scripture is used figuratively to individuals and nations. Christ is as a lion in the sense of being majestic. The reference to Satan as a lion depicted in 1Peter 5:8 warns that he walks about as a roaring lion, an adversary, laying in ambush to ruthlessly, destructively and voraciously consume who is not alert, vigilant and sober. The use of the lion's predatory nature as used here is not being physically voraciously eaten as a lion eats its prey but rather Satan places a wedge between man and God and provokes his will with the end result of condemnation to eternal punishment in hell.

Satan the Accuser works 24/7trying to alienate people from God by accusations. This is why we need God's stronghold in this war with Satan in this life; you must know where to bunker down to protect yourself. I will bunker down in God's loving arms inside his fortress. Satan's stronghold is based on lies and deception. Since Satan is a spiritual being, we, as fleshly creatures, are greatly deceived if we think we can overcome these satanic strongholds without the Holy Spirit (the Paraclete).

Satan is more powerful than humans but is under the control of God. "For though we live in the world, we do not wage war as the world does. The Apostle Paul writes this in the letter to the Corinthians (II Corinthians 10:4-5 the weapons we fight with are not the weapons of the world. On the contrary, they have divine power to demolish strongholds. We demolish arguments and every pretension that sets itself up against the knowledge of God, and we take captive every thought to make it obedient to Christ").

In the book of Genesis Satan appeared in the guise of a serpent and is described as being craftier than any beast that God had created. Satan is not the serpent but a vessel of Satan just as Satan enters into humans. There are five books in the Old Testament of the Bible that fall under the category of the Major Prophets which begin with the Book of Isaiah. Many believe that Isaiah chapter 14 gives a description of the fall of Satan from heaven (v.12 How art thou fallen from heaven, O Lucifer, son of the morning! how art thou cut down to the ground, which didst weaken the nations! V.13 for thou hast said in thine heart, I will ascend into heaven; I will exalt my throne above the stars of

God: I will sit also upon the mount of the congregation, in the sides of the north: v.14 I will ascend above the heights of the clouds; I will be like the most High. 15 Yet thou shalt be brought down to hell, to the sides of the pit.

By assimilation of verses in the Bible, it is concluded that when Satan was cast out of Heaven, He took a third of the angel followers along with him. Different Biblical verses are placed together to make this assumption because there is no one verse that specifically states this. Satan is referred to as a morning star in Isaiah 14:12. So Satan is referred to as a star cast down from Heaven to earth, Revelation 12:4 states that a third of the stars were cast out with him. Whenever I ask someone, how many angels, if any, were cast out of Heaven with Satan, this verse is used for reference.

Enhanced study of the Bible often entails the use of the commentary of Matthew Henry and other Biblical commentators. This is a brief commentary by Matthew Henry on Ezekiel 28 concerning the sinful peculiarity of pride: Ethbaal, or Ithobal, was the prince or king of Tyre; and being lifted up with excessive pride, he claimed Divine honours. Pride is peculiarly the sin of our fallen nature. Nor can any wisdom, except that which the Lord gives, lead to happiness in this world or in that which is to come.

Satan, originally an angel with perfection and beauty, was called Lucifer before he was cast out of Heaven the first time. The Bible first mentions Satan in Genesis 3 as the *Temptation and Fall of Man* is described here if you are reading the Bible from the first chapter. Angels in Heaven, just as humans on earth, were given free will to make a choice between doing the will of God and doing things outside the will of God. It seems to me that Angels have the advantage in making this choice because we humans have the most difficult task of giving up earthly or worldly things those angels never experienced.

We grieve instead of rejoicing even when we believe that the deceased person has walked in the ways of a Christian believer and has gone home to be with the Lord. Christian believers should never believe that this world is their home. This is a difficult concept for humans because we experience the earthly environment from the time we are born until we die. It takes faith and not sight to believe that we become heirs to Heaven and will eventually have eternal life when we believe and accept the fact that the redemptive work of Jesus on the cross was for our salvation. All possessions are left behind, yet sometimes we act as if we can take them with us. It must also be noted that we are saddened even when a loved one takes an extended leave such as going into military service. In this example, there is a chance that we might not see them again in this world. But if a fellow Christian leaves this world and we live according to the Word, we will see them again when we join them in Heaven.

The rich young man or the rich ruler in the Bible is describing the same person Jesus is communicating with concerning discipleship with Him. Depending on which New Testament synoptic gospel you are reading, Matthew, Mark, or Luke, this particular individual is referred to as a rich young man or rich ruler. Matthew, Mark, and Luke are referred to as the synoptic gospels because there are similar stories concerning the same occurrences which are unmistakably the same but from a different point of view. It is like several individuals observing a traffic accident and is asked to describe what happened. Even though the information might be somewhat different but, none the less it is an accident. They are describing what they saw from their point of view. Of the four New Testament Gospels, the Gospel of John is not included as a Synoptic Gospel because what he relates from his mind's eye concerning his discipleship with Jesus is different from the others.

While the approximate total versions of the Bible are about 1368 in approximately 1006 languages, we can easily see how certain events of the Bible about the same events and information, with slight variations, do occur. Encyclopedic sources indicate that in the year 2014 there were 531 versions of the full Bible and 2,883 languages that have at least some portion of the Bible translated from the original languages of Hebrew, Aramaic, and Greek. A variation of translations, cultures, and languages presents variations in the texts.

The four Gospel writers of the New Testament described Jesus the Messiah from each of their perspectives. In the arrangement of the

Gospels in the Bible, the first Gospel of Matthew, written by a former tax collector from the City of Capernaum located on the northwest shore of the Sea of Galilee (This was the city Jesus chose as the base of operations when He began His ministry where likely several of Jesus' chosen disciples were from there including Peter, John, James, and Andrew). Matthew in the first Gospel shows Christ as King. The second Gospel of Mark (written by John Mark) portrays Christ as the servant who is to suffer for us. The third Gospel of Luke, which is the longest book in the New Testament, shows Christ as a human who was born of a human virgin woman and walked and lived among humans which might be typical for a physician (written by Luke a Gentile physician who also wrote the Book of Acts). The Gospel of John which was mentioned earlier as not being included in the three synoptic Gospels depicts Christ as God.

The Bible warns and teaches us the improbability of overcoming the worldly influence of Satan by relying on our own resources. It is so important and necessary to remove the thought that this can be done by relying on our own resources instead of the Holy Spirit. One of many teachings by Jesus concerning giving up worldly thoughts and possessions is written in the synoptic Gospels but not in the Gospel of John. As mentioned previously there can be slight variations in the way the writer saw the event but never the less the context is the same. This is how the occurrence happened in KJV version of the Gospel of Matthew 19:16-26: 16 Now a man came up to Jesus and asked, "Teacher, what good thing must I do to get eternal life?" 17 "Why do you ask me about what is good?" Jesus replied. "There is only one who is good. If you want to enter life, obey the commandments." 18 "Which ones?" the man inquired. Jesus replied, "'Do not murder, do not commit adultery, do not steal, do not give false testimony, 19 honor your father and mother,' and 'love your neighbor as yourself.'" 20 "All these I have kept," the young man said. "What do I still lack?" 21 Jesus answered, "If you want to be perfect, go, sell your possessions and give to the poor, and you will have treasure in heaven. Then come, follow me." 22 When the young man heard this, he went away sad, because he had great wealth. 23 Then Jesus said to his disciples, "I tell you the truth, it is hard for a rich man to enter the kingdom of heaven. 24 Again I tell you, it is easier for a camel to go through the eye of a needle than for a rich man to enter the kingdom of God." 25 When the disciples heard this, they were greatly astonished and asked, "Who then can be saved?" 26 Jesus looked at them and said, "With man this is impossible, but with God all things are possible."

There are two things going on with this rich man, First, it is wrong to assume that by doing all these righteous things (works) qualifies one to enter into the kingdom of God or be saved for all eternity. Secondly, it depicts how difficult it is to give up earthly possessions while still living. Everything belongs to God. God created everything as is stated in the first chapter, first verse and first book of the Holy Bible, Genesis. It could be said that he was avaricious, seeking to hoard his riches. The rich man apparently had been taught and practiced from the Torah, the Ten Commandments, but he ignored the tenth one which says do not "Covet". Although covet means also to intensely desire or lust for something that belongs to someone else.

Jesus said we should give special attention to not be caught up in the extravagant amount of worldly possessions (Luke 12:15). This avariciousness easily becomes idolatry when one becomes too devoted to something or anything physical. The Apostle Paul wrote about this aptly in the epistle to his companion and son he never had, Timothy: I Timothy 6:7-9 KJV 7 for we brought nothing into the world, and we cannot take anything out of the world. 8 But if we have food and clothing, with these we will be content. 9 But those who desire to be rich fall into temptation, into a snare, into many senseless and harmful desires that plunge people into ruin and destruction.

We are told in the synoptic Gospel of Mark (Mark 10:21 KJV) that Jesus beheld this rich man and loved him and did give him a solution by telling him to go away and give away whatsoever he had to the poor and he would receive wealth in Heaven. Did he do this, we are not told. Becoming attached to earthly things is so easy since we are born into this world in a sinful state. It is not easy to give up earthly things especially when Satan's goal is to keep us for himself in his worldly kingdom. Eventually, his kingdom will become eternal also, eternal damnation and suffering. Earthly human beings cannot defeat this spiritual being without deciding to believe the promises of God and asking for divine intervention by the Paraclete (Holy Spirit).

Even though Satan no longer has a domain in Heaven but only on earth, He was allowed visitation rights. In the twelfth chapter of Revelations, He was kicked out of Heaven again by Michael and his angels who fought the dragon Satan and his angels. Satan and his angels were defeated and no longer allowed in Heaven. He was thrown down to earth (Revelations 12-7:9).

Satan appears in the first book of the Bible, Genesis chapter three called *"The Fall"*, to present a falsehood to deceive the first woman, Eve.

Evil was first exhibited by Satan for it was evil for him to want to exalt himself thinking that he had parity with God or perhaps, even greater than God. The Bible associates this name with evil. The word "Satan" is not his actual name, it is merely his title. According to Strong's Hebrew Lexicon, the word "Satan" is defined as follows

> Word #Satan saw-tan' a primitive root; to attack, (figuratively) accuse :–(be an) adversary, resist.

> According to the Bible, Satan's personal name is actually "Beelzebub"*. In Milton's "Paradise Lost" Beelzebub was one of the fallen angels, second only to Satan. In the OT of the Bible in the book of Judges 10:6, states that the Philistines worshipped most of the Canaanite gods but the most popular were Dagon, same as the Hebrew word for grain, and Baal-Zebub which meant "lord of the flies as early as 2000 B.C. The followers of Yahweh (Lord) made a deliberate change of the word Baal-Zebul (Baal the Prince) to Baal-Zebub as a protestation by these idol diet worshippers. In the NT of the Bible, Matthew 12:24 Jesus was referred to as Beelzebub by the Pharisees (One of the three major religious societies of Judaism at the time of the New Testament, the Pharisees, the Sadducees, and the

Essenes) when they heard that he healed a man that was possessed of the devil, blind, and dumb. All of the witnesses to this healing were amazed and said: "Is this not the son David"? The Pharisees were dismissing this miracle healing as one that is done by the prince of the devils.

Satan is also called Lucifer once in the Bible by the Major Prophet Isaiah (Isaiah 14:12 King James Version). Through the free will that God allows all to have, some will follow righteousness while others will follow sin. Lucifer, along with the third of angels that he brought down with him, knowing this, uses all of his cunningness to gather unto himself earthly followers.

*Be-el-ze-bub in the Bible Expand (Gr. form Beel'zebul), the name given to Satan, and found only in the New Testament (Matt. 10:25; 12:24, 27; Mark 3:22). It is probably the same as Baalzebub (q.v.), the god of Ekron, meaning "the lord of flies," or, as others think, "the lord of dung," or "the dung-god." Easton's 1897 Bible Dictionary

Satan was narcissistic in every respect, appealing and attractive to his own self. (From Greek mythology, the word narcissism, from the myth of Narcissus, means "inordinate fascination with oneself; excessive self-love; vanity" in casual usage) In the year 1968 Narcissistic personality disorder (NPD) was formulated. It is a personality disorder in which a person is excessively preoccupied with personal adequacy, power, prestige, and vanity. This condition affects one percent of the population, it was historically called megalomania and is severe egocentrism. But we know that Satan is defeated from the start.

Satan made his boast five times as is written in the book of Isaiah 14:12-14. Satan (Remember Lucifer means "day star" in Hebraic when you read the book of Isaiah) proclaimed that he would ascend to Heaven, raise his throne above all of God's highest creations in Heaven. (Isaiah 14:13-14 ESV 13 You said in your heart, "I will ascend to the heavens; I will raise my throne above the stars of God; I will sit enthroned on the mount of assembly, on the utmost heights of Mount Zaphon. 14 I will ascend above the tops of the clouds; I will make myself like the Most High."

There is no Holy Biblical Scripture evidence that there are different levels in Heaven. The closest thing scripture says about there being levels in heaven is mentioned in the letter to the church at Corinth by the Apostle Paul (See II Corinthian12:2) Jewish intertestamental literature, which is the period of the four hundred and fifty years between the OT and NT. There were no canonical writings recorded for biblical transcription. This literature began after the last OT prophet Malachi, about 450 B.C. and before the birth of Christ, about 4 B. C. The ancient cosmologists described paradise or heaven as being multi-layered. The Jewish literature, during this time, speculated seven as the number usually mentioned. Satan wanted God's glory. But God will not yield his glory to anyone else Isaiah 42:8 NIV 8 "I am the LORD; that is my name! I will not yield my glory to another or my praise to idols". He is God. Satan attempts to input his selfish desires in us, James 4:1 NIV What causes fights and quarrels among you? Don't they come from your desires that battle within you?

An earnest petition made to God must not be about your own selfish desires. One might wonder why God has not responded to his or her prayer(s) perhaps you might consider because you are making a request for selfish reasons of which Satan has devised in your mind. An example could be of praying asking the Lord to allow you to win the Lottery. There is no specific scripture pertaining to gambling. The Bible warns us to not covet money. Proverbs 13:11 ESV tells us:

"Wealth gained hastily will dwindle, but whoever gathers little by little will increase it" and Ecclesiastes 5:10 ESV: He who loves money will not be satisfied with money, nor he who loves wealth with his income; this also is vanity.

Many say I will give one tenth in tithing to the church or some other charitable organization. In reality, very few winners uphold this promise. God with His supreme power will supply the church by honest means. No church of Christ will, knowingly, accept money that is obtained dishonestly.

Prayer is communicating with God alone without Satan's input. Prayers are made as submissions to God's will and never your own (1John 3:21-22, 5:14-15.)

During the creation of the heavens and the earth, Satan witnessed God bringing into existence all things by merely speaking them into existence by His Word. Satan has no divine word or power whereby he can emulate God. Satan is limited to only do what is allowed by God. After God created man in his own image, (Genesis 1:27) Satan goes into the Garden of Eden clothed in the form of one of God's creatures, a serpent, and cunningly portrayed rebellion against God as a good thing and an innocent self-interest. The knowledge that he professed to Eve would be the same knowledge that God has. The most profound statement that changed the course of mankind's history and certainly brought sin and death into the world was made by the crafty serpent (Satan) in Genesis 3:1-5.

Satan is known as a liar. Just as he lied to Eve in the Garden, He tempted, tested, and lied to Jesus. The Holy Scripture relates that after Jesus was baptized by John the Baptist in the Jordan River He was full of the Holy Spirit (The Paraclete) and was led away by the "Spirit" into the Judean desert where he prayed and fasted for forty days. The temptation of Jesus by Satan the devil is recorded in the three Synoptic Gospels. The Gospel of Luke (Luke 4:1-15) gives a few more details concerning this event than the Gospel of Matthew (See Matthew1:1-13), and the Gospel of Mark (Mark 1:12-13) The Gospel of Luke states that Jesus was full of the Holy Spirit when He was led by the Spirit into the Judean wilderness (Luke 4:1). The gospel of Matthew states that He was led by the "spirit" into the wilderness (Matthew 4:1). The Gospel of Mark states that He was driven into the wilderness by the "spirit immediately after being baptized (Mark 1:12-13). Mark also states that wild beast was present along with angels that ministered to him. The Gospel of Luke indicates that Jesus was being tempted the whole forty days by Satan in the wilderness whereas Matthew and Mark state that He was tempted by Satan after the forty days of fasting. Jesus was tempted by Satan just as we are today. The only difference is that Jesus was without sin and remained sinless. For all three of the propositions that Satan made to tempt Jesus, he was rebuked by the spirit of God's Word. Immediately after Satan departed from Jesus, the "spirit" remained with Him as He departed from the wilderness to Galilee where the commencement of His ministry began. He began to teach in the synagogues.

Adam had authority over the woman God had created for him for companionship in the Garden of Eden. God also went so far in the complexity of creating mankind that the father determines the sex of a child. Yet Adam forfeited his authority to Eve and blamed God for his and her disobedience concerning eating the forbidden fruit. (Genesis 3:11-12)

God prepared and provided everything for Adam before he created him and all was lost to all mankind by the deception of a warring Satan. To this day since the time he fell from the grace of heaven, he has roamed the earth looking for disciples.

Adam and Eve were driven out of the beautiful Garden of Eden at once, Genesis 3-23-24. Fellowship with God was lost. Satan caused them to bring sin and death into the world and upon all future generations of mankind.

Now by God's grace, He blessed Adam and Eve to have children (Genesis 4:1-2). Adam and Eve apparently taught their two sons about God, because in the course of time, both brought sacrifices unto the Lord. In the course of time, Abel raised flocks of animals and brought the firstborn from this flock as a sacrifice to the Lord who was pleased with the offering. Cain brought some of the fruits of the soil as an offering to the Lord which He was not pleased with. Cain's anger was shown in his face which was easily recognizable by the Lord. Seeing Cain's anger the Lord provided him with a chance to make up for his bad choice of the offering, otherwise, he would become overcome by sin (Genesis 4:4-7).

We know that Cain did not try to make the acceptable offer to the Lord. He was overcome by sin and committed the first murder by becoming insanely jealous killing his brother Abel. This is the same sort of pride and jealousy that the serpent left as an inheritance for mankind.

Because of this curse, we needed someone to redeem and bless us. To receive this blessing as was earlier stated in John 3:16 that God truly did send his Son to save us because of our sinful nature. Many are yet in unbelief of this fact. The Apostle Paul indicated the attitude and fate of unbelievers in his epistle to the church of God that was in Corinth. His letter indicated that they were taking lightly what Jesus had accomplished by His sacrifice for us on the cross. The apostle is most likely directing his comments to the Jewish and Gentile teachers there in Corinth because they engaged in foolish debates because they lacked the knowledge concerning the meaning of Jesus's crucifixion. These debates caused division of the church there.1Cor1:18-21 AMP 18 For the story and message of the cross is sheer absurdity and folly to those who are perishing and on their way to perdition, but to us who are being saved it is the [manifestation of] the power of God. 19 For it is written, I will baffle and render useless and destroy the learning of the learned and the philosophy of the philosophers and the cleverness of the clever and the discernment of the discerning; I will frustrate and nullify [them] and bring [them] to nothing. 20 Where is the wise man (the philosopher)? Where is the scribe (the scholar)? Where is the investigator (the logician, the debater) of this present time and age? Has not God shown up the nonsense and the folly of this world's wisdom? 21 For when the world with all its earthly wisdom failed to perceive and recognize and know God by means of its own philosophy, God in His wisdom was pleased through the foolishness of preaching [salvation, procured by Christ and to be had through Him], to save those who believed (who clung to and trusted in and relied on Him).

Verse 19 of Paul's epistle to the church at Corinth is a partial quote from Isaiah 29:14. Paul often indicates in his epistles that he is quoting from the Septuagint* when he states *"it is written"* so that he could quench any thoughts by the recipients that he was using false doctrines of his own origin.

Septuagint Latin word for "seventy" (also known as LXX) in this application were seventy or seventy-two Jewish scholars who were asked by the Greek King of Egypt, Ptolemy II Philadelphus, to translate the Torah from Biblical Hebrew into Greek, for inclusion in the Library of Alexandria.

After King Ptolemy gathered the 72 elders, he placed them in 72 chambers, each of them in a separate one, without revealing to them why they were summoned. He entered each one's room and said: "Write for me the Torah of Moshe, your teacher". God put it in the heart of each one to translate identically as all the others did. Philo of Alexandria, who relied extensively on the Septuagint, says that the number of scholars was chosen by selecting six scholars from each of the twelve tribes of Israel.

The date of the 3rd century BCE is supported (for the Torah translation) by a number of factors, including the Greek being representative of early Koine, citations beginning as early as the 2nd century BCE, and early manuscripts datable to the 2nd century.

This particular critique in this epistle was warnings to those who considered themselves wise that had not been saved and were preaching falsehoods. He warned that the wisdom of the wise would be destroyed. The understanding of the prudent will be brought to nothing.

Many of those wise and mighty men were led by the flesh instead of the Holy Spirit (The Paraclete) (See 1 Cor1:26- 27) Therefore God takes the things you call foolish and confounds the wise. The base despised things of the world He has chosen. God is getting angry with Nations again in this present time because of the lack of dispensation. A dispensation is the method which God carries out His purpose towards mankind which would otherwise remain a mystery of His will. Dispensation as defined by the Easton Bible Dictionary: The method or scheme according to which God carries out his purposes towards men is called a dispensation. There are usually reckoned three dispensations, the Patriarchal, the Mosaic or Jewish, and the Christian. The word dispensation is not found with this meaning in Scripture. Also from the King James Dictionary also found in the Easton Bible Dictionary: An arrangement of things; a scheme: Having made known unto us the mystery of his will, according to his good pleasure which he hath purposed in himself: that in the DISPENSATION of the fullness of times he might gather together in one all things in Christ, both which are in heaven, and which are on earth; even in him. (See Ephesians 1:9-10)

I am not a theologian, so I don't know how many dispensations there really are. Theologians don't seem to agree either because they have the number of dispensations somewhere between seven and thirty-something. Presently we are living under the "New Covenant" and this dispensational period is supposed to be the sixth dispensation. This period is called the "Dispensation of Grace." All the people in the world are to believe that Jesus is the Son Of God. The provisions made by Jesus' request to His Father concerning the assistance of the Holy Spirit (The Paraclete) for believers can be found in John 14:16-26.

He sees things happening today, as they did centuries ago. Time changes but He is the same God today as he was the same God of Moses. Satan is also the same. In the New Testament, the apostle Peter warns against the wiles of Satan (I Peter 5:8-11).

# CHAPTER 2

# The Five Fold Ministry

SATAN IS CUNNING AND CONSTANTLY looking for those that he can devour. Satan's influence can be observed inside and outside of the Christian church. His influence causes churchgoers to start complaining and getting angry on the church parking lot about someone's car parked in their perceived reserved parking space. Entering the worship center, they fume again because someone is sitting in their perceived reserved seat. Satan causes division in the church which causes some attendees to go from church to church seeking what they want to hear from the ministers.

Satan even sometimes enters the pulpit with improvised righteousness deviating from the word of God. Satan's temptations have not seen much improvisation over the centuries. He still uses the same promises for tempting someone as he did from the beginning with Adam and Eve promising either satisfaction, pleasure, happiness, might, and material things. Jesus was tempted by Satan in the Judean wilderness with the same hedonism, egoism, and materialism, but refused him by speaking the Word of God causing Satan to make a quick exit (Matthew 4:1-11, Mark 1:12-13, or Luke 4:1-13) When Satan is rebuked, he doesn't give up but waits for another opportunity to try again (Luke 4:13 ESV).

Satan attempts to flood the Five Fold Ministry" with his own disciples masquerading as Apostles of Christ. There is a doctrine called the "angel of light doctrine" which is influencing many followers and leaders. Satan tries to imitate the "Light" provided by the "Holy Spirit". Satan's portrayal as an angel of light doctrines can be hard to detect because there are many ministers who profess the saving power of the Gospel and believe they are genuine men of God while being manipulated by Satan. It is not difficult to discern when the evil and wicked actions of Satan are on display in someone most of the time. It becomes difficult to discern Satan's influence on someone when he uses the guise of righteousness or posing as an "angel of light" to that person (II Corinthians 11:14-15).

God is in control of Satan and His will is that we all receive salvation. Repentance to God negates all accusations and lies Satan presents to God. Paul shows in his epistle to the church at Ephesus how to rebuke Satan by provisions given to the church there from God so that they could live and work together in unity and grow in maturity. There were rules established so that everyone would have the wisdom of the qualifications of the "Five Fold Ministry". People are to take positions according to the essential needs of the Church. These groups of gifted people's assignments are to make the church grow through edification. (Ephesians 4:11-14)

Many Biblical scholars today believe that the cornerstone work of the apostles and prophets has been completed. They believe that Satan has intervened in these righteous positions with false doctrines and have caused humans to present themselves as God sent apostles or prophets. We should stay close enough to God in the "Spirit" so that we will be able to identify the camouflaged individuals who claim to be apostles and prophets for Christ.

*Acts 20:29-30 ESV 29 I know that after my departure fierce wolves will come in among you, not sparing the flock; 30 and from among your own selves will arise men speaking twisted things, to draw away the disciples after them* (See also 2 Cor. 11:12-15 and2 Peter 2:1-3).

Many, certainly not all, are seeking to gain wealth by building mega-churches to gain more people for the monetary profitability of the church thus they make themselves rich in the process. This is not saying that church leaders should not be prosperous. The bible does not say being wealthy is a sin. If someone is devoted to obtaining wealth is sinful. The bible tells us that no one can serve two masters. The verses about this can be found in the Books of Luke and Matthew (Luke16:13, also Matthew 6:24) and are explicitly speaking of serving God or serving money. James, one of Jesus's brothers and also the prominent leader of the council at Jerusalem, wrote in his letter in the book of James in the Bible, that one that makes friends with things of the world are actively opposed to God (James 4:4). If your treasure is things stored up on earth that is where your heart is (Matthew 6:19-21). Some of the prophets of today are no more than fortune tellers and soothsayers carrying out Satan's wicked plans.

The subject of financial wealth is a highly debatable topic. In the Old Testament of the Bible, God allowed Abraham, the father of faith) to become rich in material things (Genesis 13:2). Others in the book of Genesis such as His nephew, Lot, and his son Isaac, etc., became wealthy. There are many passages in the bible that proponents and opponents use to make their case concerning financial prosperity. God appeared to King Solomon in a dream and asked him what He shall give him. Solomon confessed to the Lord that he did not have the wisdom to rule the Israelites. He asked God to give him the understanding on how to rule the people and be able to discern between good and evil. God was pleased with what he unselfishly asked for and gave him understanding, riches, and honor (1 Kings 3:1-15). My belief is that spiritual wealth, which is eternal, is the riches that one should pursue and the bible says all other things will be added unto you (Matthew 6:33).

The Holy Spirit enters those that love Him, while evil spirits enter those who love the world and its pleasures.

The fivefold ministry or five-fold ministry is a Charismatic and Evangelical Christian belief that five offices mentioned in Ephesians (Ephesians 4:11), namely that of apostles, prophets, evangelists, pastors (or "shepherds") and teachers, remain active and valid offices in the contemporary Christian church. Non-charismatic Christians may also consider these roles, and others, active and valid, but the term "fivefold ministry" is particularly associated with Pentecostal beliefs. Adherents of this ecclesiology may also affirm the continuation of the charismatic gifts in the modern church, or may hold to the concept of a "Latter Rain" outpouring of Holy Spirit gifts, while opponents commonly hold to cessationist beliefs.

## Five offices in the New Testament

Ephesians 4:11 refers to five offices in the church: apostles, prophets, evangelists, pastors, and Teachers. Other passages also refer to these things as spiritual gifts. Romans 12:4-8, for example, includes teaching and prophesying as spiritual gifts, and 1 Corinthians 12 lists apostles, prophets, and teachers in the context of spiritual gifts. 1 Corinthians 14 provides instructions on the proper use of "Prophecy and Tongues" in the edification (building up) of the church body.

## Qualifications

Paul refers to the "signs" of an apostle in 2 Corinthians 12:11-12, and notes that he performed these "with signs and wonders and having seen Jesus is a qualification of being an apostle while opponents to this belief argue that he is merely defending his authority to make the statements from the mighty works" (NIV). Some argue that in 1 Corinthians 9:1, Paul suggests that previous chapter regarding sin and grace. Paul also notes in 1 Corinthians 9:1-2 that even though some at Corinth questioned his apostleship, he certified that he had seen Jesus and was to be considered an apostle by the fruits of his labor developed from the encounter.

The qualifications of pastors or overseers are listed in 1Timothy 3:2-7 and Titus 1:6-9. These are mainly moral, with the additional qualification of being "able to teach".

## New Testament people

A number of people in the New Testament are said to hold one or more of these offices:

Apostles: The Twelve (See Luke 6:13-16), Matthias (Acts 1:24-26), Paul (See Galatians 1:1), Barnabas (See Acts 14:14), Andronicus and Junia (See Romans 16:7)

Prophets: The company from Jerusalem (Acts 11:27-28), Agabus (See Acts 21:10-11), Judas and Silas (Acts 15:32) and the daughters of Philip (Acts 21:9)

Teachers: Apollos (Acts 18:25), Paul (II Timothy 1:11)

Evangelists: Philip (Acts 21:9)

In addition to this, Acts 13:1-3 lists some "prophets and teachers" in Antioch: Barnabas, Simeon called Niger, Lucius of Cyrene, Manaen and Saul.

After the close of the Apostolic Age, Christian writers still referred to the existence of prophets. For example, Irenaeus wrote of second-century believers with the gift of prophecy, [1] while Tertullian's writing of the church meetings of the Montanists (to whom he belonged), described in detail the practice of prophecy in the second-century church. [2] It is, however, the teaching of Edward Irving an advent of the Catholic Apostolic Church in 1832 that marks the earliest known movement of what could be properly labeled as fivefold ministry. The church ordained twelve apostles and had specific understandings of the roles of prophets, evangelists, pastors, and teachers.

This trend picked up steam in 1948 with the Latter Rain Movement giving renewed emphasis to fivefold ministry, and soon after with the Charismatic Movement and Third Wave movements, led by figures such as C. Peter Wagner, who is now the leading figure in what is known as the New Apostolic Reformation, which emphasizes the specific need for apostolic leadership in the Church, among the other fivefold anointing's.

After the first century, the Christian churches developed three-fold ministry positions that have stood the test of time and are still familiar today. They are the bishops, priests, and deacons.

# CHAPTER 3

# Two Choices Eternal Salvation or Eternal Damnation

EVEN IF WHEN WE ARE receiving ministry that is of the Holy Spirit, we can't have it both ways. We are told to give up this life of the world and commit ourselves completely to God. We shouldn't be doing things that are beneath God's standard one moment and ceremoniously honor Him the next. (See 1 Corinthians 10:21)

There are many who claim to believe in God, but only call on Him when their situation becomes dire or their health is failing. God is not a part-time God. I heard a pastor say that he heard some elderly people who profess to be *saved* say, "The things I used to do I don't do no more." The pastor indicated that because of their age they were probably not physically fit to do what they used to do anymore because of health issues. Hopefully, this pastor was merely adding jocularity to his sermon. The thing God has informed us of is that there will be strong winds and storms in our lives. He has also told us how to weather the storm. God does not allow us to go through a situation that He cannot get us out of.

Figuratively speaking, Jesus is referred to as the rock in the Bible. A house built on a foundation of rock can weather storms. Since we know this, then it is utter foolishness to build a home on an unstable ground. (Matthew 7: 24-27 *ESV 24* "Everyone then who hears these words of mine and does them will be like a wise man who built his house on the rock. 25 And the rain fell, and the floods came, and the winds blew and beat on that house, but it did not fall, because it had been founded on the rock. 26 And everyone who hears these words of mine and does not do them will be like a foolish man who built his house on the sand. 27 And the rain fell, and the floods came, and the winds blew and beat against that house, and it fell, and great was the fall of it."

This world has many roads that can lead us to destruction (hell). With all of the temptations of this world working against us, it is not easy to get to Heaven (Matthew 7:13).

We have been warned of only two choices to make concerning our salvation. One is a narrow strait highway with very few walking therein. This one may seem difficult but it is not when you have all of the encouragement, strengthening, and guidance that are needed if we choose the path of Holiness and guidance of the spirit. The other path is very broad and leads to destruction. This one seems to be the easier of the two because of the conformity of the general populace. Because of Satan's deception, people think that if everyone is doing it then it must be right.

Morality is shifting so much that the government has to change or rewrite laws to conform and accommodate these changes. It is a shame that there are influential groups in the church that force pastors to conform to their own self-righteousness. There have been pastors ousted from churches for this reason. A strong pastor must not be deterred from the precepts of what Christ taught. It does not matter what the government says. There are so many different classifications of Christian faiths in the world today. There are an estimated 1,000 different Christian faiths in North America alone and an estimated 34,000 in the world. There are many small classifications that are not heard of often. The three larger groups, Fundamentalists, Liberals and Conservative Christians, are the ones that make the news because they often bicker over different beliefs on subjects such as abortion, homosexuality, virgin birth, atonement, Resurrection, Heaven, hell, Satan, etc.

Fundamentalism defined: 1. a usually religious movement or

point of view characterized by a return to fundamental principles, by rigid adherence to those principles, and often by intolerance of other views and opposition to secularism.2. a. often Fundamentalism, an organized, militant Evangelical movement originating in the United States in the late 19th and early 20th century in opposition to Protestant Liberalism and secularism, insisting on the inerrancy of Scripture. b. Adherence to the theology of this movement.

Liberal Christianity defined: Most define Liberal Christianity as not being a true Christian at all. They say that you cannot hold the beliefs of liberalism and the Bible at the same time. Liberal Christianity does not claim to be a religion as such and tries to define Bible scripture based on methodology. In other words, liberal Christianity tries to explain the scripture as if it can be done so by scientific inquiry. Therefore, this writer thinks "Christianity" should be removed from the term "Liberal Christianity" or Liberal from Christianity. Most liberal, so-called, Christians do not regard the Bible as inerrant, rather, Scripture to be "inspired" by man himself and not God-breathed inspiration. They believe that the miracles in the Bible can be accounted for by some rational or scientific explanation.

Conservative Christianity defined: Conservative Christianity is a term used to describe identified Christians who tend to follow conservative values, and which stands in contrast to liberal Christianity. "Conservative Christianity may refer to an opinion or advocacy position on certain political issues such as abortion, homosexuality, creationism, science education, taxation, affirmative action, and gun control, treatment of prisoners, immigration, racial segregation, public education, global warming, capital punishment, and divorce." (Conservapedia) Many disagreements between Christians are often about politics from what is known as the Christian Right and the Christian Left. Multifarious ideas exist in thinkers who have conceived of the relationship between Christianity and politics, with many arguing that Christianity directly supports a particular political ideology or philosophy.

Satan's proposal and deception for disobedience to God started with Eve in the Garden of Eden and, today has worked its way into our religious and political lives. The Apostle Paul's letter to the Romans concerning submitting to governing authorities might indicate that some believers did not want to submit to civil rulers who were not believers at the time he was writing. They might have thought that their allegiance was only to Christ. His letter was for clarity on this matter and we should apply it in our thinking today about government officials. Romans 13:1-7 *ESV* -Let every person be subject to the governing authorities. For there is no authority except from God, and those that exist have been instituted by God. Therefore whoever resists the authorities resists what God has appointed, and those who resist will incur judgment. For rulers are not terrors to good conduct, but too bad. Would you have fear of the one who is in authority? Then do what is good, and you will receive his approval, for he is God's servant for your good. But if you do wrong, be afraid, for he does not bear the sword in vain for he is the servant of God, an avenger who carries out God's wrath on the wrongdoer. Therefore one must be in subjection, not only to avoid God's wrath but also for the sake of conscience. Pay to all what is owed to them: taxes to who taxes are owed, revenue to whom revenue is owed, respect to who respect is owed, honor to who honor is owed.

Satan's path leads to false hope. The Apostle Paul warns against having false hope and reveals, without any ambiguity, those who will not enter at the "Strait Gate" (I Corinthians 6:9-11)

Homosexuality and support for the rights of gay and lesbian Americans are now widely accepted. Even some ministers, who should know better, place the same-sex marriage rights of these individuals in the same category of civil rights. As believers in the Word of God, we should not let the sinful nature of this world cause us to hate these individuals. We all are sinners and our sins may be different in nature, never the less, sin is sin. We do not have the ability to resist sin in ourselves. The Apostle Paul relates that the Holy Spirit is needed to remind him when he is straying from God's will (sinning): Romans 7:16-18 ESV 16 Now if I do what I do not want, I agree with the law, that it is good. 17 So now it is no longer I who do it, but sin that dwells within me. 18 For I know that nothing good dwells in me, that is, in my flesh. For I have the desire to do what is right, but not the ability to carry it out.

We should pray for ourselves and all sinners to have a repentant heart. In obedience to God, we should dutifully try bringing as many to the salvation provided by Jesus Christ as we can. Jesus provided His disciples with the Great Commission (See Matthew 28:19-20) whereby they were to go, baptize, and teach to make disciples of all nations. Most of us can't travel worldwide to make disciples but what is applicable for us Christians today, in our communities and cities, is be a witness for Jesus our Savior as stated earlier in Acts 1:8. But we should not let sin bring a disdain to our moral values and cause God to abandon us to a spirit of licentiousness. There are individuals that attend church every Sunday yet still harbor hatred for those of a different race than theirs. Quoting Rev. Martin Luther King Jr. "Sunday morning is the most segregated hour of Christian America." It has been stated that this segregation is not because of racism but rather people are more comfortable and relaxed around people like themselves. It is also known that certain racist organizations in America claim to be Christians. If we know God's Word and refuse to acquiesce to it, we are subject to His abandonment of us (See Romans 1:28-29)

# CHAPTER 4

# Obeying God's Laws by Keeping His Precepts

## KJV Dictionary Definition: precept*

PRECEPT I. IN A GENERAL sense, any commandment or order intended as an authoritative rule of action; but applied particularly to commands respecting moral conduct. The Ten Commandments are so many precepts for the regulation of our moral conduct. No arts are without their precepts. 2. In law, a command or mandate in writing*

Perceptive. - Giving precepts or commands for the regulation of moral conduct; containing precepts; as the perceptive parts of the Scriptures. 1. Directing in moral conduct; giving rules or directions; didactic. * Definitions from Webster's American Dictionary of the English Language, 1828.

Precepts are covenant regulations laid down by the Lord. How can we expect to get God's help if we don't obey His laws? There is nothing unfair or difficult to accomplish concerning God's precepts. We should rejoice knowing that we are pleasing God when we are obedient to His precepts. God has commanded us to keep His precepts diligently, that is to be in obedience to them: Psalms 19:8 KJV 8 statutes of the LORD are right, rejoicing the heart: the commandment of the LORD is pure, enlightening the eyes. Psalms 111:7 KJV The works of his hands are verity and judgment; all his commandments are sure. Psalms 119: 4-KJV Thou hast commanded us to keep thy precepts diligently.

Precepts that God commands us to know and keep can be found in the Old and New Testaments. We must seriously investigate the Bible as we read and study so that we will not miss any of the precepts. The second reason is that there are many preachers/teachers that are infusing their own precepts as if they are the very word of God. These are false doctrines. How can you be set free if you believe in false doctrines? (Jesus said: John 8:31-32 ESV 31 So Jesus said to the Jews who had believed in him, "If you abide in my word, you are truly my disciples, 32 and you will know the truth, and the truth will set you free.") Go word by word, line by line, to discover what the real truth is coming out the mouth of the Lord. While writing this book, I stated earlier that I am not formally educated in Theology or Divinity so I pray asking for understanding and guidance before I type one letter for this manuscript. The disciples of Jesus were not formally educated as the Apostle Paul was, yet the Gospels that were written by those that contributed to the canonized NT are inspired by God via the Holy Spirit. The Apostle John indicates that worldly people cannot receive God's precepts because there is no indwelling Spirit in them to receive this understanding in14:15-17 KJV 15 if ye love me, keep my commandments. 16 And I will pray the Father, and he shall give you another Comforter that he may abide with you for ever; 17 Even the Spirit of truth; whom the world cannot receive, because it seeth him not, neither knoweth him: but ye know him; for He dwelleth with you, and shall be in you. If you are looking for the truth and correction (as in disobedience), read the Bible.

The people in the Bible were real people that experienced many, if not every situation that we face today. The thirty-nine books of the OT were recognized during the first century as authoritative books of Holy Scripture. (Later the twenty-seven books of the New Testament were canonized.) The apostle Paul had a real close and dear friend whose name was Timothy (personal name meaning "honoring God") Timothy's mother was Jewish and his father was Greek. His father did not have him circumcised when he was eight days old as was the Jewish custom. Paul had him circumcised (Acts 16:1-3).

Some scholars think that Timothy was a teen at the time he was circumcised and converted to Christianity. This is probably because Paul referred to him as a child in the faith. (1 Corinthians 4:17). When Paul was unable to go and teach in various cities, he would send his very dear friend to represent him at the newly formed churches to ensure that the Holy Scripture was being correctly implemented. Paul wrote two letters to the young pastor Timothy to ensure that the right doctrines were being taught and to avoid senseless controversies. We have the two canonized epistles of first and second Timothy. One of the other young Gentile pastors and companion of Paul was Titus (Latin origin; uncertain meaning). The epistle to this young pastor is also canonized. Paul is thought to be responsible for the conversion of Timothy and Titus. The apostle Paul wrote thirteen epistles in the NT (Author of the Book of Hebrews is thought to be the Apostle Paul by some). Timothy is listed in the greetings in six of these epistles. Timothy might have been with Paul at the writing of these epistles, but it is not for sure that he co-authored them. The salutations, though, brings the highest regard for Timothy. All Jewish boys during the time of Timothy started studying the OT at the age of five. Timothy had been taught this by his mother, Eunice, and grandmother, Lois, at an early age.

Again, it must be stressed that the Holy Scripture must be studied to ensure that we have the right doctrines. Many pastors today have good intentions in teaching the word. They pull out scriptures during their sermons that sometimes are out of context to make a specific point. This is not necessarily pernicious because many souls have been saved while never realizing that they have heard something out of context. That is why we need to take notes, pray, read, and study for ourselves to get a complete understanding, of the scripture.

That is what Paul is relating to the young pastor Timothy in his second epistle to him while also encouraging and instructing him. Paul was imprisoned for the second time, not for normal crimes of the day, but a new crime, his faith in Jesus. He was in Rome at this writing of the second letter to Timothy thinking he would not be released. Timothy was the pastor of the church at Ephesus and had been there for some time. He told Timothy to study the text (Old Testament) to ensure he got it right for the congregation of new believers (II Timothy 3:14-17). The apostle knew that the Judaizers had come into the same region trying to undermine their teaching by introducing the reception of salvation by means of the law such as circumcision and their form of religious ceremony. Paul emphasizes in this letter that only God's inerrant Word should be taught. He urged Timothy to keep on teaching what he was taught from childhood. Don't stray to non-scriptural doctrines in your teaching and preaching. If someone suggests other doctrines correct them with the Holy Word of God and that is more than sufficient.

# CHAPTER 5

# Spiritual Wellbeing

THE FLESHLY SPIRIT OF THIS world doesn't know anything except what is limited by its own spirit. This kind of spirit thinks it is deep in the knowledge of its own deceit. The Spirit of God only abides in those whose faith is in Him. The Apostle Paul's epistle to the Corinthians in 1Cor 2- 6:10 ESV 6 Yet among the mature we do impart wisdom, although it is not a wisdom of this age or of the rulers of this age, who are doomed to pass away. 7 But we impart a secret and hidden wisdom of God, which God decreed before the ages for our glory. 8 None of the rulers of this age understood this, for if they had, they would not have crucified the Lord of glory. 9 But, as it is written, "What no eye has seen, nor ear heard, nor the heart of man imagined, what God has prepared for those who love him"– 10 these things God has revealed to us through the Spirit. For the Spirit searches everything, even the depths of God.

The fleshly spirit values things that are foolishness in this society. That is why our military troops have not met goals in recent wars such as Vietnam, Iraq, and Afghanistan. The world system, the so- called educated, the strong, and the mighty praise one another in deceit and conceit. (Jeremiah 9:23-24).

The Lord is against man's boastful kind of glory. He said to know and understand Him and the things that He exercises in loving, kindness, judgment, and righteousness. Examine yourselves and see if you are in the faith (II Cor 13: 5-9).

The morality and decency of the two major parties in America, the Democrats and the Republicans have degenerated to the point that Americans who vote in elections are voting against instead of for a candidate. Some vote strictly by party affiliation without taking into consideration the views, ideology, morals, etc., of the candidates. This partisanship has caused Americans to become more divided (Gal 5:15 NIV If you bite and devour each other, watch out or you will be destroyed by each other.)

Each party claims to be working for the American people. A divided house cannot stand. Jesus was speaking about Himself after He performed a miracle of curing a man's withered hand and next in the same chapter He healed a man possessed with a devil, blind, and dumb all seen by the religious group, the Pharisees. The Pharisees wanted to bring charges against Jesus since these healings were performed on the Sabbath. So they thought that Jesus must be the satanic demon named Beelzebub. Supernaturally, Jesus knew about their conversation and thoughts without hearing their spoken words. He said to them that Satan would not cast Himself out of a person but yet He casts out a demon that would be going against him creating a division with himself. This is what America's two-party system is doing creating a division within itself (Matthew 12:25 KJV And Jesus knew their thoughts, and said unto them, Every kingdom divided against itself is brought to desolation; and every city or house divided against itself shall not stand)

This country is gradually refraining from being led by the Holy Spirit (The Advocate). Some politicians that profess to be Christians capitulate to the political system going against their own moral values.

It has been said by a theologian, I don't recall who, but if there was only one book of Holy Scripture to rely on for the Christian doctrine and to teach the gospel of grace through faith in Jesus, that book is the Book of Romans. I would think that the epistle to Ephesus (Ephesians) would be a close second. In this modern time, the Apostle Paul would be considered a person who received a Ph.D. in Divinity after studying in Jerusalem under Rabbi Gamaliel (Acts 22:3). The apostle Paul did teach his understudies such as Timothy and Titus, but he did not have a rabbinical school. A Ph.D. degree in theology is the foundational degree program for teaching at a seminary or similar to what Gamaliel did in Jerusalem. Rabbi Gamaliel was a Pharisee and teacher who was considered as a doctor of Jewish law. The Apostle Paul was also a Pharisee. In the 5th chapter of the book of Acts, Peter and the apostles were arrested for preaching at a colonnade, portico, or porch called Solomon (See Acts 5:12-18). The high priests and the party of the Sadducees became jealous of Peter and the apostles and had them arrested and placed in a public prison. An angel of the Lord came during the night and released them from prison and told them to go preach in the temple. This enraged the High Priests and the council so bad that they wanted to kill them. Gamaliel actually spoke up for them.

The book of Romans is a basic guideline to receive salvation because all people are sinners, the Jews, and the Gentiles, according to Paul. If you are not a Jew then you are a Gentile. Paul was writing to the Christians who had formed a church in Rome. Paul uses the Greek version of Old Testament (Septuagint) quotations to convincingly present the theme of the righteousness that comes from God's Word. Scripture suggests the Apostle could speak Aramaic, Hebrew, Greek, and Latin which will be discussed later on.

This theme of righteousness is that God freely justifies condemned sinners by grace alone through faith in Jesus. The apostle Paul was explaining, that there is no difference between the way God sees people since all are sinners (The Jews and the Gentiles) Romans 3:21-26 KJV 21 But now the righteousness of God without the law is manifested, being witnessed by the law and the prophets; 22 Even the righteousness of God which is by faith of Jesus Christ unto all and upon all them that believe: for there is no difference: 23 For all have sinned, and come short of the glory of God; 24 Being justified freely by his grace through the redemption that is in Christ Jesus: 25 Whom God hath set forth to be a propitiation through faith in his blood, to declare his righteousness for the remission of sins that are past, through the forbearance of God; 26 To declare, I say, at this time his righteousness: that he might be just, and the justifier of him which believeth in Jesus.

The epistle to Romans should be studied diligently by all Christians because it reveals God's plans for us.

So we shouldn't be slandering or pointing fingers at anyone as Christians. It doesn't matter what prefix you have before your name, you should not exalt yourself to be greater than anyone else. We are all the same in God's perspective.

The major two-party political systems (Democrats and Republicans) in the United States frequently have different opinions and debates over why we have deficits with our monetary system. Disagreements on solutions for defeating terrorists, withdrawal of our military troops in foreign countries, immigration, abortion, etc., are some of the issues that cause partisanship in the political systems. These numerous issues cause them to keep bickering and finger pointing along party lines. There is hardly ever bi-partisanship unless there is some personal benefit from the same lobbyists. No one knows who is right because our different news media on television, radio, and the internet present their opinions based on partisanship.

They refuse to use the perfect and inerrant guidelines left by the Creator. All of the nations in this world need to realize that there is but one Creator, but continue to present precepts after precepts based on what man believes to be true. There is but one precept which is presented by the Holy Father, the Bible. Man has developed various adherences that are based on their own spiritual beliefs.

The CIA's World Fact Book gives the world population as 7,021,836,029 (July 2012 est.) and the distribution of religions as Christian 33.39% (of which Roman Catholic 18.85%, Protestant 8.15%, Orthodox 4.96%, Anglican 1.26%), Muslim 22.74%, Hindu 10.8%, Buddhist 6.77%, Sikh 0.35%, Jewish 0.22%, Baha'i 0.11%, other religions 10.95%, non-religious 9.66%, atheists 2.01%. (2010 EST.).

These facts indicate there are many that don't know the Savior Jesus Christ. They may know about Christianity but choose other adherences of worship.

Isaiah prophesied about nations that do not adhere to God's ordinances. (Isaiah 30:1 NIV "Woe to the obstinate children, "declares the LORD, "to those who carry out plans that are not mine, forming an alliance, but not by my Spirit, heaping sin upon sin ;). Also, Isaiah's Judgment on Nations: Isaiah 34:1-3 NIV, 1 Come near, you nations, and listen; pay attention, you peoples! Let the earth hear, and all that is in it, the world, and all that comes out of it! 2 The LORD is angry with all nations; his wrath is on all their armies. He will totally destroy them; he will give them over to slaughter. 3 Their slain will be thrown out, their dead bodies will stink; the mountains will be soaked with their blood.

If you are troubled and have not made a commitment to the Savior, now is the time to place all of your confidence in Him (See John 14:1-4). If you don't know Jesus, it is not too late to learn of Him. After you have accepted Jesus as your Lord and Savior, stand strong and obedient in faith in Him. The following is an excerpt of the doctrine of faith from a sermon given by C.H. Spurgeon in 1889 at the Metropolitan Tabernacle, Newington: "The moment a sinner believes, and trusts in his crucified God, His pardon at once he receives, Redemption in full through his blood."

If we think we can wait until the last minute and ask for forgiveness like the penitent thief that was being crucified with Jesus, we are placing our salvation at a huge risk!

Matthew Henry's commentary of Luke 23 speaks of the penitent thief, and though Jesus was under tremendous suffering, was still humble: "Here was the other of them that was softened at the last. (In the gospels of Matthew 27:44 and Mark 15:32 state that the thieves, crucified with Jesus, reviled him. The gospel of Luke 23:39-43 ESV states that one criminal railed at Jesus and the other criminal rebuked him for his railing.) Matthew Henry continues, "This malefactor, when just ready to fall into the hands of Satan, was snatched as a brand out of the burning, and made a monument of divine mercy and grace, and Satan was left to roar as a lion disappointed of his prey. This gives no encouragement to any to put off their repentance to their death-bed, or to hope that then they shall find mercy; for, though it is certain that true repentance is never too late, it is as certain that late repentance is seldom true. None can be sure that they shall have time to repent at death, but every man may be sure that he cannot have the advantages that this penitent thief had, whose case was altogether extraordinary. He never had any offer of Christ, or day of grace, before now: he was designed to be made a singular instance of the power of Christ's grace now at a time when he was crucified in weakness. Christ, having conquered Satan in the destruction of Judas and the preservation of Peter, erects this further trophy of his victory over him in the conversion of this malefactor, as a specimen of what he would do."

# CHAPTER 6

# Blessed are Those Who Walk in the Holy Spirit

ONCE YOU HAVE MADE THE commitment to give yourself to Jesus, there is no need to worry about what is next with your life. Through prayer and supplication, you will be guided by the same Holy Spirit that Peter and others experienced at the Pentecost in the upper room. You will learn to "Walk in the Spirit" (See Galatians 5:16-26). When the "Spirit is in you, you will walk in the "Spirit". You don't have to wear religious jewelry or a sandwich board sign to make yourself identifiable as being in the "Spirit". The fruit produced by your walk is easily apprehended, according to the Apostle Paul, by love, joy, peace, longsuffering, gentleness, goodness, and faith (v. 25).

Christ's message as given to us In Matthew 7:1-6 is asking Christians not to judge, hypocritically, one another.

The Beatitudes of Jesus (blessings) are the divine conditions for His Kingdom as was given on the "Sermon on the Mount". This is the quintessential prosperity and perfect spiritual happiness of those who share in the salvation of the kingdom of God (See Matthew 5:1-12 ESV).

(v.3)Blessed are the poor in spirit, for theirs is the kingdom of heaven. (v.4)Blessed are they who mourn, for they shall be comforted. (v.5)Blessed are the meek, for they shall inherit the earth. (v.6)Blessed are they who hunger and thirst for righteousness, for they shall be satisfied. (v.7)Blessed are the merciful, for they shall obtain mercy.

(v.8)Blessed are the pure of heart, for they shall see God. (v.9)Blessed are the peacemakers, for they shall be called children of God. (v.10) Blessed are they who are persecuted for the sake of righteousness, for theirs is the kingdom of heaven. (v.11)Blessed are you when people insult you, persecute you and falsely say all kinds of evil against you because of me.

(v.12) Rejoice and be glad, because great is your reward in heaven, for in the same way they persecuted the prophets who were before you.

The blessings that Jesus gave in the "Beatitudes" are basically from OT wisdom passages from the New International Version translations:

> Job 5:17 "Blessed is the one whom God corrects; so do not despise the discipline of the Almighty.

> Psalms 1:1 blessed is the one, who does not walk in step with the wicked or stand in the way that sinners take or sit in the company of mockers.

> Psalms 32:1-2. 1 Blessed is the one whose transgressions are forgiven, whose sins are covered. 2 Blessed is the one whose sin the LORD does not count against them and in whose spirit is no deceit.

> Psalms 33:12. Blessed is the nation whose God is the LORD, the people he chose for his inheritance.

> Psalms 41:1. Blessed are those who have regard for the weak; the LORD delivers them in times of trouble.

> Psalms 106:3. Blessed are those who act justly, who always do what is right.

> Proverbs 8:34. Blessed are those who listen to me, watching daily at my doors, waiting at my doorway.

Proverbs 28:14. Blessed is the one who always trembles before God, but whoever hardens their heart falls into trouble.

Wouldn't it be a different world than what it is today if everyone knew that the peacemakers and the meek shall inherit the earth (Psalms 37:11)? If nations of the world (Even Islamic and Muslim) would open their eyes and ears to the word of God, wars, and fighting would cease. We could help an individual based on the way we carry ourselves being proof of God in us by the way we live, by the indwelling Holy Spirit. We don't want someone to say, "If that person is a Christian, then I don't want to be one".

Wars and fights come from lusting. If you lust for worldly things then you receive not the kingdom of God. Remember how Satan was kicked out of heaven for lusting for the power of God. So men kill during wars and in our everyday lives, wanting to possess something that is not theirs. This avariciousness causes families, businessmen, and nations to go after that which belongs to others. The incentive is to gain the most power. You cannot love the world and what it offers and also love God. James 4:4-6 AMP 4 You [are like] unfaithful wives [having illicit love affairs with the world and breaking your marriage vow to God]! Do you not know that being the world's friend is being God's enemy? So whoever chooses to be a friend of the world takes his stand as an enemy of God. 5 Or do you suppose that the Scripture is speaking to no purpose that says, The Spirit Whom He has caused to dwell in us yearns over us and He yearns for the Spirit [to be welcome] with a jealous love? 6 But He gives us more and more grace ([a]power of the Holy Spirit, to meet this evil tendency and all others fully). That is why He says, God sets Himself against the proud and haughty, but gives grace [continually] to the lowly (those who are humble enough to receive it).

We need a threefold healing, that is, of the spirit, soul, and mind. We must stop rejecting God's knowledge. Hosea, a prophet, who preached to the idolatrous people in the northern kingdom of Israel in the 8th BC century, spoke of God's love and compassion for them. To read of the sinful ways of the people during this time and not place a date on it, you would think that he is some modern day preacher here in America. (Hosea 4:1-11 NIV 1 Hear the word of the LORD, you Israelites (Americans), because the LORD has a charge to bring against you who live in the land: "There is no faithfulness, no love, and no acknowledgment of God in the land. 2 There is only cursing, lying and murder, stealing and adultery; they break all bounds, and bloodshed follows bloodshed. 3 Because of this the land dries up, and all who live in it waste away; the beasts of the field, the birds in the sky and the fish in the sea are swept away. 4 "But let no one bring a charge, let no one accuse another, for your people are like those who bring charges against a priest. 5 You stumble day and night, and the prophets stumble with you, so I will destroy your mother — 6 my people are destroyed from lack of knowledge. "Because you have rejected knowledge, I also reject you as my priests; because you have ignored the law of your God, I also will ignore your children. 7 The more priests there were, the more they sinned against me; they exchanged their glorious God for something disgraceful. 8 They feed on the sins of my people and relish their wickedness. 9 And it will be: Like people, like priests. I will punish both of them for their ways and repay them for their deeds. 10 "They will eat but not have enough; they will engage in prostitution but not flourish, because they have deserted the LORD to give themselves 11 to prostitution; old wine and new wine that takes away their understanding.

We need to do self-evaluations routinely and compare this with the word of God so that we can make the necessary changes in our lives with the guidance of the omnipotent Holy Spirit. By the prompting of the Holy Spirit, the focus of our lifestyle should be striving to do things that are pleasing to God. 1964 to the 1970s a management program called "Zero Defects" was utilized by many industries to eliminate defects in production. A quality control manager named Philip B. Crosby was credited for starting this program. Its goal was to strive to achieve the least amount of defective products. Those industries that implemented this program knew that not all production would be without defects. This is the same attitude that Christians should strive for in their lives to have zero sins.

The only person that walked this earth sinelessly was Jesus. This is the reason for the expression that when a Christians profess to be saved, "they don't become sinless but should sin less." The new covenant did away with trying to keep all of the laws that couldn't be kept anyway. Do we think that we no longer have to adhere to the Ten Commandments because of the new covenant? You can't just do anything you want to because of the new covenant.

Jesus' Sermon on the Mount can be thought of today as the issuance of a new covenant, but many biblical scholars have defined it according to the time frame of Jesus. The coming of Jesus to earth as a mortal man and dying for our sins is the "New Covenant", because before this happened; we had no way of directly coming to the Father. The Pharisees of the day were not exactly following and preaching the Judaic Law. They were doing, as some ministers are doing today, giving definition according to their own interpretation of righteousness. If they had not strayed so far away from the actual scripture and prophecy of the OT, they would have recognized that Jesus is the Messiah. Jesus was not taking away or adding to the Laws already in existence, He was merely clarifying and contrasting the Law in which the Pharisees and scribes had misrepresented, to make it suitable for their own self-righteousness. He states this in Matthew 5:17, that He was not trying to abolish the Law or the previous prophecies but to fulfill them.

It is not as if they were not being educated according to Judaic religious laws because the Apostle Paul was educated as a Pharisee as stated earlier and as was the custom of the Hebrews, he was educated by his mother until the age of five. His father taught him scriptures and such until age ten. Since the Bible tells us he was also a Roman citizen, He also was taught Greek and the Roman culture. This is revealed in Acts 21 when Paul was arrested for teaching in the temple (See Acts 21:37-39). At this point, Paul was sent to Jerusalem to attend a rabbinical school. In Jerusalem at that time, there were only seven teachers that had reached a status higher than rabbi called Rabban. A Rabban is defined in Hebrew as a mentor, master or teacher (term of address and title of respect for a person of higher rank than a rabbi).

It was stated earlier that Gamaliel was a teacher but he was also one of these seven such master teachers in Jerusalem that had a rabbinical school. Gamaliel was one of the most highly, honored persons in this position of his time. This is why Paul (his Hebrew name was Saul at this time, Paul was his Greek name after his conversion) was sent to Gamaliel to learn Judaic religious laws. The apostle Paul could at least speak in Aramaic, Greek, Hebrew, and perhaps Latin (See Acts 21:40 22:2 all versions). Some biblical translations state that the Apostle spoke to the crowd in Aramaic (See NIV, NLT, NET Bible, etc.) while other translations say that he spoke in Hebrew (See KJV, Holman Christian Standard Bible, ESV, etc.). The majority of scholars agree that Aramaic was native tongue of Galilee and Judea during the first century (Common Era or AD1). The best that I can conclude from what scholar commentaries say about these two verses is that he could speak in either Aramaic or Hebrew. The Aramaic language is a part of the Northwest Semitic group of languages which includes Hebrew and Phoenician.

The Pharisees should have seen signs of the coming of Jesus from all OT implications of Old Testament prophecies. But, their hearts were hardened because they wanted to continue in their own self-righteousness. Well, if they had accepted him, the prophecy would not have been fulfilled. So, the Pharisees were not practicing basically what they taught and preached.

John the Baptist was baptizing the people in the Jordan River as they were confessing their sins and repenting knew the ways of the religious leaders of the day and was at odds with their hypocritical ways. The Pharisees were supposed to be keeping the Law of Moses and the unwritten "tradition of the elders". The Sadducees were worldlier and politically minded and were a theologically unorthodox religious group that denied the resurrection, angels, and spirits. John the Baptist called them something different based on their actions. One day as he was at the Jordan river and saw the religious leaders heading his way, he described them as such in the gospel of Matthew 3:7 KJV 7 But when he saw many of the Pharisees and Sadducees come to his baptism, he said unto them, O generation of vipers, who hath warned you to flee from the wrath to come?

# CHAPTER 7

# Jesus Exposes the Hypocrisy of the Religious Organizations

JESUS WAS NOT CHANGING THE Laws as previously mentioned, but correcting the actions of what the people were seeing from the two major religious parties. At the Sermon on the Mount beginning in the book of Matthew Chapter 5-7, Jesus said several times (six).

"You have heard that it was said by them of old". What was being said by those of "old" was good, but far from being adhered to. So he was trying to reverse the damage that had already been done by the Pharisees and Sadducees. These groups were more interested in propitiating the Roman leaders than God.

Pontius Pilate was the governor of Roman Judaea and Herod was the tetrarch of Galilee (see Luke 3:1). Pilate was persuaded, against his will, by the Jewish authorities, to order the crucifixion of Jesus. Under Roman authority, according to NT gospels, the Jewish authorities could not sentence anyone to death. That was the reason they had to convince Pilate ordered the crucifixion of Jesus (See John 18:31). In order to accomplish this, they had to convince Pontius Pilate to believe that the spurious charges they presented were serious enough to have Jesus put to death. The ruling body in Israel at that time that brought charges against Jesus to Pontius Pilate was called the Sanhedrin. The Sanhedrin was the supreme council or court of the Jews. They indirectly got away with stoning a helper named Stephen who was one of seven ordained by the disciples chosen to help with daily distributions to widows. They incited a mob riot to stone this young man to death, who was full of faith and the Holy Spirit. They were not punished by the Roman authority for this death since it was not an official judgment by them. The Roman authority usually gave the Sanhedrin sovereignty and authority probably because they were the judges of religious matters for the people of Israel (See Acts 6 and 7).

The Sanhedrin was comprised of 70 men, plus the high priest, who served as its president. The members came from the chief priests, scribes, and elders. The selection process is not known. The origin is traced back to the formation of the tribunal elders that Moses selected in Numbers 11:16-17 ESV 16 Then the LORD said to Moses, "Gather for me seventy men of the elders of Israel, whom you know to be the elders of the people and officers over them, and bring them to the tent of meeting, and let them take their stand there with you. 17 And I will come down and talk with you there. And I will take some of the Spirit that is on you and put it on them, and they shall bear the burden of the people with you, so that you may not bear it yourself alone. This tribunal of seventy is thought of as only being temporary to resolve the wilderness journey problems. Once the Israelites entered into Canaan-the Promised Land, it seemed to have dissolved.

The land referred to as Canaan in the OT is the modern day territory of Lebanon, Israel, Palestinian territories, the western part of Jordan and southwestern Syria. There were Jewish councils formed to administer the law as in II Chronicles 19:8 ESV Moreover, in Jerusalem Jehoshaphat appointed certain Levites and priests and heads of families of Israel, to give judgment for the LORD and to decide disputed cases. They had their seat at Jerusalem. Some Biblical scholars contend that there is no further historical correlation between the two parties of the seventy elders in Moses time and the New Testament Jewish Sanhedrin council.

Most of the precepts that Jesus taught during the Sermon on the Mount were against the hypocrisy of the religious groups. One that bears interpretation based on the laws of the OT and presented to us in the sermon is about "Swearing". This has nothing to do at this time with using profane laced language. But both definitions are about the tongue. All Christians are called upon to renounce evil because God wants all to be more like Christ. As such, Christians should not lie to one another: Colossians 3:9 ESV Do not lie to one another, seeing that you have put off the old self with its practices. Jesus urged integrity in all human speech. Christians are not to misuse the name of the Lord. Jesus elaborates on the seventh Commandment from the OT concerning oath-taking during his teaching on the Mount (Exodus 20:7). We see this again in Leviticus 19:12, there is no contrast in what Jesus taught and the OT; He is merely validating what was already the law. Let's look at two versions Matthew 5:33-37 ESV where Jesus is saying make sure your commitments and assertions are honest and truthful, therefore you shouldn't have to swear to make or take an oath. 33 "Again you have heard that it was said to those of old, 'you shall not swear falsely, but shall perform to the Lord what you have sworn.' 34 But I say to you, do not take an oath at all, either by heaven, for it is the throne of God, 35 or by the earth, for it is his footstool, or by Jerusalem, for it is the city of the great King. 36 And do not take an oath by your head, for you cannot make one hair white or black. 37 Let what you say be simply 'Yes' or 'No'; anything more than this comes from evil.

James, one of the four brothers of Jesus and the leader of the church in Jerusalem after the death of Jesus, has a verse in the Bible similar to Matthew 5:37. (James 5:12 ESV But above all, my brothers, do not swear, either by heaven or by earth or by any other oath, but let your "yes "be yes and your "no "be no, so that you may not fall under condemnation.) What James has reiterated here about making oaths is not the condemnation of a solemn oath like the one God made to Abraham. What He says is, condemnation to swearing on an oath, is the disrespectful use of God's name or any sacred objects to give assurance or credibility to what has been spoken. On superficial examination of the OT scripture versus the NT scripture, there seems to be a conflict but it is not. This is because, in the OT, even God swore oaths at useful times. The key word here is "useful" because the OT recognized that oaths could be beneficial when used at the proper time and situation. God assigned the rainbow as his covenant to mankind that He would not destroy flesh on the earth with global flooding again. From Noah on, the rainbow became a sign of God's faithfulness to His word, His promises, and His Noahic Covenant. God is not reminded of the covenant by seeing the rainbow on occasions. He remembers because He is God, the creator of the rainbow. It is He that causes this phenomenon of an arc formed in the sky. Only God can cause this multicolored arc of reflected, refracted and dispersion of light in water droplets resulting in a covenant reminder. He wants a covenant to tell us that it is something we can build hope on top of.

God makes an oath of retribution for the disobedient Israelites: Joshua 5:6 ESV For the people of Israel walked forty years in the wilderness, until all the nation, the men of war who came out of Egypt, perished, because they did not obey the voice of the LORD; the LORD swore to them that he would not let them see the land that the LORD had sworn to their fathers to give to us, a land flowing with milk and honey. Oath to King David: Psalms 89:3-4, 35 ESV 3 You have said, "I have made a covenant with my chosen one; I have sworn to David my servant: 4 'I will establish your offspring forever, and build your throne for all generations. 'Selah. 35 Once for all I have sworn by my holiness; I will not lie to David. For more "oaths" in the OT see: Isaiah 45:23 (apostle Paul quotes this verse in Romans 14:11), and Jeremiah 22:5. There may be more oaths, so this list is not complete on the subject of oaths made by God in the OT.

In the book of Hebrews chapter 6:13, there is reference to the promise God made to Abraham in the OT Genesis 22:16-18 ESV 16 and said, "By myself I have sworn, declares the LORD, because you have done this and have not withheld your son, your only son, 17 I will surely bless you, and I will surely multiply your offspring as the stars of heaven and as the sand that is on the seashore. And your offspring shall possess the gate of his enemies, 18 and in your offspring shall all the nations of the earth be blessed, because you have obeyed my voice. "Hebrews 13:6 ESV For when God made a promise to Abraham, since he had no one greater by whom to swear, he swore by himself.

The superiority of God relative to man means that no one else is at His level to validate an oath, so He swore by Himself. God knew since the disobedience of Adam and Eve in the garden that man is predisposed to be untrustworthy. Man, himself, knows that other men have a propensity to not keep an oath. For this reason, it is expected in the normal order of events, man swears to make his promise seem valid. For God to swear on an oath, He had to look at man's weakened condition and voluntarily descended from His level of authority in relation to the much inferior man's level. God did this so that His trustworthiness and dependability is greatly magnified many times over to man. God cannot lie nor can He break a promise. God is summum verum – the highest truth, there is none higher.

It was mentioned earlier that the Jewish council that wanted Jesus put to death was called the Sanhedrin and were comprised of seventy men and a high priest. The High Priest that conspired with the chief priests, scribes, and the elders to accuse Jesus of blasphemy and have Him crucified was Caiaphas. Initially, during the trial, Jesus refused to speak and remained silent as charges were brought forth against Him. Caiaphas then said to Jesus "I adjure you…, adjure means I command you to answer under oath. Matthew 26:62-65 ESV 62 And the high priest stood up and said, "Have you no answer to make? What is it that these men testify against you?" 63 But Jesus remained silent. And the high priest said to him, "I adjure you by the living God, tell us if you are the Christ, the Son of God." 64 Jesus said to him, "You have said so. But I tell you, from now on you will see the Son of Man seated at the right hand of Power and coming on the clouds of heaven." 65 Then the high priest tore his robe and said, "He has uttered blasphemy. What further witnesses do we need? You have now heard his blasphemy.

So in civil matters such as a courtroom, oath for an official position, weddings, etc., an excerpt from Matthew Henry's commentary on Matthew 5:33-37 offers this commentary: That we must not swear at all, but when we are duly called to it, and justice or charity to our brother, or respect to the commonwealth, make it necessary for the end of strife, of which necessity the civil magistrate is ordinarily to be the judge. We may be sworn, but we must now swear; we may be adjured, and so obliged to it, but we must not thrust ourselves upon it for our own worldly advantage. (Never swear on unimportant or trivial matters). Hebrews 6:16-18 ESV 16 For people swear by something greater than themselves, and in all their disputes an oath is final for confirmation. 17 So when God desired to show more convincingly to the heirs of the promise the unchangeable character of his purpose, he guaranteed it with an oath, 18 so that by two unchangeable things, in which it is impossible for God to lie, we who have fled for refuge might have strong encouragement to hold fast to the hope set before us.

## Alternative to Swearing an oath in court

Some Christians refuse to be sworn in at a courthouse based on their religious belief. Quakers believe in speaking the truth at all times, therefore, refuse to swear to an oath. In the past, this kept Quakers from holding any public office. If a person refuses to take a sworn oath, he or she can take an "Affirmation". By the law concerning an affirmation, a solemn declaration is allowed to those who conscientiously object to taking an oath. An affirmation has exactly the same legal effect as an oath, but is usually taken to avoid the religious implications of an oath; it is thus legally binding but not considered a religious oath. Some religious minorities hold beliefs that allow them to make legally binding promises, but forbid them to swear an oath before God. Additionally, many decline to make a religious oath because they feel that to do so would be valueless or even inappropriate, especially in secular courts. In some jurisdictions, an affirmation may only be given if such a reason is provided.

If you are unsure as to when it is inappropriate to swear on an oath or if you feel swearing is rebelling, forsaking, or abandoning what you believe about God's Word (apostasy), under any circumstances, then you should make an attempt to explain why you can't. The government, in many cases, has no concern about your salvation and many laws take no consideration on whether it is Holy or Unholy within the precepts of the scripture.

How many people are there who have taken an oath in the court room, placed their hands on the Holy Bible, and lied to benefit their own agenda? How many politicians are there who have lied under oath? If someone has taken an oath to tell the truth in a court of law and it is discovered that person has lied, then a criminal offense called perjury has been committed. For example, if a U.S. politician takes an oath to tell the truth during a United States congressional hearing or federal court and is caught deliberately lying, then that person has committed perjury which is a felony. The U.S. code concerning this perjury offense is taken very seriously and carries a punishment of maybe up to five years of imprisonment. How many athletes are there who have sworn under oath about not taking illegal substances? Even the ancient Greeks tried dietary methods to enhance their athletic potency. Modern athletes are informed of banned substances that they should not use and take an oath written and verbally. They are randomly tested for compliance. Anabolic steroids used for performance-enhancement is the most common banned substance. Track and field athletes were the first to take an oath for performance-enhancing drugs. Professional racehorses are tested for performance-enhancing drugs and the owners are responsible for the oath given for compliance.

Whether it is an oath or not, God commandment tells us we shouldn't lie under any circumstances. The government seems to be apathetic toward implementing Christian precepts to the populace. It becomes very important for the churches to make the populace knowledgeable about God's laws. In the book of Hosea of the OT, the prophet of the same name said the Israelites were not receiving religious instructions the priests. The priests were supposed to be the primary caretaker of the law for the Israelites. The Israelites lifestyle was similar to the idolatrous Canaanites because their priests were not providing any guidance. As a spokesman for God, the prophet, Hosea spoke out against the priests for not providing religious guidance. According to Hosea, the priests blamed the people and the people blamed the priests for their apostasy (Hosea 4).

Christian believers think that Bibles should be allowed in schools. This seems to pose a terrible problem for atheists and secularists.

The atheists and the secularists declare that if the Bible is allowed in schools then their non-Christian material should be allowed. This caused school systems such as the ones in Orange County Florida in 2015 to ban bibles because of the atheists. Because the word "God" was not used anywhere in the writings of the United States Constitution, we are now left with the separation of church and state. This fact is deemed important to non-Christian factions. They contend since "God" was not used in the Federal Constitution the country does not belong under God's care as believers think it should. There are eight states that have the word "God" in the preamble to their state constitutions. "Almighty God" appears in the preamble of 30 state constitutions. This is the reason the question was asked earlier, should God bless America? If the apostle Paul could write an epistle to America right now, he would wonder why we haven't progressed to eating solid spiritual food instead of still being on spiritual milk. It is as if we are regressing in spiritual maturity as far as the government is concerned.

God has blessed America, but how long will He continue due to our disobedience? The pastors in the churches of American are praying in the spirit, for a revival of Christian values in a political America. I don't consider the Declaration as a Religious document but the beginning of paragraph two has religious connotations: "We hold these truths to be self-evident, that all men are created equal, that they are endowed by their Creator with certain unalienable Rights that among these are Life, Liberty and the pursuit of Happiness."

America has been a light to the world of darkness. It is an accomplishment God smiled on. We were first in everything in the world such as manufacturing, technology, finance, medicine, etc. We are letting Satan make communist, non-Christian countries such as China move ahead of us. We are failing to recognize that we need God more than ever now. He called us to obey His Word from the beginning to the end. We need to be a country that continues to delight in Him.

If we loved each other as Jesus loves us then a multitude of our sins would be covered by the new covenant. We can't do that as a world because we still have multiple wars going on in the world all the time.

God has allocated two chapters in the Bible by the major prophet, Ezekiel, (Ezekiel 38-39) prophesying a major irreversible war after Israel has re-gathered in her land as a nation. Some Biblical scholars call this prophetic battle the battle of Armageddon (Armageddon in prophecy depicts the location of armies gathered for a battle during the end times. Armageddon is also used generically to refer to any end of the world situation) or a major war before the Armageddon. Armageddon is described in The Book of Revelations (Revelations 16:16), which coincides with the second coming of Christ (Rev 16:15), as the final and decisive battle of good and evil on earth. The Bible says the Messiah will return to earth and defeat the Antichrist, (the beast) and Satan the Devil in the Battle of Armageddon(Rev 19:11-21) Then Satan will be put into the "bottomless pit" or abyss for 1,000 years, known as the Millennium. After being released from the abyss, Satan will gather Gog and Magog from the four corners of the earth. They will encamp surrounding the "Holy Ones" and the beloved city, Jerusalem. Fire will come down from God, out of heaven and devour the instrument of evil called Gog and Magog. The Devil, death, hell, and those not found written in the Book of Life are then thrown into Gehenna (the lake of fire burning with brimstone).

# CHAPTER 8

# Apostacy in the Christian Churches

ACCORDING TO THE PEW FORUM on Religion and Public Life December 18, 2012, there are approximately 2.2 billion Christians (32% of the world population) in the world. That makes it the largest religion in the world by far. But in the United States, Christianity is most definitely in decline.

Nations are going up against nations and continually in a war over seemingly irresolvable issues. The disciples of Jesus had heard him prophesying of the doom to come and they really got interested. So when they got a chance with Him alone on the Mount of Olives, they inquired of Him these things known as the Olivet Discourse in the parallel Gospels of Matthew, Mark, and Luke. Matthew writes more about these discourses than the other two parallel Gospels. Jesus told them that the temple in Jerusalem, that they thought was so magnificent, would be destroyed. In 70 A.D. the Romans burned it completely down. The Olivet discourse is the last of the Five Discourses of Matthew and is about the seven-year tribulation period and the second coming of Christ at the end of the tribulation. During that time, God will complete His chastisement and purification of Israel and judge the entire world.

*Jesus first warns them about things that would happen that should not be interpreted as signs: Some would claim to be Christ, most likely, Antichrist. It was a general belief that if the Jewish Messiah arrived in Jerusalem, it would mean that the Kingdom of Heaven was imminent.

It is a shame that we can't all adhere to the "Word of God". People are falling into the trap that the adversary Satan has prepared. There is nothing about the Word that is not advantageous for all. The main reason that people, who don't like the Word, hate it is that they don't want to follow the course it presents. They prefer to stay with fleshly and worldly things. The Apostle Paul's epistle to the church at Ephesus warns them to prepare for Satan's schemes. Satan is not human but he uses human beings to carry out his evil. He describes Christians as needing to don the facsimile of equipment that he saw used by Roman soldiers that he came in contact with while in prison to battle the spiritual powers of evil: Ephesians 6:10-13 ESV 10 Finally, be strong in the Lord and in the strength of his might. 11 Put on the whole armor of God that you may be able to stand against the schemes of the devil. 12 For we do not wrestle against flesh and blood, but against the rulers, against the authorities, against the cosmic powers over this present darkness, against the spiritual forces of evil in the heavenly places. 13 Therefore take up the whole armor of God that you may be able to withstand in the evil day, and having done all, to stand firm.

We have our polarized congressmen in the Whitehouse being utilized by Satan lying and criticizing each other. They are proposing wars that will benefit them without thinking of the mourning of parents, who might lose their sons or daughters. They may argue about globing warming which is caused by too much carbon dioxide in the atmosphere. Carbon dioxide in the atmosphere traps heat that would, otherwise, escape from the planet. Companies that flare off various chemicals in the atmosphere say it is too costly to upgrade equipment to control toxic releases. Whether burning fossil fuels increases climate change is debatable, it is known that toxic chemicals released, at high concentration, into the atmosphere or ground is definitely the cause of health hazards to humans and animals causing respiratory illness, cancer, deformities, etc...

It is more about the profitability of the shareholders and the Chief Executive Officers (CEOs) than the people suffering the consequences of governmental allowances of these practices. They hide behind democracy and propose they are preserving it. Bipartisan politicians receive kickbacks from lobbyists such as the National Rifle Association and don't seem to care much about the mass killings of innocent children at schools. We shouldn't label these people heroes. The real heroes are those individuals who place their faith in God and go on mission trips around the world sometimes to places where the mention of Christianity is forbidden. They are carrying out the Great Commission (See Matthew 28:16-20). The heroes are those who have a national voice and still express, by their principles and actions, faith in Christ. We must keep the faith in that which we cannot see (Hebrews 11:1-2).

God's assessment of man in Psalms 14 succinctly points out that none are righteous and that none seek after Him. (Psalms 14:1-2 NIV 1The fool says in his heart, "There is no God." They are corrupt, their deeds are vile; there is no one who does well. 2 The LORD looks down from heaven on all mankind to see if there is any who understand, any who seek God. The apostle Paul reiterated this statement from Psalms in Romans 3:10 NIV as it is written: "There is no one righteous, not even one."

After the death of the Messiah, there were false prophets that renounced the teachings of the true Word of God. Today, Christians are holding revivals, crusades, etc. to ameliorate apostasy in America. We no longer live under the "Law" but by the new covenant. That is why the Pharisees and the Sadducees brought charges against Jesus because they wanted to continue to claim their righteousness in the old covenant of the Mosaic Law. The old covenant was not perfect. All of the blood and gore in the Old Testament, all of the blood sacrifices did not allow for intimate and direct communion with God.

Approximately one year after the Israelites left captivity in Egypt [being delivered by God] on their wilderness journey to the Promised Land, they constructed a tabernacle. This was done so that they could make sacrifices for the atonement of their sins to God through the high priests. These instructions for the priests are given to us in the third book of the Old Testament, Leviticus (instructions for priest and worship), and the part of the OT which is called the Pentateuch (first five books of the OT). The authorship of the Pentateuch is attributed to Moses. Chapters 1-5 of Leviticus are about how the Israelites were to make five different atonement offerings to God which was overseen by the appointed priests for people could not communicate directly with God:

1.  They made a "Burnt Offering" which was the burning of an animal from the herd or flock. This animal should be without defect. Leviticus Chapter 1

2.  "Grain Offering", the only bloodless offering and it accompanied the "Burnt Offering". This was made of a grain or finely milled flour. A handful was sprinkled on the fire along with the burning of the "Burnt Offering" and the rest was baked without yeast for the priests to eat with the "Burnt Offering" at their holy meal. Leviticus 2

3.  "Peace Offering" this was also an unblemished male or female animal from the herd sacrificed to symbolize peace between God and the people as well as inward peace. Leviticus 3

4.  "Sin Offering" was unintentional sins committed by the anointed priests, the whole Israelite community, the leader, or a member of the Israelite community. A Young bull without defect was used for this offering. Leviticus 4.

5.  "Guilt Offering" any wrongdoing against God. Lev 5: 15 NIV "When anyone is unfaithful to the LORD by sinning unintentionally in regard to any of the LORD 's holy things, they are to bring to the LORD as a penalty a ram from the flock, one without defect and of the proper value in silver, according to the sanctuary shekel. It is a guilt offering.

From the Glo Bible Study Text: The inner part of the tabernacle was reserved for the priests, who kept up the order in the Holy place. The innermost part, the Holy of Holies was the place where God's glory dwelt and only the high priest was allowed to go in there to make atonement, which was a picture of Christ who made one final atonement on the cross.

I was looking at a dictionary word knowledge game and I came across the word "Umbra" which stated that it is a shadowy apparition, as of someone or something not physically present. That is what the law of the Old Testament was. It can also be said that the Old Testament is a shadow of the coming of Jesus Christ. Thus, I thought of this verse while doing the dictionary definition game: Hebrews 10:1 NIV 1 The law is only a shadow of the good things that are coming—not the realities themselves. For this reason, it can never, by the same sacrifices repeated endlessly year after year, make perfect those who draw near to worship.

# CHAPTER 9

# The Old Covenant Revealing Sin as was Given to Moses

THE OLD COVENANT LAW IN the OT was an imperfect and faint representation of the new covenant brought forth by Jesus Christ. The Israelites needed the old covenant laws to reveal to them how sinful they had become. Jehovah was the primary God that the Hebrews worshiped throughout history. While in captivity, many worshiped the ten gods of the Egyptians along with Jehovah. So you can say that they practiced polytheism. The number ten is a significant number in biblical numerology. It represents a fullness of quantity. Ten Egyptian Plagues Means Completely Plagued. Just as the "Ten Commandments" become symbolic of the fullness of the moral law of God, the ten ancient plagues of Egypt represent the fullness of God's expression of justice and judgments, upon those who refuse to repent. God gave Moses the old covenant laws to educate the Israelites to the fact that He, indeed, was the true and only God as they embarked on their wilderness journey. They had been enslaved and oppressed in Egypt.

Moses was the greatest of all the OT prophets. He was given the 10 commandments written on two stone tablets with the finger of Almighty God. He is the only prophet in the OT that communicated directly with God. Other prophets received messages from God through visions and dreams. By God's instructions, He caused Moses to be directly responsible, eventually, for the establishment of the nation of Israel. Even though Moses, who was Hebrew, was adopted and reared by an Egyptian princess. This happened because, the Hebrews who were brought to Egypt by Joseph, son of Jacob, had favor with the Pharaoh of his time and allowed him to bring his family there. The contemporary Pharaoh of Joseph not only allowed Joseph to bring his family but he also gave them the best land in Egypt in the land of Goshen. The Easton Bible Dictionary says that Goshen has been identified with the modern Wady Tumilat, lying between the eastern part of the Delta and the west border of Palestine. Scholars are not really sure if this is the correct location so they are divided (Genesis 47:11).

Moses was an ancestor of these Hebrews. Four hundred years had passed in Egypt when Moses was born. In that course of time, there were many other Pharaohs. The Pharaoh of Moses time was not aware of what Joseph had done and had no respect for these descendants of Joseph. So he forced them into slave labor so that he could subdue and suppress them. The Hebrew slaves built two cities, Pithom and Rameses (Rameses is also known as Goshen (Genesis 47:27). The population of Hebrews in Egypt had grown so large that he was alarmed and afraid of them. He figured since he had been so cruel to them that if Egypt was attacked by another country, the Hebrews would join that country in rebellion against Egypt.

The Pharaoh informed two Hebrew midwives, Puah and Shiphrah, who delivered Hebrew babies, to kill the male babies in an attempt to control the Hebrew population. It is estimated that the original seventy that Joseph bought to Egypt had grown to over 2 million. He knew that women did not go to war and males would be capable of going to war against him. In some modern nations, it is not considered a social disgrace for women to join a military branch and might be sent to war. But there are some that might oppose, but in the United States, it is the law that women can join the military.

Midwives, Puah and Shiphrah, feared God and did not carry out the Pharaoh's order to kill the male babies. Perhaps Pharaoh had ordered that he was to be kept informed on the progress of the midwives. Pharaoh found out that the male babies were being spared so he called the women into his court and asked them why? They told him that the Hebrew women were unlike the Egyptian women and were having babies faster than the two of them could keep up with. During this period of time an Israelite woman named Jochebed, who was married to her nephew Amram, gave birth to a baby boy whom they named Moses. Moses was their third child; they had a young daughter named Miriam and another three-year-old boy named Aaron. She was able to conceal the baby Moses in their house for three months. When Jochebed felt like they could no longer conceal the baby from being murdered, she placed the baby in a waterproof basket and lowered him into the Nile River and left to go back home. Miriam had accompanied her mother to the Nile but did not leave with her. She lingered a distance back from the bank of the river where nobody could see her, to see what would happen to the baby Moses.

God's plan allowed for Pharaoh's daughter to come to the river to take a bath where she spotted the basket floating there. A slave girl had accompanied Pharaoh's daughter down to the river so she ordered her to retrieve the basket. When the basket was retrieved and brought to her, she discovered baby Moses inside. She knew that her father had commanded that Hebrew baby boys were to be killed, so she reckoned this was a Hebrew baby. Miriam came out from hiding and came upon the princess and asked her, "Do you want me to help you with this baby by getting a Hebrew woman to breastfeed him?" The princess was sympathetic toward the baby and agreed to Miriam's proposal. Miriam went back home to her mother and told what had happened to the baby. So Jochebed went down to the river and offered her services. The princess accepted the offer immediately. You might think this was a coincidence but it was all in God's plan.

When Moses had become old enough and had been weaned, Jochebed took the boy to the princess who adopted him. Moses' Egyptian education cannot be biblically substantiated, but he must have received the best there was to offer to be the son of the princess. Somehow, when Moses became older, God revealed to him that the princess did not birth him but he was birthed by a Hebrew woman. Out of curiosity, he often went out of the luxury of the royal palace and into the streets to learn about the people of his heritage. He saw the oppression his people were going through and was very dismayed. One day he saw an isolated place where a Hebrew slave was being beaten by an Egyptian slave master. He looked around to see if anyone else was around. When he thought there was no one else around but the Hebrew slave, the slave master, and himself, he killed the slave master and buried him.

The next day, Moses went back near the site where he had killed the Egyptian. There he saw two Israelites fighting with each other. He was again dismayed, because of the two Hebrews doing violence to each other. He thought, "Don't they experience enough violence from the Egyptians, why impose this on each other?" He attempted to interpose with the two fighters, they rebuked him saying, "And how can you judge us? How can you be a mediator when we observed you killing the Egyptian yesterday? Are you going to kill us too?" Their confession scared him because he thought no one had seen his crime. Moses then started thinking that his grandfather by adoption, Pharaoh, would find out about the murder and severely chastises him, so he fled from Egypt to the land of Midian.

In that land, he found a Midianite woman named Zipporah and married her. His father-in-law, named Reuel, was also a priest in the land. Reuel's personal name means "friend of God". Elsewhere in the Bible he is called Jethro which means "excess" or "superiority" (Exodus 3:1). As Moses was tending the flock of sheep on the mountain at Horeb, he saw a bush burning out of the ordinary. Most likely Moses had seen bushes burn before in the hot wilderness region, but this one was different because the other bushes would eventually be consumed by the fire, but not this one. It continually burned without being consumed which caused his curiosity to become greatly heightened. He wondered what kind of marvel is this, I must investigate. He started moving closer to the burning bush and God called to him from the midst of the bush. (Exodus 3:3-8 ESV 3 and Moses said, "I will turn aside to see this great sight, why the bush is not burned." 4 When the

LORD saw that he turned aside to see, God called to him out of the bush, "Moses, Moses!" And he said, "Here I am." 5 Then he said, "Do not come near; take your sandals off your feet, for the place on which you are standing is holy ground." 6 And he said, "I am the God of your father, the God of Abraham, the God of Isaac, and the God of Jacob." And Moses hid his face, for he was afraid to look at God. 7 Then the LORD said, "I have surely seen the affliction of my people who are in Egypt and have heard their cry because of their taskmasters. I know their sufferings, 8 and I have come down to deliver them out of the hand of the Egyptians and to bring them up out of that land to a good and broad land, a land flowing with milk and honey, to the place of the Canaanites, the Hittites, the Amorites, the Perizzites, the Hivites, and the Jebusites.

God sympathized with the affliction Pharaoh had placed on the Israelites while in Egypt. God had heard their groans (Exodus 3:7-8). He commanded Moses to go back to Egypt and make a demand for Pharaoh to set the Israelites free so that they could worship their one and only true God. Moses made five excuses on why he was not the man for the task. He made two in Exodus 3 and three more in Exodus 4 and he was rebuked each time by God.

> Excuse 1: Exodus 3:10-12 ESV 10 Come, I will send you to Pharaoh that you may bring my people, the children of Israel, out of Egypt." 11 But Moses said to God, "Who am I that I should go to Pharaoh and bring the children of Israel out of Egypt?" 12 He said, "But I will be with you, and this shall be the sign for you, that I have sent you: when you have brought the people out of Egypt, you shall serve God on this mountain."

> Excuse 2: Exodus 3:13-14 ESV 13 Then Moses said to God, "If I come to the people of Israel and say to them, 'The God of your fathers has sent me to you, 'and they ask me, 'What is his name? 'What shall I say to them?" 14 God said to Moses, "I AM WHO I AM." And he

said, "Say this to the people of Israel, I AM 'has sent me to you.'"

Excuse 3: Exodus 4:1-3 ESV 1 Then Moses answered, "But behold, they will not believe me or listen to my voice, for they will say, 'The LORD did not appear to you.'" 2 The LORD said to him, "What is that in your hand? "He said, "A staff." 3 And he said, "Throw it on the ground. "So he threw it on the ground, and it became a serpent, and Moses ran from it.

Excuse 4: Exodus 4:10-12 ESV 10 but Moses said to the LORD, "Oh, my Lord, I am not eloquent, either in the past or since you have spoken to your servant, but I am slow of speech and of tongue." 11 Then the LORD said to him, "Who has made man's mouth? Who makes him mute, or deaf, or seeing, or blind? Is it not I, the LORD? 12 now therefore go, and I will be with your mouth and teach you what you shall speak."

Excuse 5: Exodus 4:13-17 ESV 13 But he said, "Oh, my Lord, please send someone else." 14 Then the anger of the LORD was kindled against Moses and he said, "Is there not Aaron, your brother, the Levite? I know that he can speak well. Behold, he is coming out to meet you, and when he sees you, he will be glad in his heart. 15 You shall speak to him and put the words in his mouth, and I will be with your mouth and with his mouth and will teach you both what to do. 16 He shall speak for you to the people, and he shall be your mouth, and you shall be as God to him. 17 And take in your hand this staff, with which you shall do the signs."

Moses was not excused from God's command, so he left the land of Midian and went back to Egypt. Moses approached his father-in-law and asked for his permission to return to Egypt with his wife Zipporah and their two sons Gershon and Eliezer. Gershon was the oldest. On the way back to Egypt, he and his wife and sons stayed at a lodge. The Bible does not clearly state that Moses had been circumcised up to this point. Moses's son, Gershon, had not been circumcised at this time either. It was customary for eight days old Hebrew baby boys to be circumcised which was an ancient Hebrews covenant practice started with Abraham. This covenant was made to Abraham and all of his descendants to be kept forever by all the generations of Hebrews (See Genesis 17:9-14).

Something baffling and very strange happened while Moses and his wife and sons were staying at an inn (inn–Hebrew, "a halting place for the night") on the way to Egypt. God decided to kill Moses. The reason it was so strange is the fact that God had communed with Moses on Mt. Sinai and had gone through the burning bush episode and had given Moses powerful signs (See Exodus 4). While Moses was giving all the objections or excuses why he shouldn't go back, God rebuked him each time with provisions He would make for each excuse. He could have killed Moses right then and there for making excuses not to return to Egypt. Moses had agreed to go back to Egypt, had gotten the permission from his father-in-law and just all of a sudden God decides to kill him. Was it, perhaps, because he had not been circumcised? Zipporah must have known about the Hebrew covenant because she took a sharp flint knife and quickly circumcised Gershon and she took the foreskin and placed it on Moses's feet. Exodus 4:24-25 ESV 24 at a lodging place on the way the LORD met him and sought to put him to death. 25 Then Zipporah took a flint and cut off her son's foreskin and touched Moses 'feet with it and said, "Surely you are a bridegroom of blood to me!"

She then presumably simulated a circumcision of her husband by touching him with his son's foreskin. The mention of feet is no doubt a euphemism. After Zipporah had done this, God left him alone. He sent his wife and sons back to Midian to her father and he continued to Egypt alone. Some interpretations state that God wanted to kill Moses because Moses had not circumcised his son.

Matthew Henry's commentary on the matter:

I. How God met him in anger, v. 24–26. This is a very difficult passage of story; much has been written, and excellently written, to make it intelligible; we will try to make it improving. Here is,

1. The sin of Moses, which was neglecting to circumcise his son. This was probably the effect of his being unequally yoked with a Midianite, who was too indulgent of her child, while Moses was too indulgent of her... We have needed to watch carefully over our own hearts, lest fondness for any relation prevail above our love to God, and take us off from our duty to him. It is charged upon Eli that he honoured his sons more than God (1 Sa. 2:29); and see Mt. 10:37... Even good men are apt to cool in their zeal for God and duty when they have long been deprived of the society of the faithful: solitude has its advantages, but they seldom counterbalance the loss of Christian communion.

2. God's displeasure against him. He met him, and, probably by a sword in an angel's hand, sought to kill him. This was a great change; very lately God was conversing with him, and lodging a trust in him, as a friend; and now he is coming forth against him as an enemy.... Omissions are sins, and must come into judgment, and particularly the contempt and neglect of the seals of the covenant; for it is a sign that we undervalue the promises of the covenant, and are displeased with the conditions of it. He that has made a bargain, and is not willing to seal and ratify it, one may justly suspect, neither likes it nor designs to stand to it. (2.) God takes notice of, and is much displeased with, the sins of his own people. If they neglect their duty, let them expect to hear of it by their consciences, and perhaps to feel from it by cross providences: for this cause many are sick and weak, as some think Moses was here.

The exact reason cannot be stated here because any reason would be conjecture from limited scriptural information on this subject. The conjecture may not be accurate. God alerted Moses brother, Aaron, to meet him in the desert. They met, hugged and kissed, and Moses told him all of the miracles God wanted him them to perform in Egypt while negotiating for the release of enslaved Israelites from pharaoh.

Even though the Israelites were highly disliked by the Egyptian, they wanted their slave labor. God deliberately hardened Pharaoh's heart to Moses proposition so that he would be able to demonstrate to the Israelites His power, and the truth of His Word. He wanted them to remember and commemorate, for generations to come, His supernatural abilities to free them from Pharaoh's bondage.

Ten times God, through Moses, allows Pharaoh to change his mind, repent, and turn to the one true God, each time increasing the severity of the consequence of the plagues suffered for disobedience to His request. Ten times Pharaoh, because of pride, refuses to be taught by the Lord, and receives "judgments" through the plagues, pronounced upon his head from Moses, the deliverer. The ten plagues were placed on Pharaoh because his heart was hardened about releasing the Israelites from bondage. God informed Moses that He would place the tenth and last plague on Pharaoh. It hasn't been mentioned before, but pharaoh was a title meaning "great house" for the ancient kings of Egypt. Every pharaoh, during this period of time, had five "great names" which they would take on themselves as they moved up high in office to the status of king. It was thought of as not being polite to use all five names, thus the king was just called Pharaoh. It is believed by some that the king (pharaoh) Moses had the conflict with was Rameses II based on Exodus 1:11.

God brought down on Pharaoh and Egypt a plague for each of the 10 gods that they worshipped:

| EGYPTIAN PLAGUE | EGYPTIAN GOD |
|---|---|
| 1. Water Turned to Blood | *Hapi*- Egyptian God of the Nile |
| 2. Frogs coming from the Nile River | *Heket*- Egyptian Goddess of Fertility, Water, Renewal |

| | |
|---|---|
| 3. Lice from the dust of the earth | *Geb*- God of the Earth |
| 4. Swarms of Flies | *Khepri*- Egyptian God of creation, movement of the Sun, and rebirth |
| 5. Death of Cattle and Livestock | *Hathor*-Goddess of Love and Protection |
| 6. Ashes turned to Boils and Sores | *Isis*- Goddess of Medicine and Peace |
| 7. Hail rained down in the form of fire | *Nut* –Goddess of the Sky |
| 8. Locusts sent from the sky | *Seth*- God of Storms and Disorder |
| 9. Three Days of Complete Darkness | *Ra*- The Sun God |
| 10. Death of the Firstborn | *Pharaoh*- The Ultimate Power of Egypt |

The tenth plague, "Death of the Firstborn" did not include the Israelites because God commanded Moses and Aaron to tell the Israelite families, on the tenth of that month, to prepare for it.

## THE PASSOVER SEVEN DAYS OF UNLEAVENED BREAD CHRIST, OUR PASSOVER LAMB

ICORINTHIANS 5:7:8 ESV 7 Cleanse out the old leaven that you may be a new lump, as you really are unleavened. For Christ, our Passover lamb has been sacrificed. 8 Let us therefore celebrate the festival, not with the old leaven, the leaven of malice and evil, but with the unleavened bread of sincerity and truth.

Unleavened bread: The Israelites were instructed to cook their bread without yeast to eat with the Passover meal for seven days. All yeast was to be removed for their houses (See Exodus 12:14-20).

After Moses, Aaron, the elders, and the Israelites had carried out all the instructions for the Passover, at midnight there was much wailing by pharaoh and the Egyptians because God had stricken every firstborn in every single Egyptian household. Pharaoh was humbled by God. Pharaoh summoned Moses and Aaron and ordered them to leave Egypt immediately and to go worship their God. It is not known whether pharaoh was being sarcastic when he told Moses "say a blessing for me" as they were leaving (See Exodus 12:31-32). All 2-3.5 million (depending on the source) of them, including some aliens, took their unleavened dough, livestock, and clothing and journeyed from Rameses to Succoth. They also plundered the Egyptians for their jewelry, gold, and silver which the Egyptians allowed them to do for fear of someone else dying. Moses took with him the bones of Joseph. Can you imagine that many people up and leaving at one time under only one leader, Moses?

According to Exodus 12:37-38, the Israelites numbered "about six hundred thousand men on foot, besides women and children," plus many non-Israelites and livestock. Numbers 1:46 gives a more precise total of 603,550 men aged 20 and up. The 600,000, plus wives, children, the elderly, and the "mixed multitude" of non-Israelites would have numbered some 2 million people, compared with an entire Egyptian population in 1250 BCE of around 3 to 3.5 million.

Marching ten abreast, and without accounting for livestock, they would have formed a line 150 miles long. Exodus The Book of Exodus tells how Moses leads the Israelites out of Egypt and through the wilderness to Mount Sinai, where God reveals himself and offers them a Covenant: they are to keep his Torah (i.e. law, instruction), and in return he will be their God and give them the land of Canaan. The Book of Leviticus records the laws of God. The Book of Numbers tells how the Israelites, led now by their God, journey onwards from Sinai towards Canaan, but when their spies report that the land is filled with giants they refuse to go on. God condemns them to remain in the wilderness until the generation that left Egypt passes away. After thirty-eight years at the oasis of Kadesh Barnea, the next generation travels on to the borders of Canaan. The Book of Deuteronomy tells how, within sight of the Promised Land, Moses recalls their journeys and gives them new laws. His death (the last reported event of the Torah) concludes the 40 years of the exodus from Egypt.

## THE EXODUS ROUTE:

The route that Israelites took as they left Egypt is not actually known. Archaeologists can't identify the location of Mt Sinai, where the significant event of the Israelites receiving God's Law took place. Many texts and historians have presented presumptive routes and usually have footnotes to indicate so. The Bible text actually says that the Red Sea is interpreted as "The Sea of Reeds" or the Hebrew term, "Yam Sulp". The route listed below is only conjecture. Again the Bible is inerrant and just because archaeologist can't physically identify certain geographical areas mentioned in the Bible does not, in any way, refute what the prophets wrote and became accepted as Holy Scripture.

- •DAY 1-Thursday morning of the 15th of Nisan departed from Ramses (Goshen) and arrives in Succoth

- •They encamped at Succoth Thursday night retrieving Joseph's bones

- •DAY 2-The next day, the 16th of Nisan (Friday), they traveled from Succoth and encamped at Etham on the edge of the wilderness

- •DAY 3-On the 17th of Nisan, which was Shabbat, they remained encamped at Etham

DAY 4—Sunday, Nisan18 after the couriers headed back to Pharaoh God instructs Moses to go back toward Egypt so that Pharaoh can catch up with Israel. Moses sounded the shofar and the people headed to Pihahiroth

•DAY 5-The couriers traveled for a day-and-a-half and at the end of Monday, the 19$^{th}$ of Nisan, they came to Pharaoh and informed him that the people had fled.

•DAY 6-On Tuesday, the 20$^{th}$ of Nisan, Pharaoh assembled his chariots and, gathering his army to accompany him, set out in pursuit of the children of Israel, catching up to them as they encamped on the banks of the sea...

•DAY 7-On Wednesday, the seventh night of Unleavened Bread], the beginning of the 21$^{st}$ of Nisan, Israel entered the sea and in the morning they came out and saw what God's exalted Hand had done to the Egyptians. It was then that Moses and the Children of Israel sang their song of praise [of their freedom].

They arrived at Mt Sinai on the seventh day after their departure from Egypt. The number seven in the Hebrew, 7 is shevah. It is from the root savah, to be full or satisfied, have enough of. Hence the meaning of the word "seven" is dominated by this root, for on the seventh day God rested from the work of Creation. It was full and complete, and good and perfect.

If the above days are correct and the estimated date of the Israeli exodus was somewhere around 1270 B.C., scholars indicate the pharaoh of Egypt would have been Rameses II. On the sixth day of the above scenario of the exodus, Rameses II would have been the pharaoh who wanted to capture the exiting Israelites and bring them back to Egypt for slave labor. Rameses II is described by historians as being the most aggressive and successful pharaoh of the 19th dynasty (1292 BC to 1189 BC).

Biblical historians and scholars say that he engaged the Israelites slave labor into massive building projects like no other pharaoh had done. He surmised that his building projects would almost cease with the massive loss of the slave labor that was provided by the Israelites.

The last time that God hardened the heart of the pharaoh, he, the chariots, and army would meet their demise being engulfed by the rushing water refilling the Red Sea. God wanted the Egyptians to be made aware and know of His great glory before their demise. God also wanted His chosen people and all future generations to forever have in their hearts and minds the miraculous and great glory of the one and only true God. God purposely allowed pharaoh and his horsemen and chariots to come within viewing distance before the Israelites crossed the Red Sea.

When the Israelites saw the Egyptians approaching from a distance they cried out in fear to the Lord. In a panic, they said to Moses why did you bring us out of Egypt into the wilderness to die? Was it that there were not enough graves in Egypt for us? They said we told you while we were Egypt to leave us alone. It would have been better to remain slaves in Egypt alive rather than to die in the wilderness free. They had cried out to the Lord for over 400-430 years for freedom and now with the first sign of duress they had forgotten that the Lord was providing for their salvation. Moses had to remind them that God had already made provisions for their salvation. They wouldn't even have to go into battle and die, for the Lord would do battle for them.

Even though Moses displayed and expressed great faith in God to the Israelites, he cried out to the Lord in prayer about the situation. God's response to Moses indicates that perhaps Moses should have remembered that God had provided him and his brother, Aaron, the ability to perform the supernatural earlier. God said to Moses, Why are you crying (praying) to me, lift up your staff and raise your hand and the people will see another supernatural ability of my glory that I will provide for you. The sea will part and provide a safe river bed ingression of dry land to cross through. The Bible states that an angel of the Lord moved a pillar of cloud that was in front of them to the back of them. This cloud was between the Egyptians and Israelites providing a darkness that prevented the Egyptians from seeing what was going on. Remarkably, Moses stretched out his hand over the sea all night long while a strong east wind parted the waters and dried the land of the seabed. The Israelites were then able to cross on dry land with a sea wall of water on their left and right.

The Egyptians pursued after the Israelites that morning with their army and 600 or so chariots. The Chariots bogged down in the sea bed. Moses raised his hand again and sea walls of water began to recede to its normal course covering all of the Egyptians with not one survivor. The Israelites saw the great power of the Lord. They saw all of the dead Egyptians on the seashore and they feared and believed in the Lord. (Exodus 14 Crossing the Red Sea)

## THE MURMURING OF THE ISRAELITES

Ephesians 2:14 ESV Do all things without grumbling or questioning, complaining. Being discontented with God's will is an expression of unbelief that prevents one from doing what pleases God.

Moses was the gentlest of all men and he was bombarded by continuous complaining by the Israelites even before they crossed the "Sea of Reeds ("The Red Sea" or "Yam Suph"). Their first murmuring was because they felt that they would be slaughtered by the approaching Egyptians. Their rationale was that it would have been better to die and be buried in Egypt rather than a foreign land they were unfamiliar with. (Exodus 14:10-14 KJV 10 and when Pharaoh drew nigh, the children of Israel lifted up their eyes, and, behold, the Egyptians marched after them; and they were sore afraid: and the children of Israel cried out unto the LORD. 11 And they said unto Moses, because there were no graves in Egypt, hast thou taken us away to die in the wilderness? Wherefore hast thou dealt thus with us, to carry us forth out of Egypt? 12 Is not this the word that we did tell thee in Egypt, saying, let us alone, that we may serve the Egyptians? For it had been better for us to serve the Egyptians, than that we should die in the wilderness.

Murmuring after they crossed the "Sea of Reeds"

Next the Israelites complained about the food. They complained that they didn't have the same meat and bread that was familiar to them in Egypt (See Exodus 16:7-12).

The next complaint was that they didn't have any water to drink. They were like babes in the wilderness that depended on Moses for everything (Exodus 17:1-3).

The list of murmuring and complaining went on throughout this wilderness journey. (See: Exodus 32:1, Numbers 11:1-3, Numbers 11:4-6, Numbers 14:10-12, Numbers 17:12-13, Numbers 20:2-5, Numbers 21:4-7, GLO Bible notes: 21:5 we detest this miserable food! The people's impatience (v. 4) led them to blaspheme God, to reject his servant Moses and to despise the "bread from heaven" (Ex 16:4). This is the most bitter of their several attacks on the manna. Just as Moses' attack on the rock was more than it appeared to be, so the people's contempt for the heavenly bread was more serious than one might think. Rejecting the heavenly manna was tantamount to spurning God's grace.

Works of God on the courtship journey to the rendezvous at Mt. Sinai:

1. The miracle of the pillar of cloud and fire.
2. The parting of the Yam Suph and God's victory over the Egyptian army.
3. The sweetening of the bitter water at Marah.
4. The miracle of the quails.
5. The miracle of the manna 'bread from heaven.'
6. The miracle of the life-giving water from the rock.

The wandering wilderness Israelites complained, tried to go back to their old ways and worshipping of idols as they had done in Egypt. God continually revealed to them His preeminence over any obstacle they faced, starting with Pharaoh. God even sent them an angel to protect them from any harm With all of the supernatural works of God revealed to them, they still rebelled.

God is doing this for us today; still, some are like the rebellious Israelites. God had promised Abraham, five centuries earlier that He would give his posterity a land of rest, a "land flowing with milk and honey" but they should keep his statues. In good fertile land, cows produce more milk. Honey is the nectar from the fruit trees of that land. Figuratively speaking the "land flowing with milk and honey" means a land of abundance. Many of the Israelites of the first generation that left Egypt threw away their salvation by their disobedience. Some heard and saw but failed to mix faith with their hearing, as a result, they did not enter into their rest. God has given us another day today. We are warned not to harden our hearts in disbelief. The lesson from the wilderness journey, scripturally warns us not to fail in believing God's Word. Hebrews 4: 1-3 ESV 1 Therefore, while the promise of entering his rest still stands, let us fear lest any of you should seem to have failed to reach it. 2 For good news came to us just as to them, but the message they heard did not benefit them, because they were not united by faith with those who listened. 3 For we who have believed enter that rest, as he has said, "As I swore in my wrath, 'they shall not enter my rest,'" although his works were finished from the foundation of the world.

John 6:32-33 AMP 32 Jesus then said to them, I assure you, most solemnly I tell you, Moses did not give you the Bread from heaven [what Moses gave you was not the Bread from heaven], but it is My Father Who gives you the true heavenly Bread. 33 For the Bread of God is He Who comes down out of heaven and gives life to the world.

Jesus is correcting a crowd that was referring back to when Moses had given manna to the Israelites in The OT that the manna (bread) was given by God not Moses to feed the Israelites, but in the very present tense He is also offering bread, true bread from God, the Father.

The whole Old Testament prefaces the coming of Jesus Christ. When Moses struck the rock at Horeb, the "Rock" is symbolic of Jesus and is Jesus. I Corinthians 10:4 KJV 4 and did all drink the same spiritual drink: for they drank of that spiritual Rock that followed them: and that Rock was Christ. (Notes from GLO Bible on1 Corinthians 10:4 that rock was Christ. The rock, from which the water came, and the manna are here viewed by Paul as symbolic of the spiritual sustenance God's people experienced already in the desert through Christ, the bread of life and the water of life). God created everything and God provides everything.

The area where the Israelites were traveling to reach Canaan was a southern desert area with very little, if any, rain. The Hebrew term for this wilderness area is called "Midbar". This area is to the east and south of Palestine. This entire southern desert region is called "The Wilderness of Sinai". They traveled in this desert area to a place called Shur (See Exodus 15:22). From there they went into a desert area oddly named "Sin" (Exodus 16:1)

There were nomadic people in the desert who would raid anybody passing through, and also, the surrounding farmers. There were several tribes of nomadic people there, the Amalekites, who were descendants of Amalek, the grandson of Esau (Genesis 36:12), the Midianites, personal and clan name meaning "strife" were descendants of Midian who was the son of Abraham by his concubine Keturah (See Genesis 25:1-2), and the Ishmaelites- the progenitors of Ishmael (meaning "God Hears") who was the son of Abraham by the Egyptian concubine Hagar (See Genesis 16:11) Remember that the Ishmaelites were the ones who bought Joseph, son of Jacob, from his brothers and sold him to the Egyptians. Moses wife, Zipporah was a Midianite.

Exodus 17:1 ESV All the congregation of the people of Israel moved on from the wilderness of Sin by stages, according to the commandment of the LORD, and camped at Rephidim, but there was no water for the people to drink. It was at Rephidim (A station in the Wanderings, between the wilderness of Sin and the wilderness of Sinai) that the corporeal Israelites began to complain again. This is a place where water was usually found but the streams had dried up. The nomadic Amalekites possibly used this place for rest and watering also, so they were protective of this area. Rephidim is also called Massah (test) and Meribah (quarrel). Rephidim is a large wilderness area of about 1000 sq. km. There are two different places called "Meribah" in the exodus route: The first is here at Rephidim before they got to Sinai. The second is at Kadesh Barnea (See Numbers 20:11-13) forty years later when the Israelites complained a second time about no water. God became angry with Moses because he sinned in striking the rock. God told him this time to speak to the rock instead of striking it.

Rephidim and the Wilderness of Sinai are believed, by scholars, to be on the east side of Mt. Sinai, or in close proximity.

On This latter occasion, Moses took the glory and made it appear to the Israelites that it was he and not God to cause the water to come out of the rock at Kadesh-Barnea.

As soon as Moses had resolved the water problem, the Israelites were attacked by Amalek (See Exodus 17:8-16).

Moses built an altar at the place where they had defeated the Amalekites (Exodus 17:14-16).

The Amalekites were the first nation to go to war with the Israelites during the wilderness journey.

One of the messages that we should get from this is to hold up and support one another. We should, especially, support God's leaders. Even though the battle was under the command of Joshua, Moses, who was a daunting eighty year old, well respected leader, at the time of this fight with the Amalekites, watched and encouraged the soldiers. He would live another 40 years or so; we might be able to say that he was an early middle age man for this time frame. Joshua was a descendant of the Ephraim tribe and was a slave in Egypt prior to the Exodus. He was a military genius, however, in the battle with the Amalekites, it was a battle fought by men and won by God. God lifted up the Israelites symbolically with the staff of Moses representing God called. The victory was God's just as today when He lifts us up. Effectual calling on the Lord always produces positive results. Just as it did then, when believers that love him call and the call is for His purpose, circumstances are changed for the good (See Romans 8:28). Moses and Joshua were called for God's purpose. So by faith, we should wait in anticipation of future glory just as they did. We need to realize His purpose in our election when we call upon Him. We can be more than conquerors in this earth if we ask for His will to be done.

There are few military leaders in the Bible that placed their faith in God completely, but none exceed the faith of Joshua. Much attention is given to Moses, the writer of the Pentateuch, the first five books of the OT. Immediately following the Pentateuch is the book of Joshua. Joshua became an understudy of Moses as described in the book of Exodus. He was with Moses when he came down from Mount Sinai with the two tablets containing the Ten Commandments and heard the Israelites rejoicing over the golden calf made by Aaron. Moses gave Hosea son of Nun his new name: Joshua (Yeshua in Hebrew), which means "the Lord is Salvation." This name selection was the first indicator that Joshua was a "type," or picture, of Jesus Christ, the Messiah.

Joshua was the perfect example of complete obedience and faith in God. Moses sent twelve spies into the land that God had promised Abraham, Isaac, and Jacob. Joshua and Caleb were the only two of the Israelite spies that came back with a good report. The other ten spies are like so many today that face obstacles in life thinking that they are too big for God to handle. The "giants" are the things in our life that require prayer and supplication today. The "giants" are the problems and worries in our lives that Satan tries to convince us that God has turned his Back on us. Nothing is too big for the creator of everything. The ten reported that the land was well fortified and had giant men, which caused them to surmise that it would be unfeasible to try to conquer that land.

Caleb, who was forty years old at that time, was in complete agreement with Joshua that the people should not rebel against God and should invade and take the land. God became very angry with the rebellious Israelites. They treated Him with condescension by refusing to believe in the Lord's power, especially in view of all the wonders they had experienced, the people of Israel were holding him in contempt. The people were in an uproar and wanted to hurl stones at Joshua and Caleb. God got fed up with this rebellion and appeared at the "Tent of Meeting" with the intent to kill all of the rebels. Number 14:10-12 AMP 10 But all the congregation said to stone [Joshua and Caleb]. But the glory of the Lord appeared at the Tent of Meeting before all the Israelites. 11 And the Lord said to Moses, How long will this people provoke (spurn, despise) Me? And how long will it be before they believe Me [trusting in, relying on, clinging to me], for all the signs which I have performed among them? 12 I will smite them with the pestilence and disinherit them, and will make of you [Moses] a nation greater and mightier than they.

Moses had to intercede for the people so that God would not kill them. God listened to Moses plea and agreed not kill them but there had to be consequences for their rebellion. The twelve spies that went into the land to spy were there for forty days. God told all the rebellious Israelites that they would wander, haplessly, for forty years in the wilderness until all of the bones initial former slaves had dried up there in the wilderness. Anyone over twenty years old that grumbled would be included with those that would not see the land flowing with milk and honey. Numbers 14:31-34 AMP 31 But your little ones whom you said would be a prey, them will I bring in and they shall know the land which you have despised and rejected. 32 But as for you, your dead bodies shall fall in this wilderness. 33 And your children shall be wanderers and shepherds in the wilderness for forty years and shall suffer for your whoredoms (your infidelity to your espoused God), until your corpses are consumed in the wilderness. 34 After the number of the days in which you spied out the land [of Canaan], even forty days, for each day a year shall you bear and suffer for your iniquities, even for forty years, and you shall know My displeasure [the revoking of My promise and My estrangement].

Even though Joshua is the focus here, God also thought very highly of Caleb as indicated in Numbers 14:24. Remember Caleb was forty years old when God made this proclamation.

"During the 40 years the Jewish people wandered in the wilderness, Joshua served as a faithful aide to Moses. Of the 12 spies sent to scout out Canaan, only Joshua and Caleb had confidence in God and only those two survived the desert ordeal to enter the Promised Land. Against overwhelming odds, Joshua led the Israelite army in its conquest of the Promised Land. He apportioned the land to the tribes and governed them for a time. Without a doubt, Joshua's greatest accomplishment in life was his unwavering loyalty and faith in God.

Some Bible scholars view Joshua as an Old Testament representation or foreshadowing, of Jesus Christ, the promised Messiah previously stated. What Moses (who represented the law) was unable to do, Joshua (Yeshua) achieved when he successfully led the people of God out of the desert to conquer their enemies and enter the Promised Land. His accomplishments point to the finished work of Jesus Christ on the cross—the defeat of God's enemy, Satan, the setting free of all believers from captivity to sin, and the opening of the way into the "Promised Land" of eternity." Obedience, faith, and dependence on God made Joshua one of Israel's strongest leaders. He provided a bold example for us to follow. Like us, Joshua was often besieged by other voices, but he chose to follow God, and he did it faithfully. Joshua took seriously the Ten Commandments and ordered the people of Israel to live by them as well. Even though Joshua was not perfect, he proved that a life of obedience to God bears great rewards. Sin always has consequences. If we live according to God's Word, like Joshua, we will receive God's blessings.

# CHAPTER 10

# Israelites Given the Law

THROUGH FAITH AND OBEDIENCE TO God, Joshua was able to lead the Israelites out of the wilderness of Sinai and into the Promised Land. God's laws had been revealed to the Israelites while they trekked through the wilderness. The revelation was not adhered by them all of the time because they would flip-flop between worshipping the God of Moses and idolatrous gods of the tribes they came in contact with. Hosea 6:4 demonstrates the faith of these people whose faith and obedience is temporary like dew that burns off by the morning sun.

When Moses had finished communing with God on Mt. Sinai for forty days, God gave him two tablets of stones with five commandments on each. God told Moses to go back down to his people that he brought out of Egypt because they had corrupted themselves and reverted back to their old ways. The people thought Moses had probably died since he was gone for so long. Without a strong spiritual leader; they caused a weak Aaron to acquiesce to their will which was to make a god like idolatrous statue. They apparently had (a pluralistic spiritual association with God and idolatry) while in captivity in Egypt. They collected the golden earrings that they had plundered from the Egyptians before their exodus and Aaron melted the gold and made a golden calf to serve as a god for their worshipping.

The churches of modern times need strong spiritual leaders. If the spiritual leader is not strong, they will concur to the will of the people like Moses', brother Aaron did. Exodus 32:1-4 AMP 1 When the people saw that Moses delayed to come down from the mountain, [they] gathered together to Aaron, and said to him, Up, make us gods to go before us; as for this Moses, the man who brought us up out of the land of Egypt, we do not know what has become of him. 2 So Aaron replied, take the gold rings from the ears of your wives, your sons, and daughters, and bring them to me. 3 So all the people took the gold rings from their ears and brought them to Aaron. 4 And he received the gold at their hand and fashioned it with a graving tool and made it a molten calf; and they said, these are your gods, O Israel, which brought you up out of the land of Egypt!

(The Apis bull of Memphis came to be associated with the solar deity *Ra*, the oldest as well as the father of all the Egyptian gods. *Ra* was often thought to have been a golden calf, born in the morning from a heavenly cow, and growing into a bull by day). *Ra* is the ninth Egyptian god in the chart above).

How could the Israelites even dare think of creating an idol after all the supernatural miracles of powers God had displayed before their departure from Egypt? After arriving at the vicinity of Mount Sinai, they had trembled with great fear when God made his presence known by thunder, lightning, the sound of the trumpet, and smoke coming from Mount Sinai. They had been told if they approach the mountain they would perish. No one but Moses, Aaron, or priests that had been consecrated could approach God on Mt. Sinai. Moses had received the word of the Ten Commandments and spoke to them because they were fearful that they may die if God spoke to them directly. Moses verbally gave them God's commandments. The very first one given was that they should worship no other Gods nor create or carve the likeness of another god (Exodus 20: 4-6).

The Israelites came perilously close to being annihilated by God Himself because of what transpired with the Golden Calf or RA." It is very puzzling that they would bring themselves so close to extinction by God Himself by committing this sacrilege (Exodus 32:9-14).

God forgives and takes whomever He chooses to do His will. When Moses came down from Mt. Sinai and saw the golden calf and people in a frenzy, partying, orgies, dancing, etc., he was more than furious. He was so furious that he threw down and broke the two stone tablets containing the Ten Commandments.* He asked Aaron where did this evil abomination come from and he lied and placed the blame on the people. He essentially said that some gold was given to him; he threw it into the fire and poof, out jumps this golden calf. We know that this is a lie because the Bible states that he fashioned the golden calf with an engraving tool in glaring violation of the Fourth Commandment (Exodus 20:4). (See also Exodus 32:4 and 32:21-24)

All of the old covenant sacrifices could not do away with sin. All of the blood sacrifices under the old covenant were an adumbration (vague foreshadow) of the ultimate blood sacrifice of Jesus on the cross (Hebrews 10:1).

This is why when we read and complete the reading of the OT, the NT is a continuation and reality of the coming of the Messiah according to the prophecies of the OT. The whole OT is the foretelling of the coming of Jesus Christ. Helen Cadbury and her popular gospel singer husband, Charles McCallon Alexander, distributed free pocket-sized New Testaments Bibles while evangelizing on the street starting in 1908. This made it possible for all wanting to read the NT to be able to transport the word of Jesus around in a small shirt pocket sized Bible. During my elementary school days all of the students were given one of these small pocket bibles which are now prohibited by law*.

*On June 25, 1962, the United States Supreme Court decided in Engel v. Vitale that a prayer approved by the New York Board of Regents for use in schools violated the First Amendment by constituting an establishment of religion. The following year, in Abington School District v. Schempp, the Court disallowed Bible readings in public schools for similar reasons. These two landmark Supreme Court decisions centered on the place of religion in public education, and particularly the place of Protestantism, which had long been accepted as the given American faith tradition. Both decisions ultimately changed the face of American civil society, and in turn, helped usher in the last half-century of the culture wars.

# CHAPTER 11

# Inauguration of a New Sacrificial Lamb

FORTY YEARS AFTER JESUS PROPHESIED the destruction of Jerusalem and the temple, it happened as He had warned. The animal sacrifices performed by priests in compliance to the Old Testament covenant were stopped in A.D. 70 when the Roman army decimated Jerusalem.

For the Christian community, animal sacrifices stopped with the death and resurrection of Christ. There were some who were persecuted or pressured by the Jewish community to continue to offer sacrifices either because they rejected Jesus or felt his death was not enough. The book of Hebrews actually deals with this and shows that the Old Testament sacrificial system (the Old Covenant) was temporary until the coming of Christ who was the fulfillment of all that the sacrificial system anticipated. The Apostle Paul teaches us the same thing in passages like Colossians 2:16. It was Paul who specifically pointed to Christ as our Passover who was sacrificed for us: 1 Corinthians 5:7 AMP Purge (clean out) the old leaven that you may be fresh (new) dough, still uncontaminated [as you are], for Christ, our Passover [Lamb], has been sacrificed. In keeping with the Lord's Supper, instituted just before His death, Jesus also celebrated what was actually the last legitimate Passover by which He also pointed to Himself as the sacrifice for our sin.

Today, when Jews observe the Passover they cannot offer sacrifices because sacrifices are only to be offered in Jerusalem and in the temple. Prophetically, many believe that in the future during the time of Daniel's 70th week, the temple will be rebuilt and sacrifices will again be offered, but only because the Jews continue to reject Jesus as their Messiah. The sacrifices will once again be stopped by the beast of Revelation 13 the Jews will be persecuted until Messiah returns at which time they will turn to Him "whom they have pierced," to put it in the words of Zechariah."

Now we can enter the Holiest through the blood of Jesus! Hallelujah!

The first and only use of the "New Covenant" in the OT is in Jeremiah 31:31 NIV 31 "The days are coming," declares the LORD, "when I will make a new covenant with the people of Israel and with the people of Judah.

Jesus did not say that He would abolish the Old Testament scriptures (The Pentateuch 1st five books of the OT), God's Law, or the Prophets of the old covenant (See Matthew 5:17-20, Luke 16:17, and John 7:19 on this subject). Jesus told the religious leaders that while they were concerned about keeping laws, they didn't adhere to them.

The new covenant will be different from the covenant received on Mt. Sinai. The new covenant allowed for an intimate relationship with God's people. The Pharisees claimed to hang onto the Law given to Moses at Mt. Sinai (Oral Law) along with the written law (Torah). The Sadducees rejected the Oral law and hung onto the written law. They did not believe in the after-life since it was not written in the Torah.

The historical source of the word "inauguration" stems from the Latin augur, which refers to the rituals of ancient Roman priests seeking to interpret if it was the will of the gods for a public official to be deemed worthy to assume office. The Sermon on the Mount was Jesus' inaugural address for the members of his heavenly kingdom. This sermon was an appraisal in respect to the differences between His moralistic values and the legalistic (laws) doctrines of the Pharisees and the Sadducees. The introduction of the "Sermon on the Mount" begins in chapter 5 of St. Matthew and continues through chapter 7. Jesus also introduced in his inaugural address on the Mount, his commands for righteous living not only in His kingdom but how to choose between moral and immoral living for our daily lives.

Now that we know of Jesus' sacrifice for the atonement of our sins, we need to put our faith and trust in God. The first covenant of God was written on 2 stone tablets. Now the perfect covenant has been written in the hearts and minds of His people. (Hebrews 8:10-13 NIV 10 This is the covenant I will establish with the people of Israel after that time, declares the Lord. I will put my laws in their minds and write them on their hearts. I will be their God, and they will be my people. 11 No longer will they teach their neighbor, or say to one another, 'Know the Lord, 'because they will all know me, from the least of them to the greatest. 12 For I will forgive their wickedness and will remember their sins no more." 13 By calling this covenant "new, "He has made the first one obsolete; and what is obsolete and outdated will soon disappear.)

Many people are destroyed for lack of knowledge of God. They have rejected the knowledge of God that is there before them. The Lord says I will also reject thee. The Lord said I will also forget your children. We must humble ourselves and pray. God will hear us if we humble ourselves and turn from our wicked ways, seeking his face. That is the problem, so many of us want to do as we please and not humble ourselves taking things into our own hands. We are following our emotions, feelings, and our own minds instead of letting God direct our paths.

# Seek Help from None Other than God

EVEN THE GREAT KING DAVID (described as a man after God's own heart) was guilty of following his own mind instead of relying on God. The first king of the Israelites was King Saul. At first, King Saul was pleased with this shepherd because he had killed the Philistinian nemesis to Israel, Goliath. Later on King Saul wanted to kill David because of jealousy. David was a much-admired leader of the Israelites. This angered King Saul especially when he was taunted by a song by the Israelite women who sang and played on their timbrels (tambourines): 7....... "Saul has struck down his thousands and David his ten thousands." (I Samuel 18:7-8 ESV). Saul became so embittered that he attempted to kill David which caused David to flee from him.

While David and his 600 men were hiding from Saul, he and his men became hungry. They were near a large landowner named Nabal (his name means "Fool" or "rude, ill-bred"). Nabal was married to a very wise woman named Abigail. David sent 10 of his messengers to Nabal's place to ask for food. Nabal was holding a feast for his sheepherders and he had become very intoxicated and was very rude to David's men. He refused to give them any food. David in his own mind decided to kill Nabal. Nabal's wife anticipated David's reaction and loaded up donkeys with food to send to David and his men.

I had wished to condense the content of these verses of 1Samuel into my contemporary interpretation of the encounter of King David with Nabil's wife as she eloquently spoke to ameliorate the hostile feelings of the king. Her presentation is so very convincing in the Scripture as written by the Prophet Samuel that it is self-explanatory (I Sam. 25: 23-34 AMP 23 When Abigail saw David, she hastened and lighted off the donkey, and fell before David on her face and did obeisance. 24 Kneeling at his feet she said, Upon me alone let this guilt be, my lord. And let your handmaid, I pray you, speak in your presence, and hear the words of your handmaid. 25 Let not my lord, I pray you, regard this foolish and wicked fellow Nabal, for as his name is, so is he—Nabal [foolish, wicked] is his name, and folly is with him. But I, your handmaid, did not see my lord's young men whom you sent 26 So now, my lord, as the Lord lives and as your soul lives, seeing that the Lord has prevented you from blood guiltiness and from avenging yourself with your own hand, now let your enemies and those who seek to do evil to my lord be as Nabal. 27 And now this gift, which your handmaid has brought my lord, let it be given to the young men who follow my lord. 28 Forgive, I pray you, the trespass of your handmaid, for the Lord will certainly make my lord a sure house, because my lord is fighting the Lord's battles, and evil has not been found in you all your days. 29 Though man is risen up to pursue you and to seek your life, yet the life of my lord shall be bound in the living bundle with the Lord your God. And the lives of your enemies—them shall He sling out as out of the center of a sling. 30 And when the Lord has done to my lord according to all the good that He has promised concerning you and has made you ruler over Israel, 31 This shall be no staggering grief to you or cause for pangs of conscience to my lord, either that you have shed blood without cause or that my lord has avenged himself. And when the Lord has dealt well with my lord, then [[a]earnestly] remember your handmaid.*32 And David said to Abigail, Blessed be the Lord, the God of Israel, Who sent you this day to meet me.33 And blessed be your discretion and advice, and blessed be you who have kept me today from blood guiltiness and from avenging myself with my own hand.34 For as the Lord, the God of Israel, lives, Who has prevented me from hurting you, if you had not hurried and come to meet me, surely by morning there would not have been left so much as one male to Nabal.

Footnotes:

*a.1 Samuel 25:31 Whenever God's inspired Word says "[earnestly] remember," one is certain to miss something if he does not stop, look, and really listen to what the Holy Spirit is wanting to tell him—or her. "[Earnestly] remember" Abigail, the woman whom God has specifically held up as a pattern of right behavior in an unfortunate marriage. Here a dozen vital questions are answered through Abigail's example. She could not have known that thousands of years later people in similar circumstances would become "more than conquerors" because of her, but God knew. Study her until you know her God-given secrets of success; then pass them on to the people who are letting an unfortunate marriage wreck them rather than sanctify them for service.

You can see from the preceding passages that Abigail had to remind David that he was a man of God. She turned David's evil thoughts into good. She kept David from shedding blood and avenging his own self. So David humbled himself and listened to the word that God had sent him through the wise Abigail aided by the Holy Spirit.

The text relates that the next morning when Nabal sobered up and heard that David planned to kill him, he had a heart attack and led to what we, in modern terms, call a stroke or coma and was paralyzed like a stone. Ten days later he died and David took his widow Abigail as his wife, the second of eight wives (I Sam 25:36-42).

Look at God's wrath and his vengeance. We need to be in prayer begging God to please bring those who wrong us into repentance. But instead, so many of us do our own thing like David's first inclination and place God's word on the back burner. When David learned to allow God to choose the battles, many were won. God actually gave instructions on how to organize and when to go out for battle, just as He instructed Joshua at Jericho (Joshua 6:2-5). Many times actual battle was unnecessary and only required meeting together with singing and praises to God. Earlier, we saw how God fought for King Jehoshaphat without the military of his kingdom lifting a finger.

# CHAPTER 13

# The Shekhinah Dwells in the Heart of Believers Producing "Fruits of the Spirit"

IN THE NEW TESTAMENT OF the Bible Jesus speaks of all of His actions and authority was directly caused by God living in Him performing His works. In the King James Version of the Bible, the text informs us Jesus and God are selfsame in divinity while not being the same persons (John 10:30 KJV). Christians must have faith and belief that Jesus is one with God (John 14:10, 17 KJV). Believers know that God lives in them by the Spirit that He gives which is exemplified by the "Fruits of this Spirit" (1John 3:24 KJV)

1John 4:15 KJV If anyone acknowledges that Jesus is the Son of God; God lives in them and they in God.

We all are commanded to bear "Fruit of the Spirit". Galatians 5:22-26 NIV 22 But the fruit of the Spirit is love, joy, peace, forbearance, kindness, goodness, faithfulness, 23 gentleness and self-control. Against such things there is no law. 24 Those who belong to Christ Jesus have crucified the flesh with its passions and desires. 25 Since we live by the Spirit, let us keep in step with the Spirit. 26 Let us not become conceited, provoking and envying each other.

Jesus said that we can identify false prophets by the fruit they produce (Matt. 7:15 -20).

Is this not true of our two American political parties today, the Democrats and the Republicans? Don't they do all of the things the Bible clearly tell them not to do?. Where is God in their hearts? All we hear of them are disputes based on dislike (s) of each other instead of what is right. It has become such that if you belong to one party or the other you are predisposed to hate the other party. This disposition is a carry-over from the people who elect them into office. They say they are trying to do the will of the constituencies. They claim to be doing the work the American people wishes, but they are so divided, that they never accomplish anything. Or should it be said that what they do accomplish has little significance to the welfare of the whole country? They claim to be following what is written in the constitution but hardly use any of the principles in the true, best, and only book, the Bible. The best book for guidance (God's word) has been taken out of the ruling parties of this country.

Again, a divided house cannot stand. Don't you see the fear in America? How long can America continue to be headed into a reduction of morality and down this rocky road? When we say "God Bless America", do we really think God has a purpose for our blessings? We hear politicians use this phrase after every speech.

The phrase is actually from a song by the songwriter/composer Irving Berlin who wrote the song in 1918 while in the army. Berlin was a first generation Jewish immigrant. While in the army his camp officer at Camp Upton in Yaphank, New York, had heard that he was fooling around with writing songs. Berlin's talents as a song-writer were used for the composing music for an all-soldier comedy show. During preparation for this production, he wrote "God Bless America", but for his own reasons, did not use the song.

If you are not familiar with Berlin as the writer of this song, you might have heard of his songs "White Christmas" written in 1942 and the most popular "Easter Parade" written in 1933. The "God Bless America" song lay dormant until 1938 until a popular singer and radio host by the name of Kate Smith asked Berlin if he had any patriotic songs. She wanted a song to sing on Armistice Day (Today called Veterans Day) November 11, 1938. He pulled out the song and gave it to her. There was a war going on in Europe with the rise of Adolph Hitler that threatened the entire world peace and she wanted to sing something to memorialize the soldiers and also to remind everyone how much America means to each and every one of us. It has been written that Berlin borrowed six notes from a 1906 Jewish dialect novelty song called, "When Moses with His Nose Leads the Band" for use in "God Bless America".

Both the Democratic and Republican parties used the song as their 1940 convention themes. And as the United States entered the Second World War, the song became a beacon of hope for soldiers and sailors overseas – and for their families at home.

After the war, "God Bless America" was used briefly as a protest song by groups ranging from veterans breaking up a Communist Party rally in 1947 to civil rights workers sitting at lunch counters in Texas in the early 1960s. But by the mid-'60s the song had begun an inexorable rightward drift, becoming a staple of pro-Vietnam War rallies and of demonstrations by whites against integration.

Christian conservatives used this song in particular here in America in the 1960s during the controversial war when the United States was engaged in warfare with North Vietnam. This was to signal their opposition to secular liberalism and to silence dissenters who were speaking in favor of communism or in opposition to the U.S. involvement in the Vietnam War. It seems to be almost un-American today not to utter "God Bless America" after a political speech or rally. A big deal is made about politicians who don't wear American flag lapel pins on their dress coats. If we honor anything more than we do God it is idolatry. Anything created by man that is given divine devotion over God is idolatry. There are other forms of idolatry, such as nature worship, hero worship, and etc.

The American flag cannot bring salvation but the obedience to the words of the Bible will because it is the only inerrant truth. Bless America with the intercession of the Holy Spirit if it is the will of God. We should be pledging allegiance to God first and pay due respect to the flag when the occasion arises. The initial early use of this song was different from what is intended today hopefully. It was a seventh inning stretch song at baseball games and other sporting events early on. We should be using it in a prayerful manner today. "God Bless America in Jesus Name, Amen." I hope that is what our politicians intend.

Yes, America certainly needs God's blessings. Will God bless America if it doesn't follow the precepts given to us by His Word? High officials are being selected to offices of government by promises to improve the lives of their constituents which are found to be chocked with lies once they are elected. Some promises become unintentional lies when a politician is not given financial support, lack of a majority vote, or by some other political reason. The rejections of good ideas by some are because of partisanship. There is an old joke that asks the question "How can you tell when a politician is lying? The answer is when his lips are moving. I don't place all politicians in this category because I believe some, from both parties, have the will of the people at heart and are good Christians trying to do good. I am unaware of who authored this joke, I just know that it has been around for a long time.

It is perceived and mostly true that promises which have the highest priority to the elected official(s) are those for lobbyists, donators, and those that show loyalty to that official. People in this century vote for candidates, not based on their integrity and honesty, but rather who is the lesser of two evils. It has been said that high political officials of the country have promoted wars on foreign countries to subsidize and create business for defense contractors. Sometimes God allows the will of people of nations to teach them a lesson and bring them back to Him.

Historians have recorded the religious beliefs of American founding fathers, the individuals of the thirteen British colonies in North America. These individuals led the revolt against the British Crown which led to the establishment of the United States of America. The individuals that gathered to participate at the 1787 Constitutional Convention had various religious affiliations. They were mostly Protestants (including Episcopalians) (49), but also consisted of Roman Catholics (2), Presbyterians (8), Congregationalists (7), Lutherans (2), two each of Lutherans, Methodists, and the Dutch Reformed, etc.

One of the most prominent members of this assembly was Thomas Jefferson who was anti-Clerical. Jefferson's belief was that the clergy or the church should have no influence on issues related to secular or public affairs.

"Separation of church and state" is a phrase used by Thomas Jefferson and others expressing an understanding of the intent and function of the Establishment Clause and the Free Exercise Clause of the First Amendment to the Constitution of the United States which reads: "Congress shall make no law respecting an establishment of religion, or prohibiting the free exercise thereof..." The intent of this clause was to limit the power of the Federal Government in regard to religion thus ensuring freedom of religion in the United States of America. The phrase "separation of church and state" is generally traced to a January 1, 1802, letter by Thomas Jefferson, addressed to the Danbury Baptist Association in Connecticut and published in a Massachusetts newspaper. Jefferson wrote, "I contemplate with sovereign reverence that act of the whole American people which declared that their [Federal] legislature should 'make no law respecting an [State]establishment of religion, or prohibiting the free exercise thereof,' thus building a wall of separation between Church & State."

In the 1800 presidential election opponents labeled Thomas Jefferson a "howling atheist." It is said that although he was devoted to teaching about Jesus Christ he considered the Four Gospels in the Holy Bible to be untrustworthy. So Jefferson took a sharp object and cut out portions of the Bible (NT) he disagreed with and made his own 84 page Bible published in 1820.

The following is a letter that Thomas Jefferson wrote to John Adams in 1823:

1823 April 11. (Jefferson to John Adams). "The truth is that the greatest enemies to the doctrines of Jesus are those calling themselves the expositors of them, who have perverted them for the structure of a system of fancy absolutely incomprehensible, and without any foundation in his genuine words. And the day will come when the mystical generation of Jesus, by the Supreme Being as his father in the womb of a virgin will be classed with the fable of the generation of Minerva in the brain of Jupiter. But we may hope that the dawn of reason and freedom of thought in these United States will do away with all this artificial scaffolding, and restore to us the primitive and genuine doctrines of this the most venerated reformer of human errors." Ibid, 412-3. Recipient's copy at the Library of Congress.

Mister Jefferson I know of your reputed worldly intelligence and contribution to the formation of America. You were the second vice president and third president of America. You helped to write the Declaration of Independence and also wrote your own bible, so you are suggesting that the Four Gospels are errant. The many verses of scripture describing the infallibility of God's Word don't use the word inerrant. However, if believers accept the fact that God is irreproachable, those that wrote the Bible wrote inerrantly as they were carried along by the Holy Spirit and not by their own interpretations. There are verses in the OT that we can refer to such as Psalms 12:6 KJV 6 The words of the LORD are pure words: as silver tried in a furnace of earth, purified seven times. Proverbs 30:5-6 ESV 5 Every word of God proves true; he is a shield to those who take refuge in him. 6 Do not add to his words, lest he rebuke you and you be found a liar.

Using the metallurgical process of refining the silver seven times (completeness) in a furnace as to make the silver perfect and without blemish in this correlation speaks of God's Word provided by the Holy Spirit to the Biblical authors as being inerrant. The Holy Bible was not written by the spirit of human wisdom which applies to both the OT and NT. The writers received the Spirit of God while writing the Bible: I Corinthians 2:12-13 ESV 12 Now we have received, not the spirit of the world, but the spirit which is of God; that we might know the things that are freely given to us of God. 13 Which things also we speak, not in the words which man's wisdom teacheth, but which the Holy Ghost teacheth; comparing spiritual things with spiritual.

The prophets didn't just decide to write the scriptures by their own wisdom, it was by the Spirit of God in them that provided the wisdom in which they wrote and spoke. Jesus did not go to the temple and ask the Sanhedrin, the high priest, or the Pharisees to allow Him to interview for disciples to follow Him. Those at the temple were highly opposed to the teaching of Jesus and He knew it. There at the temple were men who had been taught the Hebrew law even though they didn't adhere to it as was mentioned earlier. Jesus chose fishermen such as Peter and John, a tax collector (Matthew), and others who had no formal rabbinical training to be His disciples.

After the crucifixion, resurrection, and ascension of Jesus, it was customary for the disciples, John and Peter, to go to the temple to pray and teach what they had been taught by Jesus. The priests, the captain of the temple, and the Sadducees arrested them for speaking to the people there, which were about five thousand men. The Sadducee's were a sect of Jews who were the upper echelon of the priests and the Jewish society. They maintained the temple by the rules of Moses's Torah. The function of the Sanhedrin, that was mentioned earlier on, included the participation of the Sadducees. What really aggravated them is that the apostles preached about Jesus's resurrection from the dead in which the Sadducees totally disavowed. They especially did not believe in the resurrection, especially of Jesus, and did not want anyone preaching or speaking about it.

Peter and John were brought before the council of the High Priests and all of their kindred in Jerusalem to question them. This courthouse type of interrogation was to find out by what power had been given to them to authoritatively speak and teach about Jesus' resurrection on the temple grounds. Peter had no rabbinical training and they knew this, but his knowledge came about as he was filled with the *"Holy Spirit"*. He boldly responded that they preached based on the power given to them by Jesus of Nazareth whom the Sanhedrin had the Romans to crucify earlier*.

(*During the time Jesus was crucified, around 33 AD (some scholars say 30AD), the Romans had control of the Palestinian territory. The Roman General Pompey conquered the land of Israel in 63 B.C.E and brought Palestine into the Roman Empire.

As two Apostles stood and testified about Jesus before the high priest and other educated men that were experts of the Torah Law, they perceived that these men were uneducated. They knew that Peter and John had not attended rabbinic schools so they marveled that the Apostles spoke with such boldness and authority(Acts 4:13 KJV13 Now when they saw the boldness of Peter and John, and perceived that they were unlearned and ignorant men, they marveled; and they took knowledge of them, that they had been with Jesus). There was also a lame man with them that had been healed earlier in Acts 3:2-9 by them just speaking the name of Jesus of Nazareth. This healing marveled many witnesses who were present where the healing took place at the entrance to the temple at a Gate called Beautiful. If these two apostles could heal a lame man just by doing it in the name of Jesus of Nazareth, this same God provided the same power of His spirit for canonically inerrant writings of the Holy Bible (II Timothy 3:16-17 ESV16 All Scripture is breathed out by God and profitable for teaching, for reproof, for correction, and for training in righteousness, 17 that the man of God may be competent, equipped for every good work.

The problem in the mind of those who reject the Holy Bible and find it untrustworthy is because it was written by men (At least 40 of them). The Holy Spirit communicated the message of God through these biblical authors. These writers acted as transcribers for God.

We know the reasons we study history is because history tells us where we came from and came to be as a society. Most important is the fact is that history repeats itself so history can actually be a preview of the future. How long can America prosper in the direction that we are headed? It is not intended here to refer to the bible as a history book. We know that God revealed his precepts to the forty-plus writers in the Bible. God's revelations came by visions, dreams, sometimes direct communication to the Old Testament writers by theophanies*, by Jesus, New Testament apostles, and disciples.

*The term theophany used by Christians and Jews, in regard to the Holy Bible, refers to the manifestation of God to man not necessarily in human form. There are a small number of theophanies found in the Old Testament Bible.

We have been given God's word which tells us how to find the life he intended for us. During the Test of Jesus by Satan, who was actually trying to tempt Jesus to use His supernatural powers for his (Satan) own good, Jesus quoted from Deuteronomy in Matthew 4:1-4

ESV 1 Then Jesus was led up by the Spirit into the wilderness to be tempted by the devil. 2 And after fasting forty days and forty nights, he was hungry. 3 And the tempter came and said to him, "If you are the Son of God, command these stones to become loaves of bread." 4 But he answered, "It is written, 'Man shall not live by bread alone, but by every word that comes from the mouth of God.'"

The denial of this world as our home is a difficult thing to do. Along with this denial, we may and will encounter sufferings. If we study our bibles we are made aware of things that we may encounter in this world that we can prepare for and pray for guidance to get us through the rough times.

Jesus spoke of denying oneself of this world to become citizens of God's kingdom. Now Jesus was speaking to those of us who join His discipleship which we all should be striving to do. When *any* individual becomes consumed with acquiring worldly treasures focus is taken away from Jesus and the soul is loss. There is no treasure on earth greater than the Kingdom of God. What ones obtain on earth is only temporary compared to making the choice for eternal life offered by Jesus the Savior (Matthew 16: 24-26 ESV). Verse 26 is frequently quoted concerning where one's priority should be: "For what will it profit a man if he gains the whole world and forfeits his soul? Or what shall a man give in return for his soul?)

As citizens of God's kingdom, we have to be able to overlook many sinful things that are thrown our way. If someone curses you out with profanity-laced speech, we are to ignore this and move on. What would you do if someone curses at you? It is best to pray for that individual and move on.

There was a member of the first Jewish King Saul's clan named Shimei who had it in his mind that David was trying to usurp Saul's kingdom. Shimei saw David passing on a road as he was trying to escape from his son Absalom (Absalom was the third son of King David and the only one of his sons with royal blood, His mother was Maacah, daughter of Talmai, king of Geshur).

This is a brief description of why King David was trying to escape from his son Absalom. King David also had a beautiful virgin daughter named Tamar who was the full sister of his son Absalom. King David's dysfunctional family situation became filled with turmoil. King David's firstborn son, Amnon, developed an intense sexual desire for his half-sister. Amnon told his first cousin, Jonadab, of his desire to be with Tamar. Jonadab advised Amnon that he should pretend to be sick and request of his father David to allow Tamar to cook a meal and bring it to Amnon's residence.

Tamar went to his residence and was raped by her half-brother. After raping her he became filled with guilt and couldn't stand the sight of her and had his servant to force her out and bolt the door. The love he thought he had for her was only a carnal feeling. Tamar performed the biblical Israelite custom of tossing dust on the head and tearing off clothing as a sign of humility and repentance to God. She tore off the long, beautiful robe she was wearing in which king's virgin daughters wore (2Sam 13:19). Tamar went to her full brother, Absalom, and related what had happened. He convinced her to remain silent about what had happened so she would not be subject to disgrace. Absalom devised a plan that he would kill Amnon, his brothers, and King David. This was the hate he felt in his heart because of his hatred for what Amnon had done to his sister. She remained at her brother's house and became a desolate woman living in shame.

The bible does not say how long she remained at her brother's house but it was probably the remainder of her life. King David found out about Amnon raping Tamar. He became angry but did not chastise Amnon. The Israelites had laws concerning rape in chapter 22 of Deuteronomy. (Deuteronomy 22: 28-29 ESV "If a man meets a virgin who is not betrothed, and seizes her and lies with her, and they are found, then the man who lay with her shall give to the father of the young woman fifty shekels of silver, and she shall be his wife, because he has violated her. He may not divorce her all his days).

Tamar begged Amnon not commit this rape but rather go to King David and he would surely allow them to marry. Amnon was the oldest of King David's sons and was in line to become king after the king's death. Tamar told him that he would be considered to be an outrageous fool by the Israelites if he committed the act of rape but he raped her anyway (II Samuel 13:13).

Absalom waited two years before he implemented his plan to murder King David, and his sons, especially Amnon whom he had concealed his hatred for because of the rape he committed to his sister. King David still had not addressed the rape of his daughter after two years. Absalom invited the king and his sons to attend a sheep shearing event where he kept his flock in a place approximately eight miles east of Jerusalem which was near Ephraim, a city of Judah, named Baal-hazor. King David refused the invitation so Absalom begged the king to let Amnon attend along with the other brothers. Absalom provided wine at the event and commanded his servants to kill Amnon after he had consumed enough wine to become inebriated and they did so. When the other brothers realized what was going on they mounted their mules and fled. Word got back to King David that Absalom had murdered all of his sons. King David tore his clothes and lay on the ground in grief. David's brother, Jonadab informed him that it had been in Absalom's heart all along, for two years, to kill Amnon for raping his sister. David other sons escaped Absalom's murder plans.

Absalom fled to his grandfather, Talmai, who was the king of Geshur. Archaeologists think that the ancient biblical city of Geshur location was territory along the eastern shore of the Sea of Galilee and south up to the Yarmuk River and today is southern Golan Heights. This was Absalom's mother's homeland.

Talmai's daughter, Maacha, was the wife of King David and Absalom's mother. Absalom stayed there in exile from Jerusalem for three years During this period of time King David had gotten over the death of Amnon and his heart yearned for Absalom to return to Jerusalem (II Samuel 13:37-39).

Absalom returned but King David refused to see him for 2 years. Joab, the general of King David's national army and the chief counselor had the greatest influence of decisions made by the king. He connived to have Absalom to be reconciled by his father so that their isolation from each other would cease. Absalom took advantage of this reconciliation and plotted to take over his father kingdom. Absalom

111

made efforts to gain the support of the people so that he could cause an insurrection and proclaim himself as king. When King David realized that Absalom had gained the support of the people and was ready to take over as king, he fled his household and left ten concubines to manage the palace.

Absalom came to Jerusalem with his army and took possession of the king's palace. Ahithophel who was one of King David's chief advisers and the grandfather of Bathsheba, one of King David's wife and mother of the king to be, Solomon. Ahithophel may have secretly held the death of Bathsheba's first husband, Uriah, against the King for many years and this gave him the opportunity to exact revenge. This is not in the Bible but reasonable speculation. He joined Absalom's insurrection against King David. When King David fled from Jerusalem it was Ahithophel who advised Absalom to display his scorn for the king by pitching a tent on the palace roof and sleeping with King David's ten concubines for all Jerusalem to see (II Samuel 16:22).

This act would certainly display complete alienation from his father. In today's society, this would be a deplorable act of rape but the concubines sleeping with Absalom was probably accepted as consensual. The thought process of Ahithophel advice would show that Absalom had taken away power from King David's reign over the Israelites. He saw it as retribution for the adultery of King David with his granddaughter, Bathsheba, and the murdering of her husband. Ahithophel also requested twelve thousand men from Absalom to search for the fleeing King David and kill him. The taking of King David's ten concubines was a rebuking prophecy by Nathan, King David's adviser and prophet, for having Bathsheba's first husband, Uriah, killed (II Samuel 12:9-12).

King David, his servants, and his mercenaries consisting of Cherethites, Pelethites, and six hundred Gittites fled Jerusalem traveling east and came to a village named Bahurim as they were being pursued by Absalom's army (II Samuel 15:18 and 16:5-13). A Benjamite of the house of Saul named Shimei started cursing and throwing stones at David and his entourage alongside the road they were traveling He called King David a man of blood. He shouted that God had given his son, Absalom, the kingdom because He was avenging the blood of the house of Saul. Saul and his three sons died in the battle with Philistines on Mount Gilboa (1Samuel 31). David's nephew, Abishai son of Zeruiah, requested of David to decapitate Shimei for his behavior toward God's anointed king.

King Saul stopped obeying the commandments of the Lord. He usurped the duty and authority of the Jewish priests by offering up sacrifices. He made his soldier go without food until they had won a battle. He offered to have his own son executed for disobeying a trivial rule. He fell out of favor with God because of his disobedience and it was God's decision to replace him with David (See I Samuel 15 and 16). Because the Holy Spirit left Saul and an evil spirit entered him, he started behaving like an insane man.

When the Israelite kingdom was taken from Saul and given to David, this angered Shimei. He profanely disrespected God's anointed king. This is how the Holy Scripture relates how King David responded in II Samuel 16:5-13 AMP 5 When King David came to Bahurim, a man of the family of the house of Saul, Shimei son of Gera, came out and cursed continually as he came. 6 And he cast stones at David and at all the servants of King David; and all the people and all the mighty men were on his right hand and on his left.7 Shimei said as he cursed, Get out, get out, you man of blood, you base fellow! 8 The Lord has avenged upon you all the blood of the house of Saul, in whose stead you have reigned; and the Lord has delivered the kingdom into the hands of Absalom your son. Behold, the calamity is upon you because you are a bloody man! 9 Then said [David's nephew] Abishai son of Zeruiah to the king, Why should this dead dog curse my lord the king? Let me go over and take off his head. 10 The king said, what have I to do with you, you sons of Zeruiah? If he is cursing because the Lord said to him, Curse David, who then shall ask, why have you done so?11 And David said to Abishai and to all his servants, Behold, my son, who was born to me, seeks my life. With how much more reason now may this Benjamite do it? Let him alone; and let him curse, for the Lord has bidden him to do it.12 It may be that the Lord will look on the iniquity done me and will recompense me with good for his cursing this day.13 So David and his men went by the road, and Shimei went along on the hillside opposite David and cursed as he went and threw stones and dust at him.

Shimei was aware of the reason David was fleeing from his son, Absalom, so he continued taunting David on the roadside and up the hillside telling him that his kingdom had been given to Absalom by God. This is an issue that many of us have faced today. People can see when you are down and out and hurting, instead of helping or praying for you, they gossip behind your back and actually rejoice at your calamitous situation.

Is the word you speak profitable and enlightening, with edification and correction? Or is your throat an open sepulcher? Does your tongue use deceit? Are your lips poisons, full of cursing and bitterness? Or, you may be just the opposite of these things and called by God to do a job of ministering to someone, by mercy and meekness, restore them. But you must be worthy of the vocation in which God has called you for. Let god dress you up in the "Robe of Righteousness" (Isaiah 61 10-11 ESV 10 I will greatly rejoice in the LORD; my soul shall exult in my God, for he has clothed me with the garments of salvation; he has covered me with the robe of righteousness, as a bridegroom decks himself like a priest with a beautiful headdress, and as a bride adorns herself with her jewels.

# CHAPTER 14

# God's Revelations and Allowances are for His Purpose

We must always have an alert and open mind because God allows some things to happen always to benefit us. His thoughts are so much greater than ours that we don't even have a starting point to compare. (Isaiah 55:8-9 NIV 8 "For my thoughts are not your thoughts, neither are your ways my ways, "declares the LORD. 9 "As the heavens are higher than the earth, so are my ways higher than your ways and my thoughts than your thoughts.

Some things are God's secrets and He does not want us to know. He reveals as he pleases for He is Lord Almighty (Deuteronomy 29:29 ESV "The secret things belong to the LORD our God, but the things that are revealed belong to us and to our children forever, that we may do all the words of this law).

It must be realized that God allowed Satan to come to His high throne. Why? God allows everything for His own purpose. But Satan's stay is temporary and can only happen if God has summoned him. In the book of Job mentioned earlier, angels come before the Lord to hold counsel and Satan is with them. God asks Satan what he has been up to as if He didn't already know. Satan informs God that He has just been going to and fro on earth trying to find some soul to possess.

God is proud of the fact that He has other believers like Job that He knows that Satan can't influence or possess. Satan keeps God updated on backsliders because he is known as the accuser. Satan still believes that the only reason God has loyalty from believers is because of the well-being provided. Satan, to this day, believes if the well-being provided by God is taken away, then he can possess that soul. Let not your prayer to God change through the peaks and valleys of life. Sometimes there are valleys in life because He wants you to call on Him.

The cross was God's judgment of the world. Satan was defeated. The prince of this world who is the angel of death's time had come for him to be cast out of the world that he thought he had dominion over. John 12:28-33 ESV 28 Father, glorify your name. "Then a voice came from heaven: "I have glorified it, and I will glorify it again." 29 The crowd that stood there and heard it said that it had thundered. Others said, "An angel has spoken to him." 30 Jesus answered, "This voice has come for your sake, not mine. 31 Now is the judgment of this world; now will the ruler of this world be cast out. 32 And I, when I am lifted up from the earth, will draw all people to myself." 33 He said this to show by what kind of death he was going to die.

Satan's usurpation of the world that he thought he had dominion and power over has been exposed as being merely an assumption. He has no power even over the disobedient ones of this world, unless they, willingly, yield to his subjection. Look at it this way, the evilness of Satan brought about the greatest good that could have happened to mankind, which is the Cross.

When God allowed Job to be in Satan's power, the poor man lost everything including seven sons, three daughters, and became inflicted with severe sores as was related to earlier. His friends presumed that Job had committed some act of sin that angered God. The truth is that God becomes angry when someone brings false presumptuous charges against one of his servants. (Job 42:7-8)

For us, If Christ dwells inside us; we do not have to worry about having our own assumptions or false presumptions.

The prophet Zechariah revealed in the OT book of the same title that he had visions concerning Israel. His fourth vision listed in Chapter 3 is about Israel, which had become a sinful (unclean) nation after going into exile in Babylon and would again return to be a priestly nation despite, the prosecutor, Satan's accusations. Zechariah uses the name Joshua, which is the Aramaic equivalent of "Jeshua" (the Greek equivalent is spelled "Jesus", the Lord Saves, in English), as a high priest coming before God in unacceptable dirty garments. Satan tags along as an accuser ready to pounce on the fact that this high priest (the nation of Israel and the Priesthood) is not presentable before God. (Christ washed us clean with His own blood, washed away our sins and made us presentable to the Lord). God rebukes Satan. An Angel of the Lord discords Joshua's filthy rags and cleans him up from head to toe indicating that Israel will be restored as a sacerdotal nation (Zechariah 3:1- 5).

We must listen and obey whenever God commands us to do. We will never be victorious until we learn this. We are not perfect and will make mistakes in life. But, we must come to God in repentance to be forgiven. John the Baptist prepared the way for the coming of Jesus by preaching the need for repentance and baptizing people in the Jordan River. (Luke 3: 2-4 NIV 2 during the high-priesthood of Annas and Caiaphas, the word of God came to John son of Zechariah in the wilderness. 3 He went into all the country around the Jordan, preaching a baptism of repentance for the forgiveness of sins. 4 As it is written in the book of the words of Isaiah the prophet: "A voice of one calling in the wilderness, 'Prepare the way for the Lord, make straight paths for him.'"

After Jesus was tempted by Satan and overcame all the temptations that Satan could offer, Satan left Jesus and the angels from Heaven came to attend him and take care of His needs. Immediately after this happened, Jesus began His ministry in Capernaum preaching and thus fulfilled the prophecy of Isaiah in the Old Testament. Jesus spent most of his ministry in the area of Zebulun and Naphtali (Matthew 4:12-17). Matthew was relating to the prophecy of Isaiah from the Old Testament (Isaiah 9:1-2). When Jesus returned to Galilee after being in the wilderness with Satan, He was in the power of the Spirit. Jesus went to Nazareth, where He was brought up and went to the synagogue on the Sabbath which was His custom (Luke 4:16). Someone in the synagogue gave him the scroll of Isaiah the prophet.

Since there were no books in Jesus's day, the ancient writings were written on rolls of material such as papyrus, parchment, or leather, etc. These rolled- up ancient writings were called scrolls, for example, the Dead Sea Scrolls which contained biblical and non-biblical writings (for the timeline of the writing of these scrolls, information can be found at websites about carbon date testing the Dead Sea scrolls). These scrolls were discovered in eleven caves near the site of Quran between 1947 and 1956. These scrolls were written on parchment made of processed animal hide known as vellum. The scroll of Isaiah found in the caves near the Dead Sea by Bedouin shepherds length is 24 feet and contains 17 sheets of sheepskin and is not the one Jesus read from.

Jesus unrolled the scroll of Isaiah the prophet and found where it was written that the Spirit of the Lord was upon Him. The scrolls did not have page numbers. Jesus read that He was the anointed with the Holy Spirit to minister to all humankind with preaching and healing (Luke 4:18). All eyes were on Him as He rolled up the scroll and sat down. Then He spoke again applying to Himself the scripture of Isaiah 61:1 ESV The Spirit of the Lord GOD is upon me, because the LORD has anointed me to bring good news to the poor; he has sent me to bind up the brokenhearted, to proclaim liberty to the captives, and the opening of the prison to those who are bound; (Also Isaiah 61:2). Jesus was sent, not only being a light for the Israelites, but also a light for Gentiles.

# CHAPTER 15

# The Egog Disposition of the Apostle Peter

THE APOSTLE PETER WAS A Galilean fisherman who had a challenging beginning under the discipleship of the Lord Jesus. Before being renamed by Jesus, his name was Simon which in Hebrew means to hear/ or to be heard. Jesus renamed Simon in John 1:42 NIV and he brought him to Jesus. Jesus looked at him and said, "You are Simon son of John. You will be called Cephas"(which, when translated, is Peter). Cephas means 'Rock' in Aramaic. Early in his discipleship, Peter was presumptuous and had little faith. Jesus came as a sacrifice for our sins and his destiny had already been prophesied and preordained by the Father.

When Jesus told His disciples about His impending death, Peter, at this time, did not have knowledge of the Old Testament prophesies of Isaiah, King David, Zechariah, Joel and other prophets (See Isaiah 53, Psalms 22, Zechariah 12:10, Joel 2:28-29, etc. – the 39 books of the OT foreshadow or adumbrate the coming of Jesus). Peter, along with the other disciples still didn't understand God's purpose. They thought that Jesus came to restore the kingdom of Israel (OT Israel See Acts 1:6). The thought of the impending death of Jesus was something that Peter rejected because he loved Him. Peter had not yet grasped the concept of resurrection.

Jesus prophesies His impending suffering, death, and resurrection to His disciples and had to rebuke Peter in Matthew 16:21-23 ESV 21 From that time Jesus began to show his disciples that he must go to Jerusalem and suffer many things from the elders and chief priests and scribes, and be killed, and on the third day be raised. 22 And Peter took him aside and began to rebuke him, saying, "Far be it from you, Lord! This shall never happen to you." 23 But he turned and said to Peter, "Get behind me, Satan! You are a hindrance to me. For you are not setting your mind on the things of God, but on the things of man."

Peter had interludes at times before Jesus' sacrifice of death, that he seemed to be ecclesiastically perceptive, but not all the time. We must remember his profession was a fisherman which indicates he might not have had a formal education like the Apostle Paul. Peter returned to his former profession as a fisherman after Jesus was crucified. This was Peter's comfort zone. You wouldn't think Peter would have returned to his old profession, but rather his new profession should have been ministering and evangelizing in the name of Jesus.

Peter was with other disciples; Thomas called Didymus and Nathanael of Cana in Galilee, and the sons of Zebedee, and two other of his disciples and decided to go fishing on the sea of Tiberias. They requested to go with Him: John 21:3-7 KJV 3 Simon Peter saith unto them, I go fishing. They say unto him, we also go with thee. They went forth, and entered into a ship (actually, a small boat) immediately; and that night they caught nothing. 4 But when the morning was now come, Jesus stood on the shore: but the disciples knew not that it was Jesus. 5 Then Jesus saith unto them, Children, have ye any meat? They answered him, no. 6 And he said unto them, Cast the net on the right side of the ship, and ye shall find. They cast therefore, and now they were not able to draw it for the multitude of fishes. 7 Therefore that disciple (John) whom Jesus loved saith unto Peter, It is the Lord. Now when Simon Peter heard that it was the Lord, he girt his fisher's coat unto him, (for he was naked,) and did cast himself into the sea.

Some expositors of the Bible concerning Peter's nakedness comment that Peter's nakedness does not refer to a total lack of clothing, but rather that he had laid down his outer garment to prevent it from becoming soiled. We can assume from different versions of John 21:3-7 that Peter and the six disciples were not pleasure fishing, but working and secondly, Peter did not recognize Jesus, who was on the shore, from the boat that they were on but the disciple John did. Anyway, Peter and the six disciples had spent the whole night fishing and had not caught any fish. Jesus asked them from the shore, whether they had caught any fish and they answered, no. He told them to cast their fishing nets again on the right side of the boat. They caught so many fish that they filled the boat and had a difficult time getting to shore.

When they got to shore Jesus already had a fire ready to cook the fish so that they could eat. Now Jesus already had bread to eat with the fish. This was the third time that Jesus had appeared to the disciples after the crucifixion. (John 21: 10-14 AMP 10 Jesus said to them, Bring some of the fish which you have just caught.11 So Simon Peter went aboard and hauled the net to land, full of large fish, and [though] there were so many of them, the net was not torn.12 Jesus said to them Come [and] have breakfast. But none of the disciples ventured or dared to ask Him, Who are You? Because they [well] knew that it was the Lord.13 Jesus came and took the bread and gave it to them, and so also [with] the fish.14 This was now the third time that Jesus revealed Himself (appeared, was manifest) to the disciples after He had risen from the dead.

At the "Last Supper", the final meal shared by Jesus and His disciples before the crucifixion, He washed the disciple's feet to demonstrate the humility expected of them. When Jesus came to Peter to wash his feet, the impulsive Peter asked, "Why?" Jesus answered Peter by saying that "he would not understand now but later. The other disciples had not asked such a question. The washing of their feet we are told was customary among Jews before entering an abode because they walked around in sandy areas. The Sadducees thought this type of cleanliness and washing was for hygiene purposes. However, Jesus was not doing this for the disciple's hygiene, for He was known to them as "Rabbi" which means "my master" and is exaltation applied to teachers and other revered positions. This was an act of teaching Holiness and humility.

Peter was the only one, we are told, and who resisted Jesus washing his feet. He was displaying a reverence for Jesus that indicated that someone of such high position should not stoop so low as to wash his feet. He was still showing off in front of the other disciples. This might indicate that he felt the other disciples, who had their feet washed before him, did not display such reverence.

Jesus rebuked Peter for telling him this process was mandatory for him to continue in His discipleship. (John 13:3-9 AMP 3 [That] Jesus, knowing (fully aware) that the Father had put everything into His hands, and that He had come from God and was [now] returning to God,4 Got up from supper, took off His garments, and taking a [servant's] towel, He fastened it around His waist.5 Then He poured water into the washbasin and began to wash the disciples' feet and to wipe them with the [servant's] towel with which He was girded.6 When He came to Simon Peter, [Peter] said to Him, Lord, are my feet to be washed by You? [Is it for you to wash my feet?]7 Jesus said to him, you do not understand now what I am doing, but you will understand later on.8 Peter said to Him, You shall never wash my feet! Jesus answered him, unless I wash you, you have no part with ([a]in) Me [you have no share in companionship with Me].9 Simon Peter said to Him, Lord, [wash] not only my feet, but my hands and my head too!

Footnotes:

a. John 13:8 Origen (the greatest theologian of the early Greek Church); Adam Clarke, The Holy Bible with A Commentary; and others so interpret this passage. Notice the "in Me" emphasis in John 15, especially in verses 4-9, words spoken concerning the same subject, and on the same evening.

Jesus finally gives an explanation of this illustrious demonstration of humbleness to the disciples and Peter. The Apostle John has the longest narrative of the gospels on what happened in the upper room that night. (John 13:12-20 ESV 12 When he had washed their feet and put on his outer garments and resumed his place, he said to them, "Do you understand what I have done to you? 13 You call me Teacher and

Lord, and you are right, for so I am. 14 If I then, your Lord and Teacher, have washed your feet, you also ought to wash one another's feet. 15 For I have given you an example, that you also should do just as I have done to you. 16 Truly, truly, I say to you, a servant is not greater than his master, nor is a messenger greater than the one who sent him. 17 If you know these things, blessed are you if you do them. 18 I am not speaking of all of you; I know whom I have chosen. But the Scripture will be fulfilled, 'He who ate my bread has lifted his heel against me.' 19 I am telling you this now, before it takes place, that when it does take place you may believe that I am he. 20 Truly, truly, I say to you, whoever receives the one I send receives me, and whoever receives me receives the one who sent me.")

This is an unimaginable event that has extreme awesomeness about it, the Creator of the Heavens and the earth washing feet. What an extreme honor Jesus intended to pass on to the world, which is not to live in the exaltation of yourself, but to live a humble life with humility.

It is suspected that Peter is the one that cut off the ear of the servant of the high priest during Jesus' arrest as Judas Iscariot had betrayed Him. If Peter was the culprit, he still had not grasped that things must be done as prophesied. Jesus had foretold the betrayal by Judas and the denial by Peter, who would proclaim he did not know Jesus on three occasions, at the "Last Supper" (Mark 14:43-47).

Peter a Galilean, spoke with a different accent than the people in Jerusalem and he could not hide this fact when he spoke.(Matthew 26:73 ESV 73 After a little while the bystanders came up and said to Peter, "Certainly you too are one of them, for your accent betrays you.")

What a wretched man was Peter with the realization of what he had done because he had claimed his faithfulness, love, and loyalty to Jesus beforehand (Mark 14:30). Was he vindicated and accepted back by Jesus after the resurrection? Yes. Before the crucifixion, Peter, whom we know was rash and impulsive, had boasted that he loved Jesus more than the other disciples. On the day of the third appearance by Jesus after rising from the dead as you recall they had a breakfast of fish and bread. After the breakfast Jesus vindicated Peter and he was restored as a faithful servant, (John 21:15-19)

Peter became the voice and leader for the twelve disciples and what a transformation for the rough and gruff fisherman! God can take anyone and anoint them making them able to do His will. As we grow in Christianity, there are some things that we innocently believed that were the correct interpretation of scripture. As we mature, as Christians, it is not uncommon to have a more enlightened revelation of God's Word. This certainly was the case with Peter. He was unlike the individuals that Paul speaks of in I Timothy who were deliberately preaching to usurp the new early Christian churches by preaching different doctrines. The apostle Paul wrote to his young preacher, Timothy, while he was on his way to Macedonia, to warn him about certain preachers who were departing from accepted beliefs in the church at Ephesus (I Timothy 1:3-7).

There were two apostates who had been teaching false doctrines at the church in Ephesus. An apostate is one who forsakes his religion. These so called-teachers of the Old Testament law were teaching false doctrines according to the apostle Paul. The content of these false doctrines was described as vain discussions that didn't seem to be about crucifixion, death and, resurrection of Jesus. The names of the men who were said to have made a shipwreck of their faith were Hymenaeus an apostate, and Alexander, a coppersmith (I Timothy 1:20). Apostle Paul informed Timothy that he was going to expel them from the church for disciplinary reasons so that they might receive remedial training concerning the gospel.

The Apostle Paul came to Ephesus and first taught in the synagogues then throughout the city of Ephesus. The church that he founded there became the head of the seven churches in Asia Minor (also see Revelation 2:1-3). The Apostle John went to Ephesus but it is difficult, even for biblical scholars, to factually discern if he was there at the same time as the Apostle Paul. It is said that The Apostle John developed Christians there and he and the Apostle Paul led different communities in Ephesus. Tradition also says that the Apostle John accompanied Jesus' mother, Mary, to Ephesus and both were buried there. In theology, traditional beliefs are believed to have Devine authority but not necessarily found in scriptures in the bible. Traditions and legends are different even though many people may believe in legends, but legends cannot be proved to be truthful.

Paul spent three months trying to join the Jews with the Gentiles in Ephesus without success. The Apostle had competition with magicians and soothsayers there. An Ephesian named Demetrius earned his living by making and selling silver statues of Mother Goddess Artemis along with other sellers in the city. Before the Christians came to Ephesus, Artemis was one of the highly sacramental Ancient Greek idols in Ephesus. Consequently, the Christians were hurting the business of these sellers in Ephesus. Demetrius and the other sellers elicited thousands of the populace to conjoin at the theatre where he tried to convince them that Artemis was greater than the God of the Christians. Apostle Paul wanted to go to the theater to rebuke them but his followers persuaded him against this. He spent two more years there and accumulated Christian followers who were Greek-speaking Jews (Hellenized) and the Gentiles. The epistle to Timothy instructed him to fight the good fight that was prophesied earlier to him and to ignore the false teaching of Hymenaeus and Alexander because they had doomed themselves to hell unless they repent and learn not blaspheme.

Years later, Hymenaeus upset the church by heretical preaching along with a different partner named Philetus. Paul mentions that they had done him and the church great harm (II Timothy 2:16-18).

The apostle Paul ascribed to preaching to the Gentiles. The apostle Peter had to learn that God equally loved the Gentiles just as He loved the Jews. His duty was to preach and teach true doctrine. He had to also unlearn some things that had become so ingrained in the tradition of the Jewish culture (Judaism) that were not biblical, and therefore not authoritative law. There were things considered clean and unclean, laws about not associating with anyone who had not been circumcised, dietary laws, etc.

Acts 10 starts out with the details of a very honorable, God-fearing, Italian centurion (Roman military officer similar to colonel) named Cornelius who had seen clearly in a vision from an angel of God requesting that he summon Simon Peter to his home. God prepares

Peter for this visit by also allowing him to have a vision on a rooftop where he customarily went to pray. This dream, at the time puzzled Peter because he didn't know that Cornelius had sent some soldiers to invite him to his home.

God sometimes does not immediately reveal all that he intends to do. The vision was preparing him to change his thinking on Jewish traditions (Judaism) that the religious leaders had taught for a long time. Now, the soldiers are on their way to find Peter: Acts 10:9-15 KJV 9 On the morrow, as they went on their journey, and drew nigh unto the city, Peter went up upon the housetop to pray about the sixth hour: 10 And he became very hungry, and would have eaten: but while they made ready, he fell into a trance, 11 And saw heaven opened, and a certain vessel descending upon him, as it had been a great sheet knit at the four corners, and let down to the earth: 12 Wherein were all manner of four-footed beasts of the earth, and wild beasts, and creeping things, and fowls of the air. 13 And there came a voice to him, Rise, Peter; kill, and eat. 14 But Peter said, not so, Lord; for I have never eaten anything that is common or unclean. 15 And the voice spake unto him again the second time, what God hath cleansed, that call not thou common. 16 This was done thrice: and the vessel was received up again into heaven.

Again, we can see Peter's rebellious nature even in a vision he recognized as being from God. Jesus had already set the stage for this before and now maybe Peter is finally getting it. Jesus had said in Matthew 15: 11 that it is not what goes into the mouth that corrupts a person. So Peter is relieved that God himself had declared that Jews and Gentiles did not have to practice segregation as in the past. Peter was puzzled but God had prepared both Peter and Cornelius for a significant event. The spirit of God will make things clearer in His own time.

The Apostle Paul writes of this in a letter, I Timothy 4:1-5 ESV, that he had received a revelation from the "Holy Spirit" that was free of ambiguity that some would depart from the faith and give attention to doctrines of Satan. He is not only speaking of future events but also what was going on presently in his time. He spoke of the hypocrisy and heresy, opinions contrary to the church at Ephesus. Paul actually said that those preaching this heresy were demons. These events will arise and fall throughout church age. Peter also would be relieved that the Apostle Paul wrote in verse 4 and 5 ESV: For every creature of God is good, and nothing to be refused, if it be received with thanksgiving: For it is sanctified by the word of God and prayer.

Peter didn't hesitate to leave or ask why he was being summoned to Cornelius' home, He just went. The apostle Peter became the first man called by God to admit uncircumcised Gentiles into the Christian church; and Cornelius, family, and friends were the first admitted. Peter preached the gospel of Christ to them and they were baptized with the Holy Spirit (The Paraclete) and then he immersed them in a water baptism. If we understand the times when this happened, it was extraordinary for a Jew to associate with an uncircumcised gentile in public let alone go into his home. They looked down on Gentiles.

The Apostle Peter's life teaches us, as Christians, valuable lessons. In Peter's case, he had a difficult time separating Judaism from the Gospel. We are to live our lives so that non-believers want to emulate our good ways. We don't want someone saying they don't want to be a Christian because of our hypocrisy. The news that Peter had been to a Gentile's house and had brought Cornelius and his family to become believers spread all over Judea. When Peter went to make a report at the church in Jerusalem, the "circumcised group" jumped all over him for visiting an uncircumcised Gentile. These were converted Pharisees. They had not yet become unlearned from the old "Law" (Acts 11:1-3).

Peter had to explain that it was not his idea but a vision he had of God's divine will which had caused him to go there. They were temporarily satisfied with his answer but still wanted the consent of the church before they would make such a similar move. God had called on the Apostle Paul to convert the Gentiles to Christianity but Peter had converted the first Gentiles. Fourteen years after the conversion of the Apostle Paul, he had to rebuke Peter for reverting back to his segregationist ways concerning uncircumcised Gentiles.

The Jews at the church in Antioch, where believers were first called Christians, still tried to publicly display a demeanor of superiority because of Judaic Law still in their hearts. When Peter was called out on this matter by the apostle Paul, he displayed no opposition because, in his heart, he knew he was wrong for his partiality. Galatians 2:11-14 AMP 11 But when Cephas (Peter) came to Antioch, I protested and opposed him to his face [concerning his conduct there], for he was blamable and stood condemned.12 For up to the time that certain persons came from James, he ate his meals with the Gentile [converts]; but when the men [from Jerusalem] arrived, he withdrew and held himself aloof from the Gentiles and [ate] separately for fear of those of the circumcision [party].13 And the rest of the Jews along with him also concealed their true convictions and acted insincerely, with the result that even Barnabas was carried away by their hypocrisy (their example of insincerity and pretense). 14 But as soon as I saw that they were not straightforward and were not living up to the truth of the Gospel, I said to Cephas (Peter) before everybody present, If you, though born a Jew, can live [as you have been living] like a Gentile and not like a Jew, how do you dare now to urge and practically force the Gentiles to [comply with the ritual of Judaism and] live like Jews?

The Apostle Paul's reprimand could be appropriate for some Christians today who have become reliant on their own self-righteousness. Note that Apostle Paul calls Peter "Cephas" (Jesus declared that Simon would be called Cephas in the book of John 1:42 which means Peter, an Aramaic name equivalent to the Greek Petros, from which Peter is derived and is defined as "a piece of rock; a stone; a single stone. Jesus named Peter "detachable stone" for what he would become by God's grace, the pillar of the Church. (See Matthew 16:13-20) The rock, Greek Petra, is Jesus. That are several interpretations, but this is what is intended here. Since our Lord Jesus spoke in Aramaic he still called him Simon in the following synoptic Gospels: Matthew 17:24-25, Mark 14:37 and Luke 22:31) and he was also speaking to Barnabas, a traveling companion, who was also involved in this indignation. It is possible that the Apostle Paul would call Peter "Cephas" in a chastising way in his presence to remind him that he had reverted back to his old way of thinking about the Gentiles, who they were trying to convert to Christianity.

The book of Acts (15:2) relates dissension and debate over the law concerning circumcision. This was probably an effort from the Pharisee group (also called the Circumcision Group) to try and hold on to the partial keeping of the Judaic laws. Teachers of the period had identified 613 commandments to keep in the Law of Moses. To memorize all these laws was just as troublesome as trying to adhere to them. Circumcision was the seal of the law. Whoever would willingly and deliberately get circumcised enter into a contract to obey all 613 commandments. To break even just one of the laws is to break them all. James 2: 10 ESV For whoever keeps the whole law but fails in one point has become accountable for all of it. (Note on 2:10: The law is the expression of the character and will of God; therefore to violate one part of the law is to violate God's will and thus his whole law) This is the very reason the Apostle Paul said that anyone who practices the contract of the law also enters into slavery.

The Apostle Paul was a rabbinical genius and used his knowledge ad zealousness to defend the legalism of Judaism. After his conversion to Christianity on the way to Damascus (See Acts 9 the conversion of Saul), he used this same brilliance to oppose the law. According to his epistle to the Galatians, he thought of circumcision or uncircumcision as not having any value for salvation. He emphatically believed that Christ has set the Jew and the Gentile free from the burden and the yoke of the law. A yoke literally is a bar made of wood placed on animals' necks, usually oxen, so that the person guiding them in fields could control the animals to work together for plowing, pulling wagons, heavy loads, etc. A yoke can also be used on a single animal. The biblical writers are referring to "yoke" as being in slavery, bondage, forced into doing something, suppressed, burdened, being in bondage to sin or the Judaic Law. The Apostle related that if one chooses to adhere to the Judaic Law then that person is placing a burden (yoke) on him or herself to follow all of the laws. The apostle's contention is that only faith, working through love is counted as righteousness by Christ. Circumcision does not afford any special advantage in the eyes of the Lord (See Galatians 5:1-6). This is a very important message for Christians in these modern ages that are still hanging on to only portions of the law such as those comprising the Ten Commandments. Some Christians, for example, who attend church once or more times a week, are good persons, pay their bills on time, don't steal, haven't killed anybody, etc., according to the Ten Commandments. They may think they are in good shape because of their good works, but may fail the law in other instances and need to rely on the grace of God instead of their works of righteousness in the keeping of the law. Jesus emphasized that the greatest of the laws is to love the Father with all your heart and soul, the second to the first law is to love your neighbor as much as you love yourself.

<br>

CHAPTER 16

# Apostle Peter Becomes a Testament of Holiness and Love

PETER GLORIFIED JESUS SO MUCH that it is held by Christian tradition that when he was sentenced to be crucified by the Romans, under Nero Augustus Caesar, he requested to be crucified upside down. Peter saw himself unworthy to be crucified upright in the same manner as Jesus (67AD). This is not in the bible but can be found in the apocryphal text, "The Acts of Peter."

It has been said that Peter was a tall slender man with a beard, as ancient Jews considered the wearing of a beard as a sign of manliness. Peter was born in Bethsaida (in Galilee, Israel.) By profession, he was a fisherman. His father (also a fisherman) was named Jona (John or Jonah); his brother, Andrew a disciple, also participated in the families' fishing business. He and his brother (Andrew), along with their partners the apostles James and John, sons of Zebedee conducted their business on the Sea of Galilee.

So firm was Peter's faith that Jesus gave him the name of Cephas, meaning, in the Syriac language, a rock (Peter is the Greek translation of Cephas.) The home of Peter that was in Capernaum is said to be turned into a church by the Byzantines. This is not conclusive.

It was Peter who preached to the masses in Jerusalem on the day of Pentecost (following Jesus' ascension to heaven.) His message is recorded in the New Testament of the Bible, the book of Acts, chapter

2. Peter prompted the disciples to choose a replacement to take over the apostolic ministry of Judas Iscariot (Acts 1:15-22). The apostle Peter healed a man, who was over 40 years of age (Acts 4:22), who had been crippled from birth, with but the words, "Silver and gold I do not have, but what I have I give to you. In the name of Jesus Christ of Nazareth, walk (See Acts 3:6). Peter was called by the apostle Paul a "pillar" of the Church.

It was also believed. By the crowds that gathered to see the apostle, that the mere casting of his shadow upon the sick was capable of bringing about miraculous healing. Peter is the one who defended the inclusion of the Gentiles (non-Jews) into the Christian Church at the Apostolic Council in Jerusalem (Acts 15:7-41). His ministry was primarily to the Jews, as the apostle Paul's was to the Gentiles. After being imprisoned several times in Jerusalem (because of his faith), Peter left with his wife and possibly others. It is believed that he ministered (in Babylon) to the Jewish colonists there. It is, also, believed to be his location when he wrote his first epistle (1 Peter.)

There are some biblical scholars that say that the apostle Peter never visited Rome while other scholars indicate that there is the historical probability that he did. The Holy Bible does not specify whether the apostle went to Rome or not. It is believed that John Mark (the writer of the Gospel of Mark) served as Peter's translator (as he preached in Rome?). There is a Church tradition which says that "Mark the disciple and interpreter of the apostle Peter wrote a short gospel at the request of the brethren at Rome, embodying what he had heard from the apostle Peter." Thus, it has been said that the apostle Peter's preaching was the source of the Gospel of Mark.

(Non-biblical)The Roman Emperor Nero publicly pronounced himself the chief enemy of God, which led in his fury to slaughter the Apostles. (Christian tradition) Concerning the last hours of his life, it is said that Peter, when seeing his own wife led out to die, rejoiced because of her summons and her return home. He called to her very encouragingly and comfortingly, addressing her by name, and saying, "O thou, remember the Lord." In the final days of the apostle Peter in Rome, Italy, Jowett wrote that Peter was cast into a horrible prison called the Mamertine. For nine months, in absolute darkness, he endured monstrous torture manacled to a post. In spite of all the suffering Peter was subjected to, he converted his jailers, Processus, Martinianus, and forty-seven others.

Legend has it that a spring miraculously started flowing through the prison. Saint Peter is said to have converted the two jailers and baptized them in the spring. It is also said that when the emperor, Nero, found out about them being converted and baptized, he had the guards arrested, tortured, and beheaded.

It is not that Peter did not make obvious mistakes; he did so because of his zealousness for Jesus. He was also repentant and knew and understood early on the holiness of Jesus. Jesus climbed aboard Peter's boat to preach to the masses that had gathered along the shore of Lake Galilee along with other disciples. After preaching Jesus revealed some of his awesome power to the disciples.

Luke 5:4-11 ESV 4 and when he had finished speaking, he said to Simon, "Put out into the deep and let down your nets for a catch." 5 And Simon answered, "Master, we toiled all night and took nothing! But at your word I will let down the nets." 6 And when they had done this, they enclosed a large number of fish, and their nets were breaking. 7 They signaled to their partners in the other boat to come and help them. And they came and filled both the boats, so that they began to sink. 8 But when Simon Peter saw it, he fell down at Jesus' knees, saying, "Depart from me, for I am a sinful man, O Lord." 9 For he and all who were with him were astonished at the catch of fish that they had taken, 10 and so also were James and John, sons of Zebedee, who were partners with Simon. And Jesus said to Simon, "Do not be afraid; from now on you will be catching men." 11 And when they had brought their boats to land, they left everything and followed him.)

Jesus did not send Peter away for his penitent confession. No one is righteous and if you claim to be, you are a liar and you make God out to be a liar because God's Word is not in us (Romans 3:10, 23). There are some people who profess to be Christians that have never repented. They believe their righteousness is sufficient, so there is no need to repent. There is a rebirth required when we repent and bury the old self and agree to allow God to take control of our lives. There is an immediate apprehended change that takes place in our lives when we repent and give ourselves to God.

A Pharisee named Nicodemus, a ruler of the Jews, who Jesus agreed to secretly meet with at night made a statement that God had to be with him to perform all of the miracles. Jesus replied in John 3:3 KJV: Jesus answered and said unto him, Verily, verily, I say unto thee, Except a man be born again, he cannot see the kingdom of God.)

Apostle Peter helped establish the Jerusalem church. Apostle Peter spread the gospel to the Jews as did apostle Paul for the Gentiles, who were not God's chosen people at birth. They were called "pagans" or "heathen" by the Jewish community. Even though Peter was the spokesman for the disciples and played an active role in the early church, it was James, Jesus' brother, who assumed the role of leadership of the early Jerusalem church.

In Acts 15 Peter and Barnabas brought before the early church in Jerusalem a debate concerning whether new "pagan" (Gentiles) converts should be circumcised. It was James who made the final decision that was agreed upon by all that no unnecessary obstacles should be placed upon the Gentiles who wanted to turn to God (See Acts 15- the Jerusalem Council).

Peter did change, as you might observe, from his two epistles in the New Testament Bible. Especially in the first epistle; he frequently admonished believers to live a life of holiness and love. This was a metamorphosis of character for Peter from being a gruff fisherman of fish to a fisherman for the salvation of men.

# CHAPTER 17

# Mosaic Laws Including Dietary Laws

REMEMBER UNDER THE MOSAIC LAW, they were not allowed to eat certain foods as listed in Leviticus and Deuteronomy. For information and interest sake, there are eighty or maybe more fish with scales and fins that are kosher and edible. The non-edible fish and other meats listed here that are kosher and biblically edible:

## Biblically Clean Fish (Must have both fins and scales)

Albacore (Crevalle, Horse Mackerel, Jack),Alewives (Branch Herring, River Herring), Anchovy, Barracuda, Bass, Black Drum, Blackfish, Blueback(Glut Herring), Bluebill Sunfish, Bluefish, Blue Runner (Hardtail), Bonitos, Boston Bluefish (Pollack), Bowfin, Buffalo fish, Butterfish, Carp, Chub (Bloater, Longjaw, Blackfin), Cod, Crappie, Crevalle (Albacore), Croaker, Darter, Flounder (Dab, Gray Sole, Yellow Tail), Frost Fish (Ice Fish, Smelt), Gaby, Grayling, Groupers (Gag),Grunts, Gulf Pike (Robalo, Snook, Sergeant), Haddock, Hake, Halibut, Hardtail (Blue Runner), Herring, Horse Mackerel (Albacore), Kingfish, Long Nose Sucker (Northern Sucker, Red Striped Sucker), Mackerel, Menhaden, Mullet, Muskellunge (Jack), Orange Rough, Perch, Pickerel (Jack), Pig Fish, Pike (Jack), Pilchard (Sardine), Pollack, Pompano, Porgy (Scup), Red Drum (Redfish), Red fin (Red Horse Sucker), Red Snapper, Red Striped Sucker (Long Nose Sucker), Robalo

(Gulf Pike), Rockfish, Salmon (Chum, Coho, King, Pink, Red), Sardine (Pilchard), Scup (Porgy), Sea Bass, Sergeant Fish (Gulf Pike), Shad, Sheepshead, Silver Hake (Whiting), Silversides, Smelt (Frost Fish), Snook (Gulf Pike), Spanish Mackerel, Striped Bass, Sucker, Tarpon, Tilapia, Trout, Tuna (Albacore, Bluefin, Yellowfin, Shipjack), Weakfish, Whitefish, White Sucker, Whiting (Silver Hake), and Yellow Perch

## Biblically Unclean Fish and Seafood

Abalone, Bullhead, Catfish, Clam, Crab, Crayfish, Eel, Krill, Lobster, Mussel, Oyster, Paddlefish (Spoonbill), Scallop, Sculpin, Shark, Shrimp, Squid, Stickleback, Sturgeon (Caviar), Swordfish, and Whale

## Clean Red Meat (Must chew the cud and have a divided hoof)

Antelope, Beef, Buffalo, Deer, Elk, Goat, Moose, and Sheep

## Clean Fowl

(Cannot be a raptor or scavenger)
Chicken, Dove, Duck, Goose, Grouse, Pheasant, Quail, and Turkey

Many still adhere to dietary laws of Leviticus 11 and Deuteronomy 14 and many see no spiritual benefit for a Christian to follow the dietary law other than the fact that in this health conscious society of today, the dietary law is followed. It should be noted that scientific tests have been done on the clean and unclean fish listed in the Torah.

Tests done under controlled environmental circumstances showed that all of the clean fish listed had no toxicity and those listed as unclean were toxic. Pork also has to be cooked properly with an internal temperature of 170 degrees to kill parasitic organisms such as tapeworms. Since pigs are known to eat all kinds of slop, it is probably better to spend a little more for pasture raised organic pork and other edible animal products. Antibiotics are used to treat animals for diseases that are usually raised in unhealthy environments. Edible organic animal products, in general, are supposed to be void of hormones, antibiotics and drugs. It has been said that eating pork (high in fat content) won't send you to hell but might send you Heaven faster.

Under the law, this one sin makes one guilty as if they had broken all ten of the Commandments. The Apostle Paul's influential epistle to the Galatians associated the freedom obtained by the redemptive work of Christ on the Cross as if one has been in slavery and is liberated. There were Jews of the circumcision group who would not let go of the initiation rite. This group felt that this led to a status of righteousness with God. This ritual of circumcision was not rebuked by The Apostle Paul but circumcision nor uncircumcision counts for nothing to obtain salvation. What counts is one's faith and conformity to His purpose obtained by the help of the Holy Spirit (The Paraclete) (Galatians 5:1-6).

Jesus teaching on the Sermon on the Mount said in Matthew 5:18-20 ESV 18 For truly, I say to you, until heaven and earth pass away, not an iota, not a dot, will pass from the Law until all is accomplished. 19 Therefore whoever relaxes one of the least of these commandments and teaches others to do the same will be called least in the kingdom of heaven, but whoever does them and teaches them will be called great in the kingdom of heaven. 20 For I tell you, unless your righteousness exceeds that of the scribes and Pharisees, you will never enter the kingdom of heaven.

(Jesus is not speaking against observing all the requirements of the Law but against hypocritical, Pharisaical legalism. Such legalism was not the keeping of all details of the Law but the hollow sham of keeping laws externally to gain merit before God while breaking them inwardly. It was following the letter of the Law while ignoring its spirit. Jesus repudiates the Pharisees' interpretation of the Law and their view of righteousness by works. He preaches a righteousness that comes only through faith in him and his work) NIV Notes from the Glo Bible.

This matter of circumcision for salvation was something that the Pharisees did not want to relinquish because it was a covenant

Abraham had made with God in Genesis Chapter 17 based on the old covenant law. Circumcision was evidence of a signifying consecration to God.

Apparently, there were Judaists at the church in Jerusalem where the disciples held council on important issues involving converts. James, one of Jesus' four brothers, was the head of the church at Jerusalem. There were some men, probably Judaist, who had gone to Galatia and were teaching the converts that they could not be saved unless they were circumcised. This was the main issue that had aroused a very heated debate when the council was held in Jerusalem.

Even apostle Peter, later on, recognized that placing the converted Gentiles, or even the disciples under the law, was like placing the yoke of bondage on one's self and testing God. Peter had moved from a realm of being spiritual, a child, to spiritual maturity. He emphasized that not even the Jewish forefathers could bear this yoke, so why would the disciples going forth converting Gentiles expect them to be able to bear this yoke of bondage. Acts 15:10-11 AMP 10 Now then, why do you try to test God by putting a yoke on the necks of the disciples, such as neither our forefathers nor we [ourselves] were able to endure? 11 But we believe that we are saved through the grace (the undeserved favor and mercy) of the Lord Jesus, just as they [are].

The question that presents itself about dietary laws in the Torah is this, is it a sin to eat foods listed as biblically unclean? The reason for these food laws was to make the Israelites distinct from all of the other nations and to make them a Holy nation of priests. It has also been previously stated that toxicity has been found in the food group listed as Biblically unclean. In Mark 7:18-19 ESV, Jesus declared all foods as clean. 18 And he said to them, "Then are you also without understanding? Do you not see that whatever goes into a person from outside cannot defile him, 19 since it enters not his heart but his stomach, and is expelled?"(Thus he declared all foods clean.)

If someone wants to adhere to dietary laws and we don't, we, as Christians should do everything in our power not to offend them. Whatever we eat we should do it in the glory of God and be thankful. Speculating that the Apostle Paul's message is to some of the Christians in Rome who wanted to adhere to the Mosaic dietary laws and placed judgement on those who didn't: Romans 14:1-4 KJV 1 Him that is weak in the faith receive ye, but not to doubtful disputations. 2 For one believeth that he may eat all things: another, who is weak, eateth herbs. 3 Let not him that eateth despise him that eateth not; and let not him which eateth not judge him that eateth: for God hath received him. 4 Who art thou that judgest another man's servant? To his own master he standeth or falleth. Yea, he shall be holden up: for God is able to make him stand.

Our ability to control ourselves in every aspect of our lives is what is important. Stay away from things that make a weak Christian fall into the same sin. For instance, it wouldn't look right for a Christian to be in a bar specifically designed for the sale only of alcoholic beverages even if he or she is drinking a soft drink. It just doesn't present the right image for a weak Christian to see you coming out of such a place.

Since the Mosaic dietary laws were meant for the Hebrews, and not Gentiles, who was considered non-Hebrews? According to the Bible, everyone who doesn't have a Jewish bloodline is considered to be a Gentile. (Does it really mean non-Hebrew people? Bible readers have accepted this definition, but further study of the etymology of the word "Gentile" indicates it should be used plurally as *Gentiles*. The word gentile is derived from the Latin word gentilis and is only one of several words that are used to translate the Hebrew word *goi* and the Greek word *ethnos* into English. Technically, the best way to define the word use is "nations").

# CHAPTER 18

# Abraham's Unique Relationship With God in Faith of the Holy Spirit Faith that Led to Friendship

THE STORY OF ABRAHAM IN the book of Genesis in the Holy Bible, chapters twelve through twenty-five, is a story of how God rewards for faith and obedience to Him and his wife, Sarah. Before God renamed Abraham and Sarah (Gen 17:5 and17:15). Their previous names were Abram and Sarai respectively. Abraham (name meaning "father of many") is a descendant of the eldest son of Noah named Shem (Genesis 5:32, 11:10-26). Shem is the father of the Semites or Semitic people which includes the Israelites. Abram and his wife Sarai lived in a land called Haran in upper Mesopotamia with his father Terah (Gen 11:26, 31). In Gen 12:1 God tells Abram to take his wife and leave his father and kindred and move to a land that I will tell you. Mesopotamia in Greek means "the land between two rivers.

Ancient Mesopotamia was located in a piece of The Fertile Crescent, in what is now southern Iraq. It covered an area about 300 miles long and about 150 miles wide. It is surmised that God wanted Abram to leave because his father and family were idol worshippers. During the time Abram lived in Haran (Harran) it was known as the major worship center for the moon god Sin (Any transgressing Israelite who was convicted for worshiping the moon was punished by stoning). God told Abram, I will make you a great nation and that he would make his name great so that he would be a blessing. Abram was seventy-five years old (based on Genesis 12:4) at the time he packed up his possessions along with his wife, his brother's son, Lot, and some servants and moved to the land of Canaan. Canaan, later on, would become the land God would make a covenant to give to Abraham and his descendants (See Genesis 15:18-21). This land is referred to as "The Promised Land" or the land of "Milk and Honey."

God did not forbid anyone that wanted to leave with Abraham from Haran. God never forbids someone who wants to follow him. God only tells us to count the cost and be willing to deny ourselves. Abraham and Sarah lived in Egypt for a short time because there was a famine in Canaan. In Egypt, Abraham feared for his life because his wife, Sarah, was beautiful and he felt that the Egyptians would kill him and take his wife. Instead of trusting that God would protect him he instructed Sarah to say that she was his sister. Even though he fabricated a lie, it was only partially untrue because she was his half-sister. Sarah was the daughter of Abraham's father Terah. She was ten years younger than Abraham.

Pharaoh requested Sarah for his wife from Abraham by giving him the form of wealth for that time period which was livestock and men and women servants. God had other plans for Abraham and Sarah. This ruse was revealed when God inflicted disease (plague) on Pharaoh's family. God's revelation to Pharaoh allowed him to accurately diagnose the root cause of the plague. Pharaoh called Abraham to ask him why he told this lie to him about Sarah being his sister. Pharaoh ordered Abraham to take his wife and go. Pharaoh gave his men orders concerning him, and they sent him away with his wife and all that he had (See Genesis 12:12-20). Abraham became wealthy while in Egypt and left there with livestock, gold and, silver (Gen 13:2).

This ruse was used again by Abraham for the same reason as he feared that he would be killed by a king who might want to take his wife, Sarah, away from him because of her beauty. The second ruse was in the court of the king of Gerar, Abimelech, who also took Sarah for his own. King Abimelech had a nightmare that sin had been brought to his land. God intervened to protect Sarah by informing Abimelech in a dream that if he touched Sarah he was a dead man. This was for the protection of the mother of the future Israelite nation. This was because of God's intervention to prevent him from taking Sarah as his own wife. He sent Abraham and Sarah away from his court with similar gifts as had been given by the Egyptian Pharaoh and allowed them to live in the land. (Details found in Genesis 20:1-18). Abraham and Sarah returned to the land of Canaan and they still did not have any children for Sarah was barren. She was grieved because of her barrenness and became impatient to have a child.

She gave her Egyptian maid, Hagar, to Abraham for consummation so that they would have an heir. They were impatient and would not allow God to complete his work. She became resentful when Hagar conceived and gave birth to a son named Ishmael. Ishmael was not the promised son of the father of many nations. The Lord and two angels came to Abraham when he was ninety-nine years old to reinforce the covenant that he had made with him. Sarah was inside the door of their tent when she heard God's messenger informing Abraham that they would be having a son. She laughed to herself because she was eighty-nine years old, well past childbearing age and Abraham, under normal circumstances, was too old. The Lord asked why did Sarah laugh, doesn't she know that God can fulfill any promise? Sarah lied and said that she hadn't laughed and the Lord told her so (Genesis 18:1-15).

While the Lord and two angels were there with Abraham at the oak trees of a town named Mamre, He informed Abraham that the sins of the people in the towns of Sodom and Gomorrah were so grave that He would have to destroy them. Later on, Sodom and Gomorrah were destroyed by sulfur and fire that rained down from the heavens. The Lord spared Lot and his two daughters. The Lord had told Lot to take his wife and daughters and leave Sodom where they lived and not look back. When they were leaving, Lot's wife looked back and was turned into a pillar of salt.

A year after God had reinforced his covenant with Abraham, he and Sarah had a son that they named Isaac. The biblical text, Genesis 21:5, states that Abraham was one hundred years old when Isaac was born and Sarah was either ninety or ninety-one and died at the age of one hundred and twenty-seven years old (Genesis 23:1).

Abraham's faith was tested more than he could have ever imagined when God asked him to sacrifice Isaac. He and Sarah had waited such a long time for the promise of this son. God told Abraham to sacrifice Isaac as a burnt offering at a place that He would show him. Isaac was God's own miracle anyway because both Sarah and Abraham were past childbearing age when he was conceived. This time Abraham obeyed and prepared to sacrifice his son. Abraham fully trusted God to be in control. Isaac was the promised heir of many nations so Abraham surely thought that if he would kill Isaac, surely God would resurrect him from the dead. Just as Abraham had raised a knife to slaughter his son, an Angel of the Lord intervened and provided a ram that had been caught in the thickets. Abraham memorialized this place and named it "Jehovahjireh": Genesis 22: 14 KJV So Abraham called that place The LORD Will Provide. And to this day it is said, "On the mountain of the LORD it will be provided."

We are told to bless the Jewish people because God still stands behind them. God is the one that has allowed them to be scattered to different parts of the earth for their disobedience and sin. God punished them many times as a parent would discipline a child. Sin never escapes the eyes of God but because of His grace, compassion, and love, through repentance He will restore them. God has a plan for all of His people and is dealing with Jews as well as the Gentiles (Luke 3:6 ESV and all flesh shall see the salvation of God). God's salvation was to be known to both Jews and Gentiles. Non-Jews or Gentiles don't have to become Jews or practice Judaism to receive salvation.

# CHAPTER 19

# Things of God are Revealed When His Spirit Dwells in our Heart

CHRIST SHOULD DWELL IN OUR hearts and as a result, we should be rooted and grounded in holiness and love. What does love do? When we love, God dwells in us and sin is cast out. When God dwells in us because of love, it brings about coverage of many of our sins. I Peter 4:8 NIV 8 Above all, love each other deeply because love covers a multitude of sins.

Love endures all things: ICorinthians13:4-7 NIV Love is patient, love is kind. It does not envy, it does not boast, it is not proud. 5 It does not dishonor others, it is not self-seeking, it is not easily angered, and it keeps no record of wrongs. 6 Love does not delight in evil but rejoices with the truth. 7 It always protects, always trusts, always hopes, and always perseveres.

The exhibition and teaching of love should begin in our homes if we wish for it to spread everywhere, not only in our homes, but also to our neighborhoods, cities, states, and to other nations of the world. God's love transcends our knowledge but if our hearts are rooted and grounded in Him and His love, He reveals some of His mysteries. As a result, we will live our lives according to the grace, patterns, and knowledge He has afforded us. We should kneel before the Father in prayer continuously and ask Him for greater revelation(s) and repentance as we seek His kingdom.

# CHAPTER 20

# Peter's Affirmation of Jesus's Messiahship Blessed, Then He is Rebuked

LEARN SOMETHING ABOUT GOD'S WORD and commit it to memory and it will not be taken away from you. We might be losing the morality of our country and all that is righteous worldwide. It will not profit us anything if we gain all that is worldly and lose our souls. During the time that Jesus was predicting his death as he spoke to the people and His disciples in the district of Caesarea Philippi.

Chapter 16 of the Apostle Matthew, Jesus acknowledges that, perhaps, the Apostle Peter had received divine revelation because neither the disciples (nor the religious leaders- Pharisees and Sadducees) seemed to grasp who Jesus really was even though they were with Him when He performed many miraculous feats. They really expected Jesus to be the "one" to lead a rebellion to free Israel from the corrupt political leaders.

Jesus and His disciples came to the district of Caesarea Philippi, 25 miles north of the Sea of Galilee and at the base of Mt. Hermon, He asked them "Who do the people say the Son of Man is?" Jesus was the incarnate God, so when He asked them "Who do they say the Son of Man is?" He is identifying with humanity or His human nature. It is not identified which of the disciples answered this question but the answers were that some thought He was John the Baptist, who was dead, beheaded by Herod. Herod, in the Gospel of Mark 6:16, superstitiously thinks that John the Baptist had come back from the dead to haunt him for the beheading. John the Baptist preached in the spirit of Elijah by preaching about repentance but he was not a reincarnation of Elijah (Luke 1-17 and Malachi 4:5). The disciples said that some thought that He was rebirthed (reincarnated) in Elijah's body, or the prophet Jeremiah, or some Other Old Testament prophet.

THE FATHER IN HEAVEN ALLOWED the Holy Spirit to come upon Peter at this moment and he answered the question by stating that Jesus is the Messiah who was prophesied as the promised savior of the Jewish people in the Hebrew Bible. Jesus also acknowledged that Peter could not have known this without the help of Devine intervention (See synoptic Gospels Matthew 16:13-20, Mark 8:27-30, and Luke 9:18-21). The reason Jesus asked this question was that He knew of the outside influences of the religious sects at the time who wanted to hear nothing of Jesus as being the Messiah, such as the Pharisees. They thought that Jesus was committing blasphemy by claiming to be the Messiah. Jesus knew that some involved with these religious sects were under the influence of Satan's Cosmic System (Cosmos Diabolicus -the devil's world). Jesus was testing to see if any of His own disciples had been influenced by these sect(s).

In the very next verses of scripture following the blessing that Jesus had bestowed upon Peter, the Bible tells us that from that point on Jesus foretold His impending death and resurrection to His disciples. Shortly thereafter, Peter reverted back to His ignorance of the Messiah's purpose and had the boldness to rebuke Jesus because he did not understand the concerns of God. Matthew 16:21-23 KJV 21 From that time forth began Jesus to shew unto his disciples, how that he must go unto Jerusalem, and suffer many things of the elders and chief priests and scribes, and be killed, and be raised again the third day. 22 Then Peter took him, and began to rebuke him, saying, be it far from thee, Lord: this shall not be unto thee. 23 But he turned, and said unto Peter, Get thee behind me, Satan: thou art an offence unto me: for thou savourest not the things that be of God, but those that be of men.

Peter was trying to dissuade Jesus from His predestined reason for leaving Heaven and taking on an earthly form of a human so that He could be crucified and resurrected for the atonement of the human race. Did Satan know of God's plan for redemption? The Bible does not specifically say that he does. Jesus addresses Satan directly that had come into Peter. Therefore if the spirit of Satan had come into Peter, thus I Corinthians 2:11 AMP for what person perceives (knows and understands) what passes through a man's thoughts except the man's own spirit within him? Just so no one discerns (comes to know and comprehend) the thoughts of God except the Spirit of God.

Jesus spoke to his disciples and the people informing them that He would be crucified, for He said to the people, if anyone wanted to be His disciple that they also would have to pick up his own cross and follow Him. This is saying to us that, as Christians, we all must carry a burden and be willing to do so for the belief and knowledge that Jesus will see us through it. Jesus does not bring us to any burden that He cannot lead us out of. If you chose to place your devotion to those things that you get possession of in this world, or how much power you possess, no matter the quantity you obtain, it means nothing if you have not committed yourself to living your life to the obedience of Jesus. We should be able to suffer and die for the sake of God.

In this century, Christians living in the Levant region are being crucified, murdered, beheaded, etc., in the name of Jesus Christ(The Levant is a geographical term that refers to a large area in Southwest Asia, south of the Taurus Mountains, bounded by the Mediterranean Sea in the west, the Arabian Desert in the south, and Mesopotamia in the east). Many Christian refugees are fleeing from the Near East and ancient Near East regions to avoid persecution and death. Al-Qaida in Iraq changed its name in 2013 to the Islamic State of Iraq and the Levant (ISIL) Syrian and Iraq has seen the proliferation of terrorist cells and has caused many to flee.

How many of us are willing to bear the cross that Jesus is speaking of for the sake of our own salvation? By denying Jesus while being questioned by an uncompromising Christian persecutor such as Saul, before his conversion, might spare your life in the physical world (See

Acts 8:1-3). The consequence this denial is to lose eternal life. Verse 36 of Mark 8 ESV is often quoted. It was what Jesus said while teaching to the gathered crowd at the villages of Cesarean Philippi. He spoke of His impending suffering and rejection by the elders and chief priests. He related during this teaching of His impending death (being killed) and resurrected Jesus said, "For what does it profit a man to gain the whole world and forfeit his soul?"

# CHAPTER 21

# Faith is the Key to the Gates of Heaven

WHY IS THE WORLD LIVING in such terror? Could it be too little faith or no faith at all? The system of faith gives us hope for a better world and the promise of eternal life. (Hebrews 11:1 KJV Now faith is the substance of things hoped for, the evidence of things not seen.)

Faith is something not made by man's hand. Faith is about God and will cause us delight in His laws. Faith will cause us to meditate day and night. By living in faith, we will be like trees planted by the rivers of water. There is a tree of life and an environment of water around this tree that does not let the leaves wither. The leaves of this tree will heal the nation. Jesus speaks of the tree of life in the last book of the Bible which Jesus revealed to the Apostle John (Revelation 22:1-5). This tree is unlike anything that is currently growing on earth. This tree yielded twelve varieties of fruit. It yields fruit every month of the year. Scholars find it difficult to determine if the Apostle is speaking of a single giant tree or series of trees. This tree or trees is alongside a river with sparkling water that flows through the center of the city referenced here. The tree of life is first spoken of in the Bible in Genesis 3:22 ESV Then the LORD God said, "Behold, the man has become like one of us in knowing good and evil. Now, lest he reach out his hand and take also of the tree of life and eat, and live forever–"

Jesus relates to the Apostle that the tree of life's purpose is for healing and restoration of the nations. The verses of the book of Revelation are speaking of future events where the sun will not be needed any longer to provide light. The Eden of Genesis 3 will be will be restored.

We will bring forth fruit from this tree. Men will see our good works of love and the glorification of God. We will never get weary of doing well. Nothing will be done out of season.

The fruit has the ability to produce within the appointed time. Being planted by the water, the roots of the tree have the ability to anchor and grow strong serving the life of the tree.

Faith is of the substance; love is the key, therefore, whatsoever it is that we do will prosper. Ungodly counsel must always be avoided. Now if we become thirsty and come to Jesus and drink, believing in Him, as the scriptures say, rivers of water will flow from out of our bellies. This is in reference to the Holy Ghost (Spirit). This is the inner man. Symbolically, the use of living water is speaking of the Holy Spirit dwelling in a person to receive salvation.

# CHAPTER 22

# The Use of Anointing Oils Symbolically

To receive the Holy Spirit under the old covenant, Holy anointing oil was used which was to symbolize receiving the blessing of God. It was applied to the head of the recipient being anointed. It was commonly used to anoint new kings, priests, and prophets. Since the olive tree was prominent in the Holy land during biblical times, liquid olive oil fat was extracted from the olive, the fruit of that tree. The use of the extracted liquid olive fat was first recorded in Exodus 27:20 of the Bible where the oil was hand squeezed by the Israelites, brought to the priests and poured into specific containers.

The priests were required to keep the lamps in the tabernacle perpetually burning with this olive oil. This oil was also used in religious ceremonies. For example, Moses consecrated his brother Aaron for the first high priesthood of the Israelites by pouring oil over his head. (Exodus 29:7 KJV Then shalt thou take the anointing oil, and pour it upon his head, and anoint him.) Aaron's sons were anointed priests and the oil was not to be used for anyone else's body The formula for this perfume is given in Exodus 30:23-25 KJV 23 Take thou also unto thee principal spices, of pure myrrh five hundred shekels, and of sweet cinnamon half so much, even two hundred and fifty shekels, and of sweet Calamus two hundred and fifty shekels, 24 And of cassia five hundred shekels, after the shekel of the sanctuary, and of oil olive an hin: 25 And thou shalt make it an oil of holy ointment, an ointment compound after the art of the apothecary: it shall be an holy anointing oil. If anyone in the Israelite camp was found duplicating this formula or using it on a stranger, they would be exiled out of the camp.

Apothecary used in verse 25 above is defined in the "Easton's Bible Dictionary". As one who makes perfume. Moses had to take this Holy anointing oil and anoint the tabernacle of the congregation, the ark of the testimony, the table and all his vessels, the candlestick and his vessels, the altar of incense, the altar of burnt offering with all his vessels, the laver (laver also in Exodus 30:18 KJV) is a washbasin made of melted down brass that came from the mirrors made of brass donated by the Israelite women in the camp (Exodus 38:8). It was used by the Levitical priest to wash before the offering of sacrifices and any other duties required by the law in the book of Leviticus) and his feet (Exodus 30.26-29).

Samuel, a prophet and, seer, who was also the last judge, anointed the first king of Israel, King Saul, by pouring oil upon his head (See 1Samuel 10:1). King Saul's disobedience to God's instructions led Samuel to anoint King David (ancestor of Jesus) as the second king of Israel (See 1Samuel 16:12-13). The Spirit of the LORD came powerfully over David, but departed from Saul, as he was anointed.

One of God's prophets named Elijah was sought after to be killed because he was considered a troublemaker by a king and queen of Samaria for actively opposing idolatry.

A woman that is considered to be promiscuous, dominating, or controlling is sometimes called Jezebel. For centuries the term was used for those that were considered to be false prophets. In the Bible, Jezebel was a Phoenician princess whose father was Ethbaal, king of Sidon. She was the wife of King Ahab (I Kings 16:31). She was a cruel queen who practiced idolatry and persecuted prophets of God. Her name is also used to describe a nefarious woman or unscrupulous woman.

The woman who called herself a prophetess at the church in Thyatira in the book of Revelation is referred to as Jezebel (Revelation

2:14, 20). This prophetess professed to be loyal to God was urging sexual immorality and the eating of foods sacrificed to idols.

Jezebel's husband, King Ahab, was a weakling, while she was a headstrong woman who dominated him and turned him away from God (I Kings 18:17-18). She grew up worshipping the idol gods named Baal (male) and his female companion, Ashtoreth (or Astarte). Baal was considered the god of the land and Ashtoreth was the god of fertility. She was determined to wipe out Jehovah worshipers. Jezebel persuaded or demanded her husband, Ahab, to build a temple next to their palace in Samaria to worship Baal and Ashtoreth. She brought 450 Baal prophets of Baal and 400 Ashtoreth prophets (I Kings 18:19) from Phoenicia to convert the people of the northern kingdom of Israel to this idolatry.

The prophet Elijah, (Hebrew for my God is Jehovah, is called Elias in the gospel of Matthew 11:14 KJV) was a ninth century BC prophet during the reign of King Ahab in Samaria. The prophet Elijah was sent by God to oppose Jezebel and her idolatrous prophets during a time of a drought in the land. Elijah presented a challenge to the people of Israel to either choose God or Baal and to stop switching back and forth between the two (I Kings 18:21). Elijah challenged the four hundred and fifty Baal prophets to prove who the true God was. After the Baal prophets could not get their god to participate in the challenge, Elijah exposed their inefficacy and had the Baal prophets killed (I Kings 18:20-40). Elijah executed the authority of the law described in Deuteronomy 17:2-5.

Elijah, in the Hebrew scripture, is second of only two men who did not die but was taken up by God. Enoch was the first man in Hebrew scripture that was taken up by God (See Genesis 5:24 and II Kings 2:1-11). Elijah anointed Elisha (means God saves) when he realized that his ministry was coming to an end. Elijah asked Elisha what he could do for him before he was taken up, and Elisha informed him that he wanted a double portion of his "Spirit". Elisha was anointed to become a prophet of God, taking Elijah's position to continue communicating the solemn blessings of God to the Israelite believers.

Elisha was to Elijah as Joshua was to Moses. As a matter of fact,

Joshua's name was similar to Elisha in the fact that it means "the Lord saves". The man, who was military commander under Ahab and Joram (Ahab's son), Jehu, was anointed by one of the sons of a prophet under Elisha's leadership (Jehu would be anointed king of Israel by a disciple of Eliseus). Customs varied in the cultures of the Middle East; however, anointing with special oil was in Israel either a strictly priestly or kingly right. When a prophet was anointed it was because he was first a priest. When a non-king was anointed, such as Elijah's anointing of Hazael and Jehu it was a sign that Hazael was to be king of Syria and that Jehu would be king of Israel.

There were others anointed in like manner in order to carry on the work of God. Many other religions of the world also use anointing oil with other aromatic variances added with the oil, such as flowers, to give the oil a pleasant and appealing smell. The use of anointing oil by Christians is also indicated in the New Testament Bible. The "Prayer of Faith" by James (Jesus' brother) indicated such use: James 5:13-15 NIV 13 Is anyone among you in trouble? Let them pray. Is anyone happy? Let them sing songs of praise. 14 Is anyone among you sick? Let them call the elders of the church to pray over them and anoint them with oil in the name of the Lord. 15 And the prayer offered in faith will make the sick person well; the Lord will raise them up. If they have sinned, they will be forgiven.

The definition of anoint means to rub with oil. Here today in America, anointing oils can be used as a symbolic representation of our faith in Jesus Christ and represents God's Holy Spirit. Whether one seeks healing by a prayer cloth or oil, it is the faith in God that provides the healing. This faith can be by an individual, by a pastor, or both. The Holy Bible speaks of the laying on of hands for healing and also the use of oil.

Olive oil was used in ancient times as a medicinal agent in a similar manner as described by the Apostle James. Was James speaking of using the oil for medicinal purposes? Keep in mind that the use of faith healing is only symbolic of the healing by faith in God's Spirit. Some televangelist promoters of oil and prayer cloths are merely charlatans, however not all. There are also some that will tell you that it has no special power in particular without prayer. The order of the Holy Spirit is not the oil poured or spread on us, but that which we receive through belief in the Holy Spirit within us.

God has sent forth His Holy Spirit into our hearts. God's tabernacle is no longer the tent or building, as was under the old covenant, but God now resides in our hearts when we receive the 'Holy Spirit'. Once we have received the 'Holy Spirit' we have guaranteed assurance against all things. We are sealed (Ephesians: 13-14 NIV 13 and you also were included in Christ when you heard the message of truth, the gospel of your salvation. When you believed, you were marked in him with a seal, the promised Holy Spirit, 14 who is a deposit guaranteeing our inheritance until the redemption of those who are God's possession— to the praise of his glory.

# CHAPTER 23

## *Modern Medicine has Biblical Roots*

HUMANS HAVE NO SPECIAL OR supernatural powers and cannot produce anything except that which is given to us by the Father in heaven. Now it may be said that doctors of modern medicine have developed procedures that save lives today. However, modern medicine has biblical roots. God gave to Moses procedures for maintaining sanitary conditions within the Israelite camp in the wilderness journey that is practiced today. *The Germ Theory of Disease* by Louis Pasteur (19th century) that infectious diseases were caused by germs that were on the outside of the body was given to Moses by God 3500 years ago and practiced by Israelites during their wilderness journey. In Numbers 19:1-22, God reveals to Moses laws of purification and laws regarding how to deal with a dead body.

God provided sanitary procedures for the Israelites in the desert to prevent them from being wiped out by infectious diseases. They were instructed in matters of clean and unclean food in Leviticus 11. Purification for women after their monthly period and childbirth was given in Leviticus 12. Leviticus 13 instructed them on regulations for defiling skin diseases and how such diseases are to be treated in Leviticus 14. Leviticus 15 dealt with unhealthy bodily discharges and how to isolate the individual and clean their bodies after the discharge ceases. Moses also gave them instructions on how to relieve themselves of bodily waste and what to do with it: Deuteronomy 23:12 NIV 12 Designate a place outside the camp where you can go to relieve yourself. 13 As part of your equipment have something to dig with, and when you relieve yourself, dig a hole and cover up your excrement. The first antiseptic was Hyssop oil and was described by the Psalmist 51:7 NIV (7 Cleanse me with hyssop, and I will be clean; wash me, and I will be whiter than snow.) Also, God gave to Moses vigorous instructions on final purification of a person who was determined unclean by a priest and had been declared ceremonially clean later on. Hyssop oil was used almost identically as we would use a spray can of Lysol today as an antibacterial/antifungal agent today to kill something like the influenza virus in a room (Numbers 19:18 NIV 18 Then a man who is ceremonially clean is to take some hyssop, dip it in the water and sprinkle the tent and all the furnishings and the people who were there. He must also sprinkle anyone who has touched a human bone or a grave or anyone who has been killed or anyone who has died a natural death).

Why did God specify that a Hebrew baby boy was to be circumcised on the eighth day after birth? Modern-day scientists have found out that blood clotting agents to stop the bleeding of a circumcised baby is at the highest level on the eighth day after birth. Finally, on this subject, a procedure called anesthesia which is used to allow physicians or dentists to perform medical procedures that, in most cases, would be too painful for the patient to endure. An anesthetic can be used locally on the body or it can be given to induce deep sleep which allows the physician or dentist to perform the procedure with no pain felt by the patient. Experts on the subject of pain have now scientifically found that pain starts at the source on the body affected, and pain stimulators at these locations release chemicals that travel to the spinal cord stimulators. The spinal cord stimulators send a pain message to the brain and that is when we know something has happened at the initial source of the pain.

The anesthesia used for major surgeries is done by intravenously injecting a short-acting medication such as Propofol which quickly sedates the patient to unconsciousness in about two minutes. After the sedative wears off and the patient gains consciousness, there is usually a lack of memory of the procedure performed. That is about as scientific as I can get on this subject.

When was the first method involving anesthetizing performed? There weren't any pharmaceuticals given to Adam by God, the Great Physician, in Genesis 2. God rendered Adam unconscious without the use of an anesthetic used by modern anesthesiologists. The procedure involved removing one of Adam's ribs to be used to make a woman.

God had allowed Adam to name all of the species that He created. Adam observed, during this naming process, that there were male and female for every species of animals. Adam did not have a companion or helper. God recognized that Adam could not propagate the species without having a female companion. Everything that God created He pronounced was good. This is the first time that God said that something wasn't good. What God said that was "not good" is that it wasn't good for Adam to be alone. God was speaking of the fact that Adam did not have another person, a female human person. Lonely can be differentiated from alone by the fact no other person is in your presence which causes a person to be sad, depressed, and unhappy, etc. A person may say I want to be alone or left alone by a matter of choice, whereas lonely is more of a bad emotional state that is not good. The state of being lonely is not usually a choice that one can make, whereas if you are alone you can by choice, find someone to be with, and then you are no longer alone.

Without a human companion, Adam didn't have anyone or anything of the same biological makeup that he could relate to. When Adam started the process of assigning names to the different species, he recognized that the animals came in pairs, that is, a male and female for the propagation of their own particular species. Adam wasn't using the formal naming process used by scientists called binominal nomenclature or binary nomenclature which is giving a name in two parts. The species binomial Homo sapiens was coined by Carl Linnaeus in his 18th century. The species binomial Homo sapiens was coined by Carl Linnaeus in the18th century. The first part gives a name to genes the species belong in (Homo- Latin meaning human, sapiens – wise man). The second part identifies the species within the genus. The formal name given to humans is Homo sapiens.

Adam, the most intelligent of the species created by God did not have a mate "Then the LORD God said, "It is not good that the man should be alone; I will make him a helper fit for him." (Genesis 2:18 ESV). When God spoke in this verse, it was not to Himself but to the triune union (God the Father, Jesus the son, and the Holy Spirit). God created a companion suitable for Adam, a woman. (Genesis 2:21-22 NIV 21 So the LORD God caused the man to fall into a deep sleep; and while he was sleeping, he took one of the man's ribs and then closed up the place with flesh. 22 Then the LORD God made a woman from the rib he had taken out of the man, and he brought her to the man).

# CHAPTER 24

# Sustenance Received from God by the Holy Spirit

MAN, BY HIMSELF, IS NOT responsible for any event or creation without God's input. It is God and God alone that gives sustenance. Psalms 127:1 ESV Unless the LORD builds the house, those who build it labor in vain. Unless the LORD watches over the city, the watchman stays awake in vain. That is why we pray, "Let thy Will be done" Matthew 6:10 KJV Thy kingdom come, Thy will be done in earth, as it is in heaven.

During Jesus' ministry on earth He said He was only presenting to the world, in His teachings and judgment, that which had been given to Him by His Father: John 8:26 KJV 26 I have many things to say and to judge of you: but he that sent me is true; and I speak to the world those things which I have heard of him.

When Jesus was baptized by John the Baptist, all three members of the Holy Trinity were present that day at the Jordan River (Matthew 3:16-17). Jesus was already without sin, so He was not doing this as we do, getting baptized after receiving salvation. A snippet quotation from a minister's sermon: "When we receive salvation, we do not become sinless but we should sin less."

God, the Father, through the Holy Spirit, empowered Him. The Bible tells us that many were empowered by the *Holy Spirit*. Here are some Biblical illustrations of the Holy Spirit empowerment: <u>King</u>

<u>David</u> I Samuel 16:13 KJV Then Samuel took the horn of oil, and anointed him in the midst of his brethren: and the Spirit of the LORD came upon David from that day forward. So Samuel rose up, and went to Ramah.

<u>Othniel</u> in Judges 3:10 KJV And the Spirit of the LORD came upon him, and he judged Israel, and went out to war: and the LORD delivered Chushanrishathaim king of Mesopotamia into his hand; and his hand prevailed against Chushanrishathaim.

<u>Gideon</u> Judges 6:34 KJV But the Spirit of the LORD came upon Gideon, and he blew a trumpet; and Abiezer was gathered after him.

<u>Sampson</u> Judges 14:6 KJV And the Spirit of the LORD came mightily upon him, and he rent him as he would have rent a kid, and he had nothing in his hand: but he told not his father or his mother what he had done.

and the <u>seventy elders</u> with Moses Numbers 11:25 Then the LORD came down in the cloud and spoke with him, and he took some of the power of the Spirit that was on him and put it on the seventy elders. When the Spirit rested on them, they prophesied —but did not do so again. (Source: 'Holy Spirit'- GLO Bible).

When we receive the 'Holy Spirit' we are also empowered and ready for "Spiritual Warfare". We pray that the nation will receive the 'Holy Spirit' and spread it around the world to those who don't know Jesus and learn to love one another as Jesus loves us, in the name of Jesus, Amen.

# CHAPTER 25

# The Perfect Sacrifice, Jesus, The Lamb of God

JESUS WAS IN COMPLETE SUBMISSION to the will of His Father and willingly offered Himself as the perfect sacrifice. There would no longer be need of animal sacrifices day after day, year after year as it was under the old covenant. God was not pleased with the old covenant sacrifices. It is impossible for the sacrificial killing of goats and sheep to take away sin for they do not present an adequate sacrifice of a human. Jesus obediently submitted Himself to the will of God and became the "Lamb of God" the perfect optimum sacrifice (Hebrews 10:4-11).

Now that we are under the new covenant we are expecting to carry righteousness to the next level. Nothing says it is going to be easy, but if we are to win this war against the evil one, then our vision should always be on Christ. We can't have retaliatory actions in our lives. In difficult confrontational situations in our lives, the question to ask ourselves is: "What would Jesus require of us?"

Matthew Henry's Concise Commentary on Matthews 5:38:42 the plain instruction is, Suffer any injury that can be borne, for the sake of peace, committing your concerns to the Lord's keeping. And the sum of all is that Christians must avoid disputing and striving. If any say, Flesh and blood cannot pass by such an affront, let them remember, that flesh and blood shall not inherit the kingdom of God; and those who act upon right principles will have the most peace and comfort.

When Jesus preached the 'Sermon on the Mount', He gave full meaning to what was spoken by the OT prophets and law. He said that He was coming to complete God's law with finality. Matthew 5 He brought clarity to subjects such as: Murder 21-26, Adultery 27-30, Divorce 31-32, Oaths 33-37, Eye for an Eye 38-42, and Love for Enemies 43-48.

These things are not new but have always been in the heart of God from the beginning of time. There is a time and season for everything (Ecclesiastes 3:1). God created time so one is not to think of time as his/her possession, it all belongs to God. So God decided to send His Son in His own time. He decided when he wanted to send a revelation of Himself to earth [His word] through His Son. The 'Ten Commandments', on tablets of stone, were given to Moses for divine instructions on His own time and by His own finger (Exodus 31:18).

God created us, we didn't create ourselves. He provided for His Creation things of need and things to consecrate ourselves to Him. The ten laws given unto Moses pointed out that the Israelites were sinful. Had they not been sinful, there would not have been a need for the law. These laws did not justify the Jewish people and arbitrarily make them righteous to God: Galatians2:16 KJV Knowing that a man is not justified by the works of the law, but by the faith of Jesus Christ, even we have believed in Jesus Christ, that we might be justified by the faith of Christ, and not by the works of the law: for by the works of the law shall no flesh be justified. Galatians 2-21 KJV I do not frustrate the grace of God: for if righteousness come by the law, then Christ is dead in vain.

The Apostle Paul uses the word frustrate here which means to abolish or nullify the sacrifice of Jesus on the Cross, a provision given to us by God. Reliance on keeping the Mosaic Law to claim the righteous acceptance of God frustrates the Holy Spirit (The Paraclete). God gave His only begotten Son for the atonement of our sins which is made ineffectual by reliance on self-righteousness.

The Apostles Paul and Joseph, a Levite native of Cyprus, (also called Barnabus by the other apostles See Acts 4:36, Barnabus is called an apostle in Acts 14:14), did not plan their first missionary journey but were sent out by the Holy Spirit from Antioch of Syria to Seleucia and then to Salamis, Cyprus (See Acts 13:4). Barnabas was born on the island of Cyprus and, because of his familiarity of the region; most likely chose the route of this first missionary journey.

The apostles went to the Jewish synagogues on the island.

After the illicit persecution and stoning death of Steven by the Sanhedrin, many of the Jewish people scattered from the church at Jerusalem to regions of Judea and Samaria (See Acts 8:1). The apostles did not leave Jerusalem but the church went underground. Some scattered as far as Phoenicia, Cyprus, and Antioch (Acts 11:19). The synagogues in Cyprus were probably built by these believers who scattered from Judea. They proclaimed the gospel of Christ only to the Jews.

The island of Cyprus is not very large being approximately 141 miles long and has an average width of 35-45 miles. The city of Salamis, Cyprus where Paul and Barnabas (John Mark assisted them-Acts 13:5) landed is located on the southeast coast of Cyprus. They traveled to the west coast to the city of Paphos, Cyprus. The Roman governor of Cyprus, Proconsul Sergius Paulus, resided in Paphos. He is described as an intelligent man, so he probably had informants providing information concerning that the apostles were ministering at the Jewish synagogues on the island. Sergius requested the apostles to come to his residence so he could learn more about Jesus and the word of God.

A Jewish magician (ESV, KJV calls him a sorcerer) named Elymas (also Bar-Jesus) was with the proconsul and heard what was requested of the apostles. Elymas did not want the proconsul to hear about the proclamation of God so he attempted to prevent the apostles from teaching about Jesus. Acts 13:9 says the apostle Paul looked at Elymas intently which probably means that he became quite animated in his speech. Apostle Paul, filled with the Holy Spirit, called this man a son of the devil, an enemy of righteousness, full of all deceit and villainy.

Then the apostle called upon the Lord to temporarily blind him. When the proconsul saw this man become blind when Apostle Paul said the hands of the Lord will be upon him and he would lose his sight for a limited time, he was convinced and even more interested to be taught the word of the Lord. He was amazed and astonished by the teaching and was converted (Acts 13:4-12).

While reading Acts 13, it occurred to me that I had been thinking that Saul of Tarsus name was changed to Paul after his encounter with Jesus on the road to Damascus. In the book of Acts, Luke describes the conversion of Saul, who had been a zealous Pharisee persecutor of the Christian churches (Galatians 1:13). He received a letter of permission from the high priests to go from Jerusalem to Damascus and arrest Christian believers and bring them back. When Saul and the men traveling with him were near Damascus, a bright light from heaven flashed around him causing him to fall to the ground. Saul heard a voice asking him why you are persecuting me. Saul found out it was the resurrected Jesus speaking (Acts 9:5-6).

I just want to mention here that I have heard a variety of ministers say that he was knocked off of his beast or the horse he was riding. I have been unable to find this in the bible. The only thing that I could find as to why they say this is from Caravaggio's famous painting titled "Conversion on the Way to Damascus" where it shows Saul laying on the ground with a horse and man in the background. The bible states that the men traveling with him stood speechless (Acts 9:7). It does not say that they got off of an animal they were riding to attend Saul.

I assumed that the conversion incident of Saul on the road to Damascus was when his name was changed to Paul. It could be assumed in Acts 13:9 that Saul's name was changed to Paul when the Roman Proconsul Sergius Paulus was converted to Christianity after being taught the word of the Lord.

Paul was a Roman citizen (Acts 16:37 and 22:25-28) and he was also a Hebrew (Philippians 3:5). Saul was his Jewish name and Paul was the name he used as a Roman citizen, a biblical Greek name. Luke suggests that he used the two names interchangeably (Acts 13:9). I suppose that when the apostle was ministering to a Jewish audience he went by the Hebrew name, Saul. When he was ministering to a Gentile audience he went by the Roman/Hellenistic name of Paul. After converting Sergius Paulus, Saul was called Paul henceforth. It is plausible that the apostle started using the name Paul after his first missionary trip where he ministered to Jews and then to a gentile Roman Governor. The resurrected Jesus in Acts 9:15 chose Saul of Tarsus to be an instrument to carry His name before the Gentiles and kings and the children of Israel.

Paul and Barnabas set sail from Paphos and went to Perga in Pamphylia. John Mark left them and returned to Jerusalem. Pamphylia was a former region in the south of Asia Minor. Today, Asia Minor comprises most of the Asian part of modern Turkey and the Armenian highland. It is a peninsula also called Anatolia.

From Perga, Paul and Barnabas went to Antioch in Pisidia (approximately 110 Miles). In the New Testament Bible there are two cities mentioned with the name of Antioch, Antioch in Syria and Antioch in Pisidia. Both were Roman colonies during the time of Paul with sufficient Jewish diaspora inhabitants. It was mentioned earlier that many of the believers scattered to various cities after the persecution of Saint Stephen in Jerusalem.

Prior to their first missionary trip, Barnabus searched for Paul and found him in his hometown of Tarsus and brought him to Antioch in Syria where they taught many disciples for a year at the church there. Antioch of Syria, the larger of the two similar named cities, is where the disciples were first called Christians (Acts 11:26)

Paul and Barnabas went to the Jewish diaspora synagogue at Antioch in Pisidia on the Sabbath day. After the rulers of the synagogue had finished reading the Law (Law of Moses- Torah) they invited the visiting apostles, Paul and Barnabas to speak if they had any words of encouragement for the congregation. The apostle Paul stood up and motioned with his hand and started his salutation to the Jewish and Gentile audience. He gave a synopsis of Jewish history. This synopsis included that the Jewish population while in Egypt, God promised a Savior for Israel that would come from the offspring of the second Israelite king. King David's offspring would provide Israel with a Savior named Jesus (Acts 13:13-40). The theme of the apostle's speech is in his conclusion in Verses 38-39: 38 Let it be known to you, therefore, brothers, that through this man (Jesus) forgiveness of sins is proclaimed to you, 39 and by him (Jesus) everyone who believes is freed from everything from which you could not be freed by the Law of Moses.

We were babes and had to be fed milk, but by now, we should be growing to the point that we can digest solid food. The Apostle Paul's epistle to the Christian people of Corinth indicated that he was disappointed that they had already had enough time to progress in Spiritual maturity concerning their knowledge and behavior of Christ, but they had not. They were so filled with the carnal or fleshly (food, milk) life that they had no room for spiritual food. Paul says that the Corinthians were sarkikos which in I Corinthian 3 means fleshly. Paul was indicating that the people were acting in more of a carnal nature than by the spirit of God. (I Corinthian 3:1-3)

A comparison can be made between the church at Corinth during Paul's time and the modern Christian church today. There were good things about the church in Corinth (I Corinthians 1:4-8 ESV 4 I give thanks to my God always for you because of the grace of God that was given you in Christ Jesus, 5 that in every way you were enriched in him in all speech and all knowledge– 6 even as the testimony about Christ was confirmed among you– 7 so that you are not lacking in any spiritual gift, as you wait for the revealing of our Lord Jesus Christ, 8 who will sustain you to the end, guiltless in the day of our Lord Jesus Christ.

And there were bad things previously addressed in I Cor 3. Paul's epistle to the church addressed the good things and then he spoke of the carnality of the church. All of the bad things fell basically under this heading. There was a division of the members. This is seen in 21st-century churches where people gather in their different sects and sometimes destroy a church. There was bigotry or sectarianism close to the border of being heretical. This is when the people were devoted to their own carnal opinions and are not acting like Christians. In their own minds, they claim to be saved Christians but their actions are divisive, contrary to the Word of God. They hold their heads high; sometimes ignore the good wishes of other members of the congregation. The healing of America in this present day depends greatly on the prayers of revival by Christians. Christians can't proselytize others if what others see is a Christian behaving in a derogatory manner. The churches will have to be on solid food (Spiritual Maturity) for this to take place.

Ephesians 4:13 NIV until we all reach unity in the faith and in the knowledge of the Son of God and become mature, attaining to the whole measure of the fullness of Christ.

The churches of the nation must exemplify the behavior of Christ: Romans 15:1-4 ESV 1 we who are strong have an obligation to bear with the failings of the weak, and not to please ourselves. 2 Let each of us please his neighbor for his good, to build him up. 3 For Christ did not please himself, but as it is written, "The reproaches of those who reproached you fell on me." 4 For whatever was written in former days were written for our instruction, that through endurance and through the encouragement of the Scriptures we might have hope.

This nation cannot continue to flourish without the nourishment of 'spiritual' food. God will not let good and faithful stewardship fail. We are required to be faithful to God first and foremost, and not to monetary or political gains. Special interest groups and lobbyists buy access from politicians for their own benefit. The politicians go so far as creating laws so money received from lobbyists does not have to be formally reported. Another disturbing trend is a practice of "soft lobbying" where the moneys received and not reported is called going "dark." It may be "dark" for man but God sees all. If the judgment of others is the hindrance then the judgment of oneself should be primary.

Apply the word of God to your own life. It is living, sharp, piercing, dividing, and powerful and knows the thought of every man (Hebrews 4:12-13 ESV 12 For the word of God is living and active, sharper than any two-edged sword, piercing to the division of soul and of spirit, of joints and of marrow, and discerning the thoughts and intentions of the heart. 13 And no creature is hidden from his sight, but all are naked and exposed to the eyes of him to whom we must give account).

This is an all seeing-eye and nothing is hidden from Him. He can see the innermost of one's being. Jesus said to the disassemblers of His day, some of the Pharisees and the scribes speak of believing in Him by word of mouth but it is in vain because their hearts are not in it. They continued to teach the doctrines created by men (See Matthew 15:8–9).

The second hypocrisy He spoke of at the 'Sermon on the Mount' is concerning judging others while ignoring your own sins we can find in Matthew 7:1-5 ESV "Judge not, that you be not judged. For with the judgment you pronounce you will be judged, and with the measure you use it will be measured to you. Why do you see the speck that is in your brother's eye, but do not notice the log that is in your own eye? Or how can you say to your brother, 'Let me take the speck out of your eye,' when there is the log in your own eye? You hypocrite, first take the log out of your own eye, and then you will see clearly to take the speck out of your brother's eye."

There is an outward appearance of virtue that is not present in the heart. How many times have we seen politicians profess things to get elected and to the contrary, we never see the results? How many times have we seen them drag out all of the dirt, true or untrue, on their opponents during an election? This quote from American comedian, Gallagher (Leo Anthony Gallagher), if "pro" is the opposite of "con", is "progress" the opposite of "congress"? From the 1985 movie The Bookkeeper.

This false virtue is contrary to the extension and revelation of the new covenant given to us by God's Son. Being in accord with the word given to us by Jesus Christ is the only way we can be justified. He is the second Adam sent by God. The first Adam was sinful. The second Adam, the anthropomorphic man, Jesus, was without sin.

# CHAPTER 26

# *Faith in a God we Cannot See (Only His Works)*

THE ONLY WAY WE CAN receive the salvation and grace that we have today is by faith in the death and resurrection of Jesus. We are charged with having faith and obedience to that which we have received. What is faith? The Bible defines faith scripturally in Hebrews 11:1-2 ESV Now faith is the assurance of things hoped for, the conviction of things not seen.

The Apostle Paul's letter to the Romans ask questions (rhetorical) that he is not eliciting answers to but is making statements that he wants to be understood concerning receiving salvation. Romans 10:14-17 ESV How then will they call on him in whom they have not believed? And how are they to believe in him of whom they have never heard? And how are they to hear without someone preaching? And how are they to preach unless they are sent? As it is written, "How beautiful are the feet of those who preach the good news!" But they have not all obeyed the gospel. For Isaiah says, "Lord, who has believed what he has heard from us?" So faith comes from hearing and hearing through the word of Christ.

To have faith, you have to have the working of the 'Holy Spirit' and Word of God and be clothed in the full armor of God to defend against the schemes of Satan (see Ephesians 6:11). There are many battlefields, spiritually and physically, that can be overcome by faith.

By faith nothing is impossible and nothing is too hard for God. Jesus' disciples apparently had faith but they wanted to increase their faith, to which Jesus indicated you can accomplish much with little faith (Luke 17:5-6 KJV And the apostles said unto the Lord, Increase our faith. And the Lord said, if ye had faith as a grain of mustard seed, ye might say unto this sycamine tree, be thou plucked up by the root, and be thou planted in the sea; and it should obey you).

A man brought to Jesus' disciples a boy who was possessed, who was epileptic. They had been given the power and authority by Jesus to cast out this malady from the boy, yet they tried and were unable to do it. They asked Jesus privately since they had been given the authority, why couldn't they heal the boy? Jesus answered with an oft-quoted verse by preachers about not needing an abundance of faith but faith the size of a mustard seed is sufficient - with enough faith to believe anything is possible even to move a mountain (Matthew 17:14-20). (The mustard seeds are very minuscule compared to other seed except for the orchid seed; they are usually about 1 to 2 millimetres (0.039 to 0.079 in) in diameter. To make a comparison, the little black specks on a strawberry are about the same size as mustard seed. Just as strawberries are not botanically a berry, the black specks are not actually a seed but are called a seed. The black specks on the outside of the strawberry are named "achenes which are the ovaries of the flower, with a seed inside it).

This had to be frustrating to the disciples to have to tell Jesus they couldn't do it because they had insufficient faith. Jesus foretold to them His impending suffering and death and the disciples were grieved because their faith was not at the level where it should have been (Matthew 17:22-23).

You cannot have a faintness of heart when placing your faith in Jesus. Satan is always at work trying to destroy your faith. That is why we pray to maintain our faith. Peter saw Jesus walking on water toward a boat he and other disciples were on. He asked Jesus to command that he also may walk out on the water. He walked out on the water where Jesus was, as the wind increased, he became afraid and began to sink. He had a sudden dissipation of faith that swished out of him.

Matthew 14:28-31 KJV 28 and Peter answered him and said, Lord, if it be thou, bid me come unto thee on the water. 29 And he said, Come. And when Peter was come down out of the ship, he walked on the water, to go to Jesus. 30 But when he saw the wind boisterous, he was afraid; and beginning to sink, he cried, saying, Lord, save me. 31 And immediately Jesus stretched forth his hand, and caught him, and said unto him, O thou of little faith, wherefore didst thou doubt? Jesus, the Rabbi, was teaching a lesson to Peter and to the other disciples about maintaining faith.

In the OT Emunah (Hebrew) basic meaning is "certainty" and "faithfulness" and the one who is faithful is the Lord Himself. One with Emunah will act with firmness toward God's will. Pistis (Greek) in the NT it basically means trust in an invisible God based on hearing of the Spiritual Word.

Many of Jesus' followers have been martyred because of their faith and never used violence to oppose it. Faith and grace belong to us. Let us use the weapons of faith that God has made available to us.

# CHAPTER 27

# War Between Nations is Normally Caused by Sinful People Absent of the Paraclete

THE CHRISTIAN IDEA IS OPPOSED to war. The cause of war is always sin. So why do we allow our troops abroad to die for something that is caused by sin? Their lives are just as important to them and their families as ours are to us. Jesus shed His blood then ordered a stop to the killing. Many of the OT wars were termed religious wars. God often ordered the Israelites to go to war with other nations (Joshua 4:13 *ESV* about 40,000 ready for war passed over before the Lord for battle, to the plains of Jericho.

The world is full of sinful people and sometimes war is necessary to protect innocent people or to prevent more powerful evil occurrences. War is never good and should be avoided if at all possible. We should not be going to war to take somebody else's land as our own to obtain natural resources such as oil, uranium, gold and, silver, etc.. Such wars are blatantly wrong.

Some countries have gone to war against multiple nations with the intent of spreading or imposing their own national interests. Two infamous names come to mind such as the French military leader, Napoleon Bonaparte, who conquered much of Europe in the nineteenth century. Or Adolph Hitler, German politician and the leader of the

Nazi Party, his aggressiveness concerning foreign policy is attributed to the commencement of World War II. Hitler is infamously known for the Holocaust in which an estimated 11 million people were murdered with estimated 6 million Jewish people included.

The History of America had its own divisions between the north and south states concerning economy and social issues, state rights versus federal rights, states that were for slavery and those that wanted to abolish slavery. Seven states seceded from the union, during Abraham Lincoln's presidency, believed that he would not support the southern states because of his anti-slavery stance. These divisions caused America's civil war from 1861 to 1865 over these issues.

The Macedonia King, Alexander the Great (356-323 BCE), who claimed to be some kind of deity or demi-god called himself the son of Zeus. In ancient Greek religion, Zeus is the sky and thunder god. Historians record that he was a great military leader and one of the most powerful rulers ever. Most of the known world at that time was conquered under his leadership.

One of America's greatest family wars in history was the war between the Hatfield's and McCoy's. One major dispute between the families involved the ownership of a hog. One Hatfield family member was killed by two McCoy brothers. Both families were members of the Church of Christ.

Evil people sometimes have to be overthrown. Sometimes it may entail going to war. Here is a list of evil people in the past history of the world absent of the indwelling Holy Spirit:

Attila the Hun. He was the ruler of the Huns from 434 until his death in 453. He killed so many people that they could not be numbered

Caligula. He is also known as Gaius, was Roman Emperor from 37 AD to 41 AD. This Roman emperor bragged about sleeping with other men's wives and bankrupted the Roman monetary coffer. He killed people for his amusement. He was an egotist who wanted a statue of himself in the temple of Jerusalem so that he could be worshipped as a god. Herod Agrippa, his friend and, king of Judea, interceded for the Jews and time persuaded him not to do this for fear of a revolt in the already volatile area. This would have broken the Jewish Law of idolatry. The Jews also would have considered the statue erected in the temple as a desecration of their temple and a large contingent of Jewish peasants was willing to give up their lives to prevent the statue from being erected in the temple. During Caligula's reign, criminals were thrown into an arena to be killed by animals. When there were no criminals to execute, he randomly chose a section of innocent people and placed them in the arena to be devoured by the animals for his amusement. Caligula was assassinated in early AD 41

Francisco Pizarro. Francisco Pizarro González was a Spanish conquistador who conquered the Inca Empire. Francisco Pizarro was one of the European explorers who went to South America to colonize it and had natives murdered so he could plunder their gold and silver.

Idi Amin. Idi Amin rose to become a brutal and utterly ruthless dictator who committed atrocities on his people. He killed as many as half a million people during his eight-year Ugandan dictatorship in the 1970s.

Ivan the Terrible- Ivan IV of Russia, also known as Ivan the Terrible, was the Grand Duke of Muscovy from 1533 to 1547 and was the first ruler of Russia to assume the title of Tsar. He was also a devout theist. He controlled the largest nation on Earth but in his later years, executed thousands and, in rage, killed his own son.

Joseph Stalin. He was the de facto leader of the Soviet Union from the mid-1920s until his death in 1953. Stalin was an atheist and tyrant who was purported to having 7 million or more people killed and placing about 50 million people under suppression. He might hold the distinction of being the greatest tyrant of all time.

Nero ruled Rome from AD 54 to AD 68. He was, perhaps, the most infamous Roman ruler. Nero had his own mother murdered. He had an obsessive dislike of the Christians. He was extremely cruel. It is said, believed and written that he started the fire at the southeastern angle of the Circus Maximus and eventually burned down ten of the fourteen Augustans regions according to the historian, Tacitus. He blamed the Christians for the starting the fire because they refused to worship him, especially the apostles Paul and Peter.

Pol Pot -Pol Pot became leader of Cambodia on April 17, 1975, and his rule was a dictatorship. One to three million out of a population of 8 million people died by execution, forced labor, and malnutrition attributed to him.

Torquemada. Tomás de Torquemada, O.P. (1420 – September 16, 1498) was a 15th-century Spanish Dominican friar and the first Grand Inquisitor in Spain's movement to restore Christianity among its populace in the late 15th century Torquemada tortured and burned thousands of innocent Spaniards and expelled Spain's Jewish population. Thomas De Torquemada was head of the Spanish Inquisition and was renowned for his cruelty.

Vlad the Impaler or Vlad Dracula. Count Dracula was the name Bram Stoker's used in his 1897 novel "Dracula" inspired by Vlad the Impaler. He is best known for the legends of the exceedingly cruel punishments he imposed during his reign. The total number of his victims is estimated in the tens of thousands.

Satan. Satan tops the list of evilness. Satan is still roaming the earth going to and fro under God's long leash as we can see from the carnal evil people mentioned above, but we know he is fighting a battle that is unwinnable. Satan is who instigated all of the evilness in the world. These people are examples of pure evil brought on by a jealous Satan. Satan is a liar and deceiver who yearn to have other disciples to commit atrocities upon the world.

Christians have made a covenant with the commandments recapitulated by the Apostle Paul in Romans 13:9. The last command in this verse which the Apostle reiterates is to love your neighbor. This command is actually an obligation to act in a way to benefit society or a social responsibility. This means that it should be something done naturally because you are a Christian. Some might say obedience to the commandments is easy, but to love your neighbor as you do yourself is the hardest. There have been so-called 'saved' Christians who maintain racist attitudes, biases, prejudices, insensitivities (especially for the poor), hatred, and so on. These attitudes are not gender or race specifically but it is a fact racial disparities exist even in the church. There is evidence that certain individuals encourage race wars here in the United States of America.

The shooting of nine black church members, who were at bible study at a two hundred year old historically black church, Emanuel African Methodist Episcopal Church in downtown Charleston, South Carolina, United States. The shootings occurred on the evening of June 17, 2015, and have been called pure evil. The shootings have been labeled a hate crime committed by a twenty-one year old white supremacist. The shooter confessed that he did it in the hope that it would ignite a racial war here in the United States.

At the commemoration service for the victims, attended by a variety of races, it asserted that the shooting would not divide the community. It had to be the love of God that caused five survivors and relatives of five of the victims who spoke to the perpetrator directly at his court hearing and said they forgave him and was praying for his soul.

Jesus asked the Father to forgive those who were crucifying Him, a sinless and guiltless man (Luke 23:34). These five, that made an intercession for the shooter, certainly followed the example of Jesus. He interceded for His transgressors. This certainly requires prayer because only God's Spirit can produce love and overcome all sins.

I try, honestly, to love my immediate neighbors, but I feel some kind of way when the neighbors allow their pets to use my yard as a latrine. We must also pray for strength within ourselves to be able to turn the other cheek so to speak. We should pray, as we ought, for love and peace throughout the world without ceasing.

Since the two planes destroyed the two World Center towers in New York and a plane flew into the Pentagon on September 11, 2001, the United States and some of its allies have been committed to the war on terrorism throughout the world. "Saddam Hussein was the fifth President of Iraq, serving in this capacity from July 16, 1979, until April 9, 2003. In 2003, a coalition led by the U.S. and U.K. invaded Iraq to depose Saddam Hussein, in which U.S. President George W. Bush and British Prime Minister Tony Blair accused him of possessing weapons of mass destruction and having ties to al-Qaeda". Al-Qaeda is a global militant Islamist organization founded by Osama bin Laden in

Peshawar, Pakistan and takes responsibility for bombing many public buildings killing innocent people among other horrendous things.

Osama Bin laden was the founder of al-Qaeda, the Sunni militant Islamist organization that claimed responsibility for the September 11 attacks on the United States, along with numerous other mass-casualty attacks against civilian and military targets. He was a member of the wealthy Saudi bin Laden family and an ethnic Yemeni Kindite. In April 2011, President Barack Obama ordered a covert operation to kill or capture bin Laden. On May 2, 2011, the White House announced that U.S. Navy Seals had carried it out, killing him in his Abbottabad compound in Pakistan" (Wikipedia).

The terrorist threat in the twenty-first century is the group, ISIS or ISIL that use an extremely radical version of Sharia law to justify the crucifixion, murder, beheading, rape, etc. of Christians. ISIS believes a prophecy from the Prophet Muhammad means the end of the world is coming. The 1,300-year-old prophecy says the Day of Judgement will come after an epic battle between Christians and Muslims. The ISIS terrorist members want an Islamic state or caliphate according to Islamic Sharia law. A caliphate is an Islamic state. It's led by a caliph, a person considered to be a political and religious successor to the Islamic Prophet Muhammad. Sharia law (Sharia literal translation "a path to life-giving water."), according to Muslims, this law believes in treating other people justly, based on the principles of the Islamic holy book, the Quran, and the life of Prophet Mohammed.

ISIS: The militant group, which began as the Iraqi branch of al Qaeda during the U.S. occupation, gained this name after it invaded Syria in 2013. ISIS is an acronym for the "Islamic State in Iraq and Syria," or "Islamic State of Iraq and al-Sham," which is an old Arabic term for the area.

ISIL is an acronym for "Islamic State of Iraq and the Levant." The Levant is a geographical term that refers to the eastern shore of the Mediterranean – Syria, Lebanon, Palestine, Israel and, Jordan.

It has been reported by reliable news sources that ISIS or ISIL has declared a war on Christians. Many Christians that survived being killed and beheaded have fled from the cities and towns of the Holy

Land because of ISIS attacks. It is difficult for organized militaries around the world to eliminate ISIS because the terrorist group is not basically a uniformed military from a specific country. The rapid proliferation of internet technology accessibility around the world has allowed ISIS or ISIL to easily achieve radicalization of individuals around the world.

The mistaken identity of terrorists by appearance causes prejudices and discrimination to be cast on innocent individuals that wear Islamic or Muslim wardrobes such as the Hijab, a modest dress worn by Muslim women, the Khimar-a face veil, the Abaya – a cloak for women common in Arab Gulf countries, other items of dress for women are, the Chador, the Jilbab, the Niqab, and the Burqa.

The women that are associated with the terror group currently don't engage in combat activities. They basically do strip searches of women that the men aren't allowed to perform and checking identification at borders. Other apparels worn by both women and men are the Shalwar Kameez, the Thobe – a long robe by Muslim men, and the Ghutra and Egal. This list does not list all of the clothing worn by Muslim and Islamic men and women.

There are people that have professed fear and are uncomfortable while flying on an airplane when someone is wearing Islamic or Muslim apparel. Not all individuals who are affiliated with the terrorist group wear any particular wardrobe. Photos of designated suicide bombers of ISIS or ISIL terror are clad in all-black jacket and trousers with the balaclava and a black ammunition belt (A Balaclava is a close-fitting garment, usually made of wool, covering the whole head and neck except for parts of the face). Others wear camouflage green or tan pants and jacket, while other members wear a black uniform consisting of a sweatshirt and baggy pants.

The United States has the right to go after and punish those who commit terrorist acts and those who are planning them. They are to do it as a unified legitimate organized body such as the country's military authority and not individually. As more people in the world become saved, conflicts diminish. Proverbs 29:2 ESV When the righteous increase, the people rejoice, but when the wicked rule, the people groan. There is no authority unless it is ultimately given by God (Romans 3:1). Voters whose candidate loses often rely on the last sentence in the preceding verse for mental comfort, nevertheless, it is true whether your candidate wins or loses and you truly believe God is king.

Leaders can govern a nation into an error which possibly could lead to loss of alliance or even war. Jesus' fifth and final exegesis on His second coming to earth includes warnings of end times; famines, earthquakes, and deception by those appropriating the name of Jesus (see Matthew 24).

While the fifth exhortation by Jesus on Mount Olive gives us hope of His return it also reveals direful events relating to events of the end times.

Titus was a young pastor and a Gentile companion of the Apostle Paul and also the recipient of the severe letter written by the Apostle to the church at Corinth. This epistle by the Apostle Paul is basically telling the Church to reject an ungodly life and that salvation by believers should lead to good works. No one knows when the end times will occur so the Apostle is telling us how to prepare ourselves and be ready at all times. The Apostle Paul wrote to one his highly respected converts named Titus from Macedonia. Titus received this epistle in AD 63 while he was in Actia Nicopolis which was the capital city of the Roman province of Epirus Vetus. Today, this location is western Greece. Titus 2:11-14 KJV 11 For the grace of God that bringeth salvation hath appeared to all men, 12 Teaching us that, denying ungodliness and worldly lusts, we should live soberly, righteously, and godly, in this present world; 13 Looking for that blessed hope, and the glorious appearing of the great God and our Saviour Jesus Christ; 14 Who gave himself for us, that he might redeem us from all iniquity, and purify unto himself a peculiar people, zealous of good works.

God will eventually take over all nations in the "end times" and destroy all rulers, authorities, principalities, etc., and all factions opposing Him (1Corinthians 15:24). (Second coming of Christ the kingdoms of earth will be handed over to the Father)

# CHAPTER 28

# Put Aside Unbelief: Have Faith in the Light Which is Jesus Christ

MANY IN THE WORLD WILL refuse to believe although Jesus had done many signs. This fulfilled the prophecy of Isaiah (John 12:36-40). Jesus said in Matthew 13: 14, 'You will indeed hear but never understand, and you will indeed see but never perceive.' (Isaiah's prophesy is found in Isaiah 6:0-10)

We need to put aside our doubt and unbelief of the 'Word' presented to us by Jesus. The present-day news presented through media sources is perplexing and difficult to determine who is telling the truth. New contemporary meanings of the news, whether true or false, have emerged such as "Alternative Facts" and "Fake News". The Word of the Lord, presented by inspired writers of the new covenant, presents "Good News" that is inerrant. This good news is called the "Gospel". The good news is concerning the death, burial and the resurrection from death by Jesus Christ for the propitiation of our sins (reconciliation by His shed blood).

The Apostle Paul preached this good news in the epistle I Corinthians 15 This whole book is concerning the Resurrection of Christ. In this letter, he states that we need to wake up to this realization and become knowledgeable of God. If we don't, (be born again) he warns that we will be walking around with a diminution of sensibility until we accept this good news.

Not all of the first century Israelites of authority, who heard the 'Word', doubted after hearing but were afraid of being kicked out of the Jerusalem temple and losing their position. Their faith was in man and not in God. Many of the Pharisees believed in Jesus and His teaching. They would not let on to this, for they preferred the exaltation they received from man more than they did the glory that comes from God (John 12:42-43).

Imagine you are an adversary in a huge Roman Colosseum or amphitheater. You are not a spectator but a participant down in the combatant area of the field. You are not there for any animal fights or gladiatorial combat. In the audience of the Colosseum are all of the ancient men and women of faith and truthfulness, written about in the Bible. They are not merely spectators, but a group of cheerleaders named "Inspiration" that are there as exemplars of the power of faith. They chant in unison, "Keep the faith and stay the course." Heretical false prophets enter the combative area of the arena intent on inducing doctrines contradictory to your faith by chasing you down. You must run because your salvation is at stake, but not so fast as to run out of breath but just fast enough where they are unable to catch you. You must run patiently as the faithful witnesses in the audience are cheering you on. You fling off all unnecessary clothing that might hinder you. You run focusing your mind on Jesus. You escape with your salvation secure because you keep your mind stayed on Jesus.

Hebrews 12:1-3 AMP 1 Therefore then, since we are surrounded by so great a cloud of witnesses [who have borne testimony to the Truth], let us strip off and throw aside every encumbrance (unnecessary weight) and that sin which so readily (deftly and cleverly) clings to and entangles us, and let us run with patient endurance and steady and active persistence the appointed course of the race that is set before us,2 Looking away [from all that will distract] to Jesus, Who is the Leader and the Source of our faith [giving the first incentive for our belief] and is also it's Finisher [bringing it to maturity and perfection]. He, for the joy [of obtaining the prize] that was set before Him, endured the cross, despising and ignoring the shame, and is now seated at the right hand of the throne of God. 3 Just think of Him who endured from sinners such grievous opposition and bitter hostility against Himself [reckon up and consider it all in comparison with your trials], so that you may not grow weary or exhausted, losing heart and relaxing and fainting in your minds.

Look to Jesus, He is the author and finisher of our faith. He paid a great price for us to receive this faith. He is alpha and omega, the beginning and the end and He will finish it. Jesus has given every man a measure of faith. We all are messengers in that we should always be able to articulate and espouse the 'Word' of God on the spur of the moment. Not all can pastor a church. We all can't be in the choir or be deacons but we have a measure of faith given to us based on the power given to us by the Holy Spirit. Now just because you are a pastor, or you can sing or you can play a musical instrument, or have good communication skills, it does not place you on a higher level of righteousness than anyone else. So you should not exalt yourself or think more highly of yourself than you should. You will stick out like a peacock in a chicken pen if you do. You cannot have an attitude of superior self-righteousness (Romans 12:3).

# CHAPTER 29

# Growing in Faith and Knowledge

TO OBTAIN A BETTER RELATIONSHIP with God, one's spiritual growth needs to increase. We must desire to know more of the 'Word' of God to enhance our spiritual growth and thus our faith. God communicates His word with us through the bible. How do you know how to be obedient to Him if you don't know what it requires? You've heard about eternal life? How can you get it? What if you bought something that cannot possibly be assembled without an instruction manual? Well, the Bible is God's instruction manual on how we ought to live to obtain eternal life.

God gave His son Jesus authority to offer eternal life. Jesus brought the 'Word' so that we might know in truth where He came from. It must be emphasized that the importance of the thirty-nine books of the Old Testament is because it is an` adumbration (shadow) and divine prophecy about Jesus Christ. Once Jesus' disciples learned the truth of his origin and genealogy, it led them to believe in Him even more (John 17:8). Jesus disciples believed in His incarnation contrary to the belief of the high priests, Pharisees, and Sadducees in Jerusalem.

## More on the Inerrancy of the Holy Scriptures

The first five books of the Bible called the "Pentateuch" or "Torah" writings were ascribed to Moses. We know that Moses wasn't around when the world was created as described in the first book of the Old Testament, "Genesis". Where did he get this information? He received it from revelation because the Bible is inerrant. He might have received the information when he was in communion with God on Mt. Sinai. We know that when Apostle Paul wrote, perhaps his last epistle, to his friend and co-worker Timothy, he said that all scripture is breathed out by God. II Timothy 3:16 ESV All Scripture is breathed out by God and profitable for teaching, for reproof, for correction, and for training in righteousness.

The New Testament was written in Greek and the Greek word used in this passage for 'God-Breathed is theopneustos (Strong's Concordance definition: God-breathed, inspired by God, due to the inspiration of God) Please be aware that the Apostle Paul was probably speaking from the Old Testament since the entire New Testament had not been written at this time although some of the writings of the New Testament were considered to be equally canonical at the time. The epistles written by Paul might have circulated among the churches. All twenty-seven books of the New Testament are believed to have been written no later than around 120 AD. There was a debate in the Early Church over the New Testament canon. The major writings are claimed to have been accepted by almost all Christians by the middle of the 3rd century AD.

The art of beautiful handwriting is called calligraphy. The ancient Old and New Testaments were written in the Greek language in a form of calligraphy called uncial. Merriam Webster defines uncial as a handwriting used especially in Greek and Latin manuscripts of the fourth to the eighth centuries A.D. and made with somewhat rounded separated majuscules but having cursive forms for some letters.

In the fourth century, the entire text of the Old and New Testaments was painstakingly handwritten using the uncial style of calligraphy. The material used to write on was Vellum (animal skin or membrane). The manuscript pages were hail together by stitching them together. A codex (plural codices) is a manuscript held together by stitching. The manuscripts that contain the entire text of the ancient Greek Bible (Old and New Testaments) are the great uncial codices or four great uncials handwritten in the fourth century. The Codex Vaticanus is one of the oldest manuscripts of the Greek Bible still in existence. The Codex Vaticanus is most highly praised by scholars to be one of the best Greek texts of the New Testament Bible. Codex Sinaiticus or "Sinai Bible" is considered a close second.

"Faith comes by hearing God's Word. That is why before Jesus ascended He said that He would send a "Comforter" (THE HOLY SPIRIT) back for all evangelists, prophets, teachers, messengers, and preachers to deliver the 'Word' by mouth (See Romans 10:17). This is Christ speaking through His messengers. This does not free us from studying the 'Word' for ourselves. Some say that the bible is just too hard to understand. Always pray for understanding prior to studying. Ask your pastor for assistant in understanding a difficult passage. The internet is chocked with biblical commentaries from numerous biblical scholars for discernment. There are many study bibles available. Since there are so many sources, with various interpretations to choose from, is the reason prayer to the Holy Spirit is necessary for spiritual direction and understanding. The same scripture can be read over and over again because sometimes this can increase discernment of the text. Bible study groups are also helpful, especially if there is a teacher who has done a diligent inquiry of that particular scripture. Pastors encourage the extracurricular reading of the Word other than what is received on Sunday.

Just as we pray outside of our place of worship, we must set aside time to study the 'Word' outside the place of worship by praying to the Holy Spirit to stay aligned with God's will. The Apostle Paul seemed to appreciate the fact that those who left the synagogue compared what he preached to what is written in the Old Testament scriptures to verify his accuracy of presentation (See Acts 17:11). The Apostle and a fellow Roman citizen like himself named Silas, who was a prominent leader of the Christian community in Jerusalem, were sent to a city in Macedonia named Berea. They found that the Berean believers there were studying the word to make sure what they were being taught was true. He spoke of them as being nobler (admirable and praiseworthy) in character as compared with the Thessalonians. With the advent of early Christianity, there were many false teachers. There are some misleaders in the churches today. It is important to find a strong religious leader who teaches the word of God without deviation. Always complement this personal prayers and study of the word.

Sugar coated sermons are used at some churches to preach what the congregation wants to hear so that members won't desert the church. Apostle Paul's letter to his young minister, Timothy, was an exhortation for him to speak the needed word in any situation and at any time because God the Father and Jesus Christ will judge everyone. It could be for encouragement, rebuking, or correction.

Apostle Paul said that a time is coming when people will have itching ears and will not want to hear sound doctrine. They will only want to hear sermons that are in accord with their own evil desires (II Timothy 4:1-5). Those members with the itching ears will leave the congregation eventually anyway.

# CHAPTER 30

## *Hall of Fame for People of Faith*

EARLIER, I SPOKE OF PEOPLE of faith in the example of being in a Roman colosseum environment offering encouragement toward obtaining faith. If there was such a thing as "A Hall of Fame of Faith in God", we could draw from names of the OT ancients in Hebrews Chapter 11. All these people of faith had to overcome a myriad of obstacles but survived by faith.

The 'Hall of Fame of Faith' recipients (names in chronological order) mentioned are: Abel –offered to God a better sacrifice than his brother Cain, Enoch – was taken up so that he would not see death, Noah – offered what was not seen, a weather report predicting a world flood and worked on building an arc for the event for almost 120 years, Abraham – was called to go out to an unknown place not knowing where he was going. He also offered up his son Isaac for a sacrifice by fire. Sarah, Abraham's wife, was sterile because of old age, received power to have a baby. Isaac –invoked future blessings on his twin sons Jacob and Esau. Jacob also called Israel – blessed both of Joseph's sons, Manasseh and Ephraim. - Joseph son of Jacob (Israel) - made mention of the exodus of the Israelites from Egypt, and gave instructions on what do with his bones. The parents of Moses hid Moses from the wrath of Pharaoh. Moses gave up the benefits of Egypt to save his people. Joshua – believed the Israelites could capture Canaan, felled the walls of Jericho. Rehab – prostitute befriended the Israelite spies and helped them escape, etc. there were many who, by faith, battled many obstacles and were successful (See the Bible)

Joseph (the first son of the patriarch Jacob with his beloved wife, Rachel) exhibited faith and forgiveness. Joseph became a magnate in Egypt and was very fundamental in preventing the death, by starvation, of the progenitors of the future nation of Israel.

Jacob married Rachel's older sister, Leah, first, beforehand, he had to work for his uncle seven years by a deceptive agreement. He thought that he was working those seven years to marry Rachel both Laban deceived him and gave him Leah in marriage. After marrying Leah, Jacob had to work for his uncle seven more years before he could marry Rachel. Jacob's uncle, Laban told Jacob that according to the custom of his land, he had to give the oldest daughter in marriage first (See Genesis 29:21-28). Both women were also cousins of Jacob, which was acceptable in ancient biblical times. Jacob's mother, Rebekah, was Laban's sister (See Genesis 27:43, 29:10) Joseph was Jacob's favorite son because he didn't ever think that he would have children in his old age with Rachel, the wife that he really loved. She was barren for many years but God finally opened her womb and she bore a son and named him Joseph. (See Genesis 30:22-24).

Jacob made a paternal mistake of showing distinguishable favoritism to Joseph over the others. Joseph had dreams that his brothers would one day pay homage to him. Instead of keeping the dreams to himself, he boasted about one of them even to his father. His father rebuked him for doing such a thing. On top of all this, he was a tattletale frequently telling his father about the misbehaviors of his brothers. They despised Joseph even more for these things, especially the dreams of his future grandeur over them (See Genesis 37:9).

Note: Jacob was on his way to make up with his estranged brother, Esau; his name was changed to Israel when he wrestled with an angel in the form of a man all night. This angel was God himself. God changed his name to Israel after this encounter. Jacob's Hebrew name means "supplanter". As the twins Esau and Jacob were about to exit their mother, Rebekah womb, Esau came out first. Jacob came out holding on to his brother's heel, so he was named Jacob. This name became known as being deceptive (See Genesis 25:24-26). After Jacob wrestled with God from night to dawn, God accepted him as being a devoted follower and changed his name to Israel (Genesis 32:22-28, 35:10).

It was easy for Joseph's stepbrothers to perceive favoritism because Jacob lavished him with a rich ornamental robe. Joseph's stepbrothers perceived that Israel (Jacob) loved him more. The scripture uses a strong description of the conflict that went so far as to say they hated Joseph (See Genesis 37:4). Jacob (Israel) made Joseph a coat of many colors and none for the other sons. This favoritism stemmed from the fact that Jacob produced a baby son at a late age with his favorite wife, Rachel.

The twelve sons of Jacob and his wives and concubines are listed here by first born to last: Reuben, Simeon, Levi, and Judah-mother and wife- Leah, Dan and Naphtali- mother and concubine, Bilhah, Gad and Asher mother and concubine, Issachar and Zebulun – mother and wife, Leah, Joseph and Benjamin –mother and wife, Leah (See details Genesis 29:31-30:24, Genesis 35:16-18). Joseph and Leah also had a daughter named Dinah (Genesis 30:21). With these many brothers in this family with different mothers probably caused bickering among them anyway. The sons hated Joseph so much that they were unable to hold a friendly conversation with him. The hatred went beyond a family feud when Joseph's brothers plotted to murder him. (See details in Genesis 37:1-36, Genesis 39:1-23)

Jealousy caused Cain to kill his brother Abel. Jealousy caused Joseph's brothers to contrive a plan to murder him. Joseph's sibling was named Benjamin, who was too young to be with the brothers at the time of the plot. Benjamin was the progenitor of the Israelite Tribe of Benjamin. He was the second and last son of Rachel and the thirteenth and last son of Jacob (Israel). Jacob (Israel) was the father of twelve sons and one daughter named Dinah. Rachel went into a painfully hard labor and her midwife informed her that is because she was having a son. Rachel died while giving birth to Benjamin. Jacob's clan was traveling from Luz (Bethel) to Ephrath (Bethlehem) when Rachel died (See Genesis 35:16-19 Bethlehem called Ephrath in Genesis).

The half-brothers went out in the fields of a place called Shechem* to feed sheep (modern name-Tell Balata, located in the Palestinian West Bank). They had to find the sheep because they were not in Shechem but in a place called Dothan. Joseph was at home when Jacob told him to go find out where they were because he must have felt that they were not where they were supposed to be. He wanted Joseph to bring back a report. When he located them in Dothan, they saw him coming from a distance and that is when they contrived a plot to murder him. The plot was to make it seem like a wild animal had killed him and this would eliminate any chance of his dream becoming a reality of them becoming obeisant to him. There was an empty pit nearby. One of the brothers, Reuben, didn't want to hurt Joseph so he proposed they cast him into the empty pit instead of having blood on their hands. So they went along with this plan and took off his fancy coat and lowered him into the pit and sat down and ate.

They saw a caravan of camels approaching in the distance. As the caravan got closer they recognized the people as being Ishmaelites accompanied by some Midianite Merchants. His brother Judah said we can be completely free of this crime of murder if we sell him to them. We'll make some money and won't have the guilt of killing our brother, hanging over our heads. They all agreed and sold him. They dipped his coat in some goat's blood so they could tell their father, Jacob, when they got back home, that Joseph had been completely ravaged by a wild beast. These are the brothers whose posterity would inherit the 'Promise Land'. Joseph's two sons, Manasseh and Ephraim, would be born to an Egyptian woman later on.

*Shechem was a prominent city in the Bible. When the Israelite kingdom divided after the reign of King Solomon, it was the first capital of the northern kingdom of Israel. Abram went there (See Genesis 12:6-7). Jacob resided there (See Genesis 33:18-19). Jacob's only daughter, Dinah, was raped there when she went out to see the women living there. The prince of the land, the son of Hamor the Hittite, saw, seized, and raped her (See Genesis 34:1-2). Her two full brothers, Simeon and Levi, killed all the males there including Hamor and his son. Then they plundered the city (ref. Genesis 34:2-29). Joseph's brothers were herding sheep near Shechem where they plotted to kill and eventually sold him to some Midianite traders (Ref. Genesis 37:12, 18-28). Rehoboam, son of King Solomon, was crowned king there (See 1 Kings 12:1). Jesus visited with a Samaritan woman at Jacob's well in Sychar, a small village near Shechem (See John 4:5-8).

(Joseph, a Christ type, was sold for twenty pieces of silver.

This circuitous route of information is merely a comparison of the ransomed pieces of silver received by Joseph's brothers for selling him into slavery and the pieces of silver Judas Iscariot received for betraying Jesus is just a symbolic analogy. This comparison between the Jesus like qualities of Joseph will be discussed in more detail later on.

The price of betrayal of Jesus was thirty pieces of silver, which Judas Iscariot, a disciple of Jesus, received prior to the "Last Supper" from the Jewish Chief Priests. After the "Last Supper" Jesus went to a garden outside the city named Gethsemane and commanded three of His disciples, Peter, John and, James, to stand watch as He prayed. Judas was aware that Jesus prayed and joined in fellowship with His disciples in this garden often. He knew that Jesus would be entering this garden He and the disciples had supped this particular night. Judas brought soldiers sent by the chief priest and elders, who were armed with swords and clubs, to Gethsemane to arrest Jesus. The soldiers didn't know Jesus' identity from the others that were there so Judas revealed Jesus' identity to the Roman soldiers by giving him a kiss. The satanic spirit departed from him and then he became full of remorse and repented about betraying an innocent Jesus.

There was nothing that Judas could have said or done that would have changed their minds about putting Jesus to death. Since the Jewish leaders refused to accept the returned thirty pieces of silver from Judas. He threw the ransomed silver pieces down on the temple floor and then departed from the temple and went out and hung himself. The hypocrisy of the Chief priests and elders caused them to refuse blood money to be placed in the Temple treasury but had no problem with having Jesus, an innocent man, crucified.

They took the silver and purchased a burial place for strangers called Potter's Field just outside of Jerusalem (See Matthew 27:3-8).

Acts 1:18 gives somewhat of a different version of Judas's death: (Now this man acquired a field with the price of his wickedness, and falling headlong, he burst open in the middle and all his intestines gushed out.) This causes a debate among scholars of the Bible on who purchased the "field of blood", Potter's Field, the Chief priests or Judas himself?

The above is only for comparison of somewhat similar ransom paid to Potiphar for Joseph as was paid to Judas for identifying Jesus. The death of Jesus was ransom that defeated Satan and sin.

Potiphar found out quickly that the silver paid for the purchase of Joseph was well spent. Joseph was very good at all that he did and was loyal and trustworthy. So trustworthy that he placed him in charge of his household. Joseph was also a handsome man. Potiphar's wife noticed this and tried to seduce him to sleep with her. After many refusals to her advances day after day, one day when Joseph came to the house to do his chores, she grabbed him and tried to make him go to bed with her. Joseph, the loyal one, pulled away from her but she pulled off the robe he was wearing as he was running out of the room and screamed to her servants to come quickly because Joseph is trying to rape me.

When Potiphar came home she showed him Joseph's robe and lied to her husband about the incident. Potiphar was furious and placed Joseph in prison. The chief prison jailer liked Joseph and placed him in charge of all the prisoners. Two high officers of pharaoh's court, the royal butler and royal baker, were placed in prison because they had done something to displease the Egyptian king. On the same night, both the baker and, the butler had strange dreams that had them visibly disturbed the following morning. Joseph was able to accurately interpret the dreams. The butler's dream indicated he would be getting out of prison in three days and the baker would be hung in three days. When the butler was being released from jail, Joseph asked him to put in a good word to pharaoh for him. The butler was so elated to get out that he completely forgot to mention Joseph to the pharaoh.

Two years went by and the pharaoh had two dreams that nobody in his court could interpret including all the magicians and wise men of Egypt. The butler then remembered Joseph as an interpreter of dreams. He was still in prison, so they told him to clean himself up to make himself presentable to the pharaoh. Joseph told the pharaoh that it was not he that could interpret dreams, but God could give him an answer that would give him peace of mind. (Genesis 41:16 ESV Joseph answered Pharaoh, "It is not in me; God will give Pharaoh a favorable answer.")

Joseph, by the revelation of God, told Pharaoh that the two dreams were one in the same. In the dreams, God was telling the pharaoh what He was about to do. There would be seven years of plenty and then seven years of famine and that the pharaoh should find a wise man to organize and store food during the good years to prepare for the bad years. The plan so pleased the pharaoh that he placed Joseph, who was then thirty years old, second in charge over all of Egypt to rule the people. Joseph was blessed because of his great faith in God. The land of Canaan where Jacob and Joseph's brothers were still living experienced the famine as interpreted by God through Joseph. Jacob heard that there was food to be bought in Egypt. This was twenty years after the brothers had sold Joseph into slavery.

Jacob (Israel) sent ten brothers from Canaan to Egypt to buy food because of a famine in the land. Benjamin, the youngest son of Jacob, was not allowed to go because Jacob thought something might happen to him. Joseph was in charge of all transactions in Egypt, including selling the grain, and he also had become fluent in the Egyptian language. The ten brothers came before him and bowed down. They did not recognize him, especially since he was communicating with them through an interpreter, but he recognized them. He remembered the dream he had as a youngster that they would bow down to him one day. They were speaking in Hebrew to each other not knowing Joseph understood them. He carried out this stratagem with his brothers proclaiming they were spies sent to find out Egypt's weaknesses.

He wanted to see his sibling, Benjamin, so he ordered them to go back to Canaan and get him. When they brought Benjamin before him, he almost gave the ruse away by breaking down and crying. He hurried out to another room and wept so loud that the Egyptians could hear him from a distance. The word about this was told to the pharaoh.

He finally told his kin who he was and asked about their father. They were completely in disbelief that this was their brother Joseph.

This happened the second year of the famine in Canaan. Joseph forgave his brothers and told them it was not them that sent him there by selling him into slavery. Rather, it was God that sent him there, to eventually, save them from the famine. Genesis 45:4-8 ESV 4 So Joseph said to his brothers "Come near to me, please. "And they came near. And he said, "I am your brother, Joseph, whom you sold into Egypt. 5 And now do not be distressed or angry with yourselves because you sold me here, for God sent me before you to preserve life. 6 For the famine has been in the land these two years, and there are yet five years in which there will be neither plowing nor harvest. 7 And God sent me before you to preserve for you a remnant on earth, and to keep alive for you many survivors. 8 So it was not you who sent me here, but God. He has made me a father to Pharaoh and lord of all his house and ruler over all the land of Egypt.

It was Joseph's faith in God that brought him from the bottom of a pit, despised by his brothers to become a great redeemer. He, indeed, became his brother's keeper. He, like Moses, had many qualities like Jesus. All of the stories of faith and the prophets point toward Jesus. That is why many stories of the ancients parallel Jesus.

# CHAPTER 31

# Christians Martyred

THROUGHOUT THE HISTORY OF THE Christian world, many have been martyred for their faith. Starting in the book of the "Acts of the Apostles" we learn of such a man named Stephen who was full of faith and the Holy Spirit. Stephen was the first of the Christian martyrs who were strong in the scripture and often refuted those who were in opposition to Jesus being the Messiah. Stephen and six other disciples broke up a dispute between the Greek converts and the Hebrew Christians by working to serve the Greek widows in the early church. This allowed the other apostles to devote themselves to prayer and ministering the Word to those who needed to be converted (Ref. Acts 6:1-7). Because Stephen was so well versed, wise, and had Great Spirit there were those in the synagogue who rose up against him.

These groups of people were called the "Synagogue of Freedmen" (Hellenists) who were people that had been freed from slavery. They were not Hebrew, spoke Greek, and came from different Greek cultures (Acts 6:8-10 AMP 8 Now Stephen, full of grace (divine blessing and favor) and power (strength and ability) worked great wonders and signs (miracles) among the people.9 However, some of those who belonged to the synagogue of the Freedmen (freed Jewish slaves), as it was called, and [of the synagogues] of the Cyrenians and of the Alexandrians and of those from Cilicia and [the province of] Asia, arose [and undertook] to debate and dispute with Stephen.10 But they were not able to resist the intelligence and the wisdom and [the inspiration of] the Spirit with which and by Whom he spoke.

Saul of Tarsus (Became the Apostle Paul) might have been one of the men who argued with Stephen. His testimony against those who charged him with blasphemy infuriated them so that during the trial they covered their ears up. When he looked up to Heaven and saw the heavens had opened up and the Son of Man was standing on the right side of God, they dragged him out of the city and stoned him to death (Acts 7:54-60 ESV 54 Now when they heard these things they were enraged, and they ground their teeth at him. 55 But he, full of the Holy Spirit, gazed into heaven and saw the glory of God, and Jesus standing at the right hand of God. 56 And he said, "Behold, I see the heavens opened, and the Son of Man standing at the right hand of God." 57 But they cried out with a loud voice and stopped their ears and rushed together at him. 58 Then they cast him out of the city and stoned him. And the witnesses laid down their garments at the feet of a young man named Saul. 59 And as they were stoning Stephen, he called out, "Lord Jesus, receive my spirit." 60 And falling to his knees he cried out with a loud voice, "Lord, do not hold this sin against them. "And when he had said this, he fell asleep.

A Christian martyr does not commit suicide or hurt anyone else but is put to death for religious faith in Jesus. Many Christian martyrs suffered cruel and torturous deaths like stoning, crucifixion, and burning at the stake. The word 'martyr' comes from the Greek word translated "witness". Martyrdom is a form of religious persecution.

The first Christian martyr was Saint Stephen as recorded in the book of Acts chapter 7; he was stoned to death for his faith. Stephen was killed (i.e., martyred) for his support, belief, and faith in Jesus of Nazareth as the Messiah. Saul (Apostle Paul) of Tarsus is mentioned as bringing many murderous threats against the disciples of Jesus (Acts 9:1).

The first Christian Martyr in England was Saint Alban, a Roman citizen, who lived in Verulamium and while sheltering a Christian priest, converted to Christianity. When he refused to worship the Roman gods, he was executed. It is believed that the executioner's eyeballs fell out. Since then, Verulamium grew and changed its name to Saint Albans.

In subsequent centuries, especially during periods of widespread inquisition and Protestant Reformation, many Christians were martyred on charges of heresy. There are many incredible stories, ancient and contemporary, of Christian martyrdom.

Early Christian martyrs

Saint Stephen was stoned and some 2,000 other Christians suffered at the time of Stephen's persecution.

James the Great (Son of Zebedee) was beheaded in 44 A.D.

Philip the Apostle was crucified in 54 A.D.

Matthew the Evangelist killed by a halberd in 60 A.D.

James the Just, beaten to death by a club after being crucified and stoned.

Matthias was stoned and beheaded.

Saint Andrew, St. Peter's brother, was crucified.

Mark was beaten to death.

Saint Peter, crucified upside-down.

Apostle Paul beheaded in Rome.

Saint Jude was crucified.

Saint Bartholomew was crucified.

Thomas the Apostle was killed by a spear.

Luke the Evangelist was hanged.

Simon the Zealot was crucified in 74 A.D.

Saint Antipas was ordained by John, the disciple that Jesus loved, as bishop of Pergamum. This was during the reign of Roman emperor Domitian (81-96 AD). Domitian was an evil man. He killed his brother and had many Roman senators slain. He commanded all ancestors of King David be put to death. He had the Apostle John boiled in hot oil (Next martyr below). Nicodemus suffered under the rage of Domitian persecution (called the Second persecution of Domitian. The first Christian persecution occurred during the reign of Roman emperor Nero 67 AD). Timothy, the disciple of the Apostle Paul, died from being clubbed when he rebuked pagans in a procession about to celebrate an idolatrous feast called Catagogion. This also is said to happen during the second persecution of Domitian. Christian tradition believes that Saint Antipas is the same person in the last book of the New Testament, Revelations 2:13. It is believed that Roman Emperor Domitian had Saint Antipas placed inside of a life-size Bronze bull or Brazen Bull, then a fire was lit underneath the Brazen Bull until he was roasted to death. Saint Antipas is said to be first Christian martyr in Asia Minor.

John the Evangelist was cooked in boiling hot oil but survived and died of old age circa 110 A.D.

# 2nd and 3rd century A.D.

- Polycarp of Smyrna, probably around 160 A.D.
- Ignatius of Antioch in 107 A.D.
- Justin Martyr of Palestine in 168 A.D.

- The Martyrs of Scili (in North Africa, about 180 A.D.) The Passio Sanctorum Scilitanorum is regarded as the oldest Christian text in the Latin language.
- Perpetua and Felicity of Carthage in 202 A.D.
- Origen of Alexandria, about 250 A.D.
- Saint Januarius of Naples, Italy in 305 A.D.
- Saint Philomena of Corfu, Greece (died in Rome) about 305 A.D.

## Middle Ages Period, 5th century to 15th century

- John Huss (Jan Huss), 1415
- Jerome of Prague, 1416
- Joan of Arc (Jeanne d'Arc), 1431

## Reformation period, 16th century

- Felix Manz, 1527
- Patrick Hamilton, 1528
- George Blaurock, 1529
- Thomas More, 1535
- William Tyndale, 1536
- Margaret Pole, 1541
- George Wishart, 1546
- Hugh Latimer, 1555
- Nicholas Ridley (martyr), 1555
- Rowland Taylor, 1555
- John Hooper, 1555
- John Rogers (religious), 1555
- William Hunter (Protestant martyr), 1555
- Lawrence Saunders, 1555
- Thomas Cranmer (Anglican martyr), 1556
- Dirk Willems, 1569
- Margaret Ball, 1584

Some were martyred for preaching a different doctrine and some were persecuted for advocating the doctrine of Jesus Christ the Messiah. One man that was charged with heretical writings and teachings was Martin Luther who went up against the corruption of the Roman church in 1517. From the above list it appears that many were martyred during the 16th century during the time of Martin Luther comparable to the numbers of those martyred in the first century.

# CHAPTER 32

# Martin Luther's Intolerance for the Sale of Indulgences

MARIN LUTHER, WHO WAS A monk and scholar, born in Eisleben, Germany, in 1483, who protested the sale of indulgences by the Catholic Church because he felt it, was a sin. After Martin Luther received his doctorate in 1512, he became a savant of biblical studies. Martin Luther's intolerance with the church was mostly about the sale of indulgences. The Catholic Church has disavowed the selling of indulgences, but the process has been reported to be active today. By paying for the indulgences, a person would no longer have to perform special acts of good deeds or say certain prayers and still, they would go to Heaven without having to go to Purgatory.

An indulgence is the full or partial remission of temporal punishment for sins after the sinner confesses and receives absolution.

Pope Urban II, who was born around 1035 or 1041 AD, depending on the source, in the northern part of France He is the first to offer indulgences to all persons who participated in the Crusades and confessed their sins. Those persons who did not participate directly in the Crusades, but made contributions to the cause, were also offered indulgences. Pope Urban II ordered the Crusades in 1095 which was a call to all European Christians to wage war against the Muslims to reclaim the Holy Land. He died approximately four years later in 1099. Pope Urban II was accorded the first step toward canonization by being beatified in 1881 by Pope Leo XIII. Beatification is performed usually five years after the person receiving the beatification is deceased and is done by a Pope who has studied this person for one year to determine if he or she has lived a Holy life or is martyred and is now residing in Heaven.

The contemporary pope during Martin Luther's time delegated this sparse privilege of granting full remission of sins. The popes deliberately used monies collected from granting full remission of sins for various purposes. Leo X, the pope in 1517, is said to have depleted the pontifical treasury because he did place enough significance to the Reformation initiated by Martin Luther. Pope Leo X also used funds from selling indulgences to complete a building in Rome named St. Peter's Basilica Leo X franchised the sale of indulgences entered into an arrangement that essentially sold indulgence franchises that he collected half the monies from for the construction of the building. Some franchisees that received this privilege advertised that their indulgences came with premium packages that would provide and bypass purgatory. In addition, a person could buy the indulgence for an already deceased person. The monarchy paid a higher rate for indulgences then the commoners.

Well distributed folklore, up until this very day, concerning Martin Luther, is that his objection to the sale of indulgences was protested, on October 31, 1517, when he obstinately nailed a copy of his 95 Theses on the door of the Wittenberg Castle church. These 95 Theses publically condemned the promise of releasing an individual(s) from purgatory by paying money or compensation to the church. He also denounced the fact that the pope was acting as a middleman for the purpose of granting the remission of sins. His action led to what is called the Protestant Reformation and caused him to be ecclesiastically sentenced (excommunicated) for exclusion from the church in 1521.

Martin Luther believed that only God could pardon sin because people were naturally sinful and should seek salvation by believing in God. Unscrupulous priests had set themselves up as being high and mighty as if they were endowed with heavenly powers to rid people, including the dead, of temporal sins for a price based on the severity of the sin. He believed that priests should be subject to the law as all people were. The priests had set themselves up among the people as being divine and identifiable by their elaborate wardrobes in which Luther opposed. He believed that people should read the Bible for themselves as the people of Berea had done in Acts 17:11 discussed earlier. The priests wanted to spoon feed the people during Luther's time because they didn't want them forming their own opinion about the church practices especially about the practice of selling indulgences. His premise was that if the priests had such powers to rid people of sin, then the Christ-like act to do was to do it at no charge.

Luther was blessed to discover the biblical book of Romans, the longest and most theological of the thirteen letters by the apostle Paul. Because of the following scriptural verse, it is believed that Tertius, the Apostle Paul's secretary, acted as an amanuensis in the writing of the Book of Romans (Romans 16:22 ESV I Tertius, who wrote this letter, greet you in the Lord.)

Luther formed his conclusion that by faith alone does one become righteous in the sight of God. The Reformation battle cry was "By Faith Alone". He was completely convinced in his reading of this epistle that justification comes to man only through faith. Luther now believed and taught that salvation is a gift of God's grace, received by faith and trust in God's promise to forgive sins for the sake of Christ's death on the cross. This, he believed was God's work from beginning to end. After this awakening knowledge, he broke ties with the Roman Catholic Church. Luther was not the first to refute the teachings of the church as being un-Biblical.

# CHAPTER 33

# Reformers Opposed the 14th–16th Centuries European Churches

PRECEDING MARTIN LUTHER, AN OXFORD professor, scholar, and theologian named John Wycliffe produced the first hand-written English language Bible manuscripts in 1380's AD. Wycliffe translated out of the Latin Vulgate because he thought the bible shown be in the native language. The Latin Vulgate translation was the only source text available to him. Wycliffe was well-known throughout Europe for his opposition to the teaching of the organized Church, which he believed to be contrary to the Bible. Wycliffe's manuscripts were eventually burned and twelve years after he died of a stroke, his body was exhumed, burned to ashes and scattered upon the sea.

John Hus who was one of the followers of Wycliffe was also a Christian martyr who was burned at the stake in 1414 AD. Wycliffe's manuscripts were used as kindling for the fire. John Hus actively promoted the idea that people should be permitted to read the Bible in their own language, and they should oppose the tyranny of the Roman church that threatened anyone possessing a non-Latin Bible with execution.

Another of Martin Luther's contemporaries is John Colet who is said to be a true Christian. He presented a sermon in 1512AD that greatly critiqued the pope.

Colet's sermon was based on the fact that a council should be established to consider a Church reformation. He did not agree with the lifestyle of luxurious living by the priests of his day. They were not setting an example as they should have by leading a Christ-like life. His sermon consisted of four evils of the corrupt priests, demonic pride, carnal concupiscence, worldly covetousness, and worldly occupations. The first evil was that they were not humble in their service but, instead, they highly exalted themselves because of the office of priesthood thinking that they were better and above everyone else. The Apostle Peter spoke of humility because he was a witness to Jesus washing the disciple's feet in the upper room prior to the Crucifixion. His teaching by example was the instruction to them to be humble always and not to think more of themselves than they ought. (I Peter 5:5 ESV Likewise, you who are younger, be subject to the elders. Clothe yourselves, all of you, with humility toward one another, for "God opposes the proud but gives grace to the humble.")

Secondly, too many of the priests were engaged in carnal activities, taking part in fleshly lusts. Many of the priests Colet was speaking of in his sermon were not adhering to I John 2:16 ESV: "For all that is in the world– the desires of the flesh and the desires of the eyes and pride in possessions–is not from the Father but is from the world." (See also the Apostle Paul epistle to the Romans 8:5-6)

Thirdly, they were breaking one of the Ten Commandments by coveting (See Exodus 20:17) Many desired evil things by their selfish motivation. Colet believed many were seeking to become priests for monetary gain. It was so prevalent that Colet called it a plague. Jesus' parable to the rich fool in Luke 12:15 ESV. 15 And he said to them, "Take care, and be on your guard against all covetousness, for one's life does not consist in the abundance of his possessions."

Finally, Colet admonishes to the clergy to return to servitude to God instead of catering to man. Colet wanted the priest to become more knowledgeable of the Holy Scripture. Colet said that the clergy must first reform their minds so that this reformation could be passed on to the church. He said that the Apostle Paul's orders were to "be reformed into a new mind".

Another spiritual Protestant reformer and leader was William

Tyndale (1494-1536). He was a Biblical translator who was fluent in eight languages and is credited for translating the Christian Bible into a primitive form of modern English from Hebrew and Greek text. He was martyred in 1536, by strangulation and then his body was burned at the stake.

The Roman Catholic Church disallowed the English translation and dissemination of the Bible during the time of Tyndale. Tyndale had the Hebrew and Greek versions of the Bible translated and printed in English. The Tyndale New Testament (1525-1525) became the first printed edition of the scripture in the English language. Tyndale would have had an almost impossible task of effectively distributing his English translation of the Holy Bible if he had to hire scribes to hand write each copy. Because of Johannes Gutenberg first commercial printing facility built in Mainz, Germany in 1450, Tyndale was able print thousands of copies of his English translated bibles which were smuggled into England and distributed throughout. All bibles that were confiscated by the wicked Church of England were burned. Anyone found in possession of the Tyndale Bible was also burned.

The English law forbade the Bible from being translated into the native tongue. Tyndale was also in disagreement with the Church's teachings and adopted much of the theology of Martin Luther as did many others during the Reformation era. These were the major causes for him to be arrested and tried for heresy.

The sixteenth century produced many reformers from different countries in Europe. Consequently, there was opposition not only to the Roman Catholic Church but differences among the reformers. The reformers disagreed among themselves about Christian doctrines which caused them to divide and establish different rival Protestant churches. In Switzerland, there was a Roman Catholic priest named Ulrich Zwingli, who had started reformation of the church years before Luther. Zwingli was against the sale of indulgences by the Catholic Church like Luther. Zwingli believed in the Bible as the True Authority. His doctrine concerning Christianity was summed up by one statement that he used: "If it can't be found in the Bible, don't believe it and don't do it."

A German nobleman named Philip of Hesse tried to get Zwingli and Luther together so that Switzerland and Germany would be united concerning the Reformation which was going on during the same time frame in both countries. It didn't work out because the two opposed each other concerning the "Lords Supper". Luther believed Christ's words; "This is my body" meant Jesus was actually present during the sacrament of communion. Zwingli said the phrase meant "This signifies my body" so that the bread and wine were only symbolic. They agreed on some things concerning the Bible but never agreed concerning communion. They departed without accomplishing what Philip of Hesse desired.

The result of the reformation by these men caused the formation of the Protestant Church which separated from the Catholic Church. The first European settlers that came to New England brought Christian Protestantism and Separatism with them in the 16th and 17th centuries. These pilgrims, the smaller group called separatists, came in 1620 seeking safety from the dissension of the English Church. King James said, "I tried to have them thrown in jail for non-participation in the Church observances". There was a larger group of several hundred that wanted the freedom to worship as they pleased. Before they left England, their intentions were to purify the Church of England, thus they were called the Puritans, also Protestants.

Another reformer that was a contemporary of Martin Luther was John Calvin, a brilliant French theologian. He was very important in the second generation of the reformation movement. Though Calvin and Luther never met, Calvin has been thought of as second to Luther concerning the starting of the Reformation. Calvin believed in the predestination of those who are saved. Luther agreed with him on this point. Both also believed in faith over works. Luther and Calvin were really not that much different in their theology. Calvin believed and taught "once saved, always saved." Today, the terminology for this doctrine is called eternal security. Calvin believed that Jesus died only for the sins of the Elect, which is called Limited Atonement or Particular Redemption. This goes along with the doctrine of predestination. Some are predetermined to go to Heaven while the rest are predetermined to spend eternity in hell. This would make one think of Judas Iscariot who had been prophetically appointed and predetermined to be the one who would betray Jesus Christ leading to His crucifixion and resurrection.

# CHAPTER 34

# Judas Iscariot's Betrayal Fulfilled the Prophesy of Jeremiah

THE ONE THING THAT IS common in both the practice of "indulgences" in the Catholic Church and Judas Iscariot is the lust for money or wealth. Judas was discussed briefly earlier concerning the comparison of Joseph son of Israel (Jacob) and Jesus both being treacherously sold with the sellers being compensated with silver pieces. The scripture clearly indicates that Judas thought that he would profit because of his relationship with Jesus. Judas was the treasurer for Jesus' ministry. He stole from the coffer. He objected when Mary of Bethany anointed Jesus' feet with some expensive oil and wiped his feet with her hair. He proclaimed that the expensive oil could have been sold for a good price and the money given to the poor. Jesus rebuked him for this and it is believed that this rebuttal hurt his feelings so bad that he went to chief priests to start a plot to betray Jesus.

Judas' betrayal is believed to be the prophecy of Zechariah. Even though it was written and predestined, Judas still acted in his own accordance (Zechariah 11:12-13 *ESV* 12 Then I said to them, "If it seems good to you, give me my wages; but if not, keep them. "And they weighed out as my wages thirty pieces of silver. 13 Then the LORD said to me, "Throw it to the potter"– the lordly price at which I was priced by them. So I took the thirty pieces of silver and threw them into the house of the LORD, to the potter).

At the "Last Supper" with the twelve disciples, Jesus said truly one of you will betray me. The apostle Peter nudged the apostle John thinking that he might be able to reveal which one Jesus was speaking of concerning this betrayal. Jesus said he is the one who I will give a piece of bread. Jesus dipped the bread and gave it to Judas Iscariot and told him to leave quickly and to do what he had to do. The other disciples, at the time, did not know what Jesus meant. They thought since Judas was the treasurer of the group that Jesus had sent him out to buy something for the Passover Festival.

Later, when Judas heard that Jesus had been condemned, he was remorseful and went to the chief priests to return the thirty pieces of silver they had given him to betray Jesus. I am not saying because he was sorrowful about his betrayal that this represented a Godly repentance. He ended up taking his own life (II Corinthians 7:10). He told them that he had betrayed an innocent man, but they didn't care about that because they had accomplished the arresting of Jesus to kill Him. Judas took the silver and threw it on the floor and left. This was blood money, by the Hebrew Law; the chief priests could not accept it into the treasury of the temple at Jerusalem. Instead, they used the returned silver to buy a cemetery plot which was used as a place to bury deceased foreigners, strangers, or the poor. This was called Potter's Field and was indirectly purchased by Judas for his burial site through the actions of the high priests. Judas hung himself and his body decayed causing his guts to gush out when he fell from the tree (Matthew 27:3-10).

Did Judas Iscariot go to Heaven, hell, or neither since he was sorrowful? There is an abundance of various opinions that can be found from biblical study sources. Many opinions are backed by scripture. The Gnostic Gospel of Judas does not portray Judas Iscariot as a betrayer of Jesus; rather he is acting at the behest of Jesus. This Gnostic gospel was said to have been composed in the second century by Gnostic Christians. There are many Gnostic gospels (fifty- four plus) which are supposed to be secret, mystical knowledge found in ancient texts based upon the teachings of several spiritual leaders written by them from the 2nd to the 4th century AD. Earlier in this text, Roman

Catholic priest Ulrich Zwingli was quoted as saying, "If it can't be found in the Bible, don't believe it and don't do it."

As discussed earlier, the sale of indulgences was profitable. It contributed to the pope's climb to the status of becoming one of the richest men in the world in the sixteenth century and led to the reformation. The Bible tells us that the love of money is the essential core of many types of evil (I Timothy 6:9-10)

## CHAPTER 35

# Religious Leader's Greed Prevented "Watching and Spiritual Intercession"

MANY PEOPLE HAVE ERRED BECAUSE of the love of money and have fallen into Satan's trap becoming inattentive to God, the Holy Spirit, and the warnings Jesus provided in the scriptures. They call themselves "Watchmen" but how could this be when they are blind? The prophet Isaiah called the religious leaders of his day a bunch of hungry dogs before or during the exilic period of Israel to Babylonia. These leaders were only looking after their own welfare and personal gain. So God, speaking through Isaiah, called them out on their irresponsibility and greed (Isaiah 56:9-12). The prophet Isaiah compared irresponsible leaders to the watchdogs that guarded sheep saying that the dogs were lazy, greedy, and spent most of their time sleeping.

The same thing was going on in the New Testament and Jesus quoted the same sentiment concerning what was going on in the temple for worship in Jerusalem. Jesus came into the temple and found money changers there and those that bought and sold doves. He overturned the tables that were blocking the ingress of the temple. The chief priests and the scribes heard about what Jesus had done and conspired to destroy Him because they felt that too many people were becoming amazed at His teaching (Mark 11:15-19)

Religious leaders have always been critiqued more than laymen because they are responsible for feeding the sheep, which are the people seeking salvation. Their actions must duplicate what they are teaching. It is understood that all have sinned and we all make ourselves liars if we say that we haven't. The apostle Paul made clear this point of the universality of sin in the epistle to the Romans 3: 9-10 NIV What shall we conclude then? Do we have any advantage? Not at all! For we have already made the charge that Jews and Gentiles alike are all under the power of sin. 10 As it is written: "There is no one righteous, not even one."

# CHAPTER 36

# Only God can Provide Righteousness

BELIEVERS ARE MADE RIGHTEOUS NOT by their own doings or works, but by the grace of God. No one can be made righteous on his own by observing the law- refers to Romans 3:21-29. The Apostle Paul wrote approximately one fourth (23.5-28% based on source) of the New Testament and is the principal writer on the idea of righteousness. Of the twenty-seven books of the New Testament, Paul is credited for the writing of thirteen of the books of the New Testament Bible which is 48% of the books not based on word count from any source. This does not include the Book of Hebrews that many ministers and New Testament scholars give him credit for writing. The author Luke wrote the Gospel of Luke and Acts accounts for approximately 27.5% (varies based on source) of the New Testament based on word count.

In the early ministry of the Apostle Paul, he attempted to preach the Word of God in Jerusalem. Although he was a persecutor of Christians prior to his conversion to Christianity, the Disciples of Christ accepted him wholeheartedly. The Jews in Jerusalem did not accept him, and argued with him, and tried to kill him. They would have succeeded had it not been for the help of believers who saved his life by taking him out of Jerusalem to the port city of Caesarea.

Paul traveled from Caesarea to the city where he was born which is Tarsus capital of the province of Cilicia. Tarsus, during Paul's day, was a large city in Cilicia and is identified today as Anatolia, Turkey. On the Sabbath, Paul spoke at the synagogue there by the invitation of the rulers of the synagogue. Paul was so influential on his message about the forgiveness of sins by Jesus that on the following Sabbath just about everyone in the city showed up, Jews and Gentiles. Upon seeing the overflow crowd there to hear Paul, the Jews again, became jealous, argued with him and tried to rattle him with insults. Because of the insults and the rejection of the Word of God by some Jews, it's most likely the reason the Apostle became a minister to the Gentiles also.

The rejection of the Word of God by the Jews happened in several places where Paul ministered about the grace of God which is a free gift that cannot be earned by works. Paul's message was that Jesus is the Messiah who was crucified and resurrected for the atonement of all believers sins. The Apostle's message on receiving justification by faith and righteousness received from God by believers is basically the emphasis of his ministry.

Paul made no distinction between Jews and Gentiles concerning the fact that all people are sinners and are in need of salvation. The only way sinners can be pardoned and liberated from sin is by the redemptive work of Jesus Christ on the Cross. The contemporary Pharisees at the time of Paul's ministry were still teaching and preaching about righteousness received by adherence to the Judaic Laws which is self-righteousness, received by one's own works and circumcision obligatory for converted Gentiles.

The Jews came to the early church at Antioch teaching that those converted had to be circumcised which caused a huge debate between them and the Apostle Paul and Barnabas. They believed that the prerequisite for receiving the Holy Spirit, one must be circumcised. This caused a controversy in Antioch that had to be settled by the Church council in Jerusalem before the apostles and elders. The Apostle Peter spoke and this issue was resolved by the head of the council, who was, James, Jesus's brother (Acts 15:1-20).

Jesus was circumcised at eight days old and so was his cousin, John the Baptist (Luke 1:59-63 & Luke 2:21). Jesus believed circumcision was fitting but rarely spoke of the Jewish religious rite allowing circumcision on the Sabbath, which is one of the Mosaic Laws. Jesus rebuked the fact that the religious leaders were very critical of Him performing miracles on the Sabbath, yet they didn't have a problem with circumcising on the Sabbath. There were six hundred and thirteen laws or commandments (called Law of Moses) that were impossible to be adhered to or even, possibly, memorized by the Pharisees or the high priests. The Sadducees were less pious than the Pharisees so it is not really known which laws they adhered to concerning their beliefs.

The Apostle Paul's letter to the Christians at Rome was that the righteousness of God is altogether different and distinct (from the Law) because it is dependent on the reliance on Jesus Christ's righteousness. Adherence to the Law has nothing to do with being justified before God. He wanted to dispel, in his letter also, the fact that God was not only for the Jews but for Gentiles alike.

To receive the righteousness of God we must confess with our tongue that God is Lord of Lords and King of Kings. There are some who know His word but do not establish a relationship with God to experience His grace. Therefore God shows His wrath against those certain individuals which are called corrupt or reprobate. Unlike humans that might throw a fit and act irrationally when things don't go as planned, God's wrath is just and of a Holy nature (Romans 1:18-20).

Satan is not going to give up his plan to sit in God's almighty seat. He uses humans as instruments to usurp God's grace and love to show him as the exalted one. God's wrath is for those who know this and allow Satan to fulfill his purpose through them. The Apostle Paul's second letter to the church at Thessalonica basically is speaking of the second coming of Jesus Christ, but he also speaks of the accelerated pace by Satan to cause great rebellion against God's supremacy.

Satan's utmost plan is the coming of the antichrist to misguide many; that is his ace card but it is a no-winner because Jesus will destroy him with the breath of His mouth. II Thessalonians 2:1-4 ESV 1 Concerning the coming of our Lord Jesus Christ and our being gathered to him, we ask you, brothers and sisters, 2 not to become easily unsettled or alarmed by the teaching allegedly from us—whether by a prophecy or by word of mouth or by letter —asserting that the day of the Lord has already come. 3 Don't let anyone deceive you in any way, for that day will not come until the rebellion occurs and the man of lawlessness is revealed, the man doomed to destruction. 4 He will oppose and will exalt himself over everything that is called God or is worshiped, so that he sets himself up in God's temple, proclaiming himself to be God.

Aaron, Moses's brother, used a graven tool to form an idolatrous "golden calf" (Exodus 32). Aaron apparently learned how to use the graving tool while in Egypt. The Egyptians often fashioned their idols, resembling an ox or a bull, using wood overlaid by gold. When Moses came down from Mount Sinai, he was so infuriated, he burnt the golden calf, ground the ashes and scattered the ashes in water and made the Israelites drink this mixture. This seems to indicate that the golden calf was wood overlaid with gold (Exodus 32:20).

Aaron apparently had seen the Egyptian bull-god, Apis or Hapis. Apis was the most sacred of all the idolatrous animal gods in Egypt. A metallurgical process such as this, gold would have to be heated to make it pliable or melted. Aaron was knowledgeable of this metallurgical process because he received gold earrings from the Israelites and made a golden calf. (The Hebrew word for graving tool is cheret). He made this "golden calf at the request of the wilderness traveling Israelites while Moses had left them for forty days as he had gone to Mount Sinai to receive God's Ten Commandments.

While he was gone they reverted back to worshiping the LORD and serving idols simultaneously (a form of polytheism). Their celebration and sacrifices to this calf were with sinful, pagan, joyous celebration, and disobedience to the Second Commandment of God (See Exodus 20:4).

Today, individuals display these rebellious, disobedient "golden calves" in their own mind and become reprobated. Ones' outward display of immoral fruits display what is going on in his or her mind just as fruits of the Holy Spirit are displayed by believers.

As mentioned when discussing the Reformation period, Martin Luther and other reformists singled out "justification by faith" as the theme of the book of Romans. Others cite the theme of "the righteousness of God" for the entire book. In reading the entire letter neither can be described as being taken out of context. The most prominent theme of the entire book is revealed in Romans 1:16-17 ESV 16 For I am not ashamed of the gospel, for it is the power of God for salvation to everyone who believes, to the Jew first and also to the Greek. 17 For in it the righteousness of God is revealed from faith for faith, as it is written, "The righteous shall live by faith."

There is no excuse available for dishonoring God even if knowledge of the Bible is lacking. Look around, the whole creation was done by his "breath" or by his "Word" (See Psalms 33:6). Nobody has a good excuse! In the Old Testament, the creation of idols could be easily seen because the people would build the idols and place them in high places.

Today, it is not as apparent to see the deities created because it can be someone's mental attitude or mindset such as revering materialistic things. It could be the exaltation of one's self. But the creation of righteousness other than that of God's is basically the same throughout the ages. Some believers are quick to redefine what righteousness is by claiming that the law given under the Old Covenant does not apply under the New Covenant.

The Apostle Paul explains in Romans 6 concerning being "dead in sin and alive to God." The Apostle sometimes to pre-states an argument or question, and then he gives an answer. The beginning of the apostle's assertion in the beginning of Romans 6 is prefaced by the last two verses of Romans 5 (v. 20, 21). Concerning the Hebrew Laws there is an increase in evil and lawfulness (apprehension of the contrast between sin and Holiness are made more evident); as evil and lawfulness increases, grace proliferates even more. Sin causes eternal damnation and grace leads to eternal life through Jesus. The Apostle asked a question that he anticipated would be asked concerning his assertion, "then should we continue in sin because grace is going to increase anyway?" He asked, rhetorically, "that in no way we are we continue to sin because we have died to sin, so how can we still live in it?"

Many have read the Bible, have heard sermons, attend Bible study, memorized and can quote many scriptures verbatim, but their carnal lifestyle has not changed or decreased. This is a quotation I heard a minister say during a sermon, "There are dry devils that go down in water to be baptized and come up out of the water wet devils after baptism." (Baptists and Dunkards have always used Baptism by immersion following the Biblical practice of John the Baptist. Dunkards is derived from the German word, dunke; dunke origin is from another German work, tunken, which means to immerse or dip.)

The realization of what compromises sin should be understood. The Apostle Paul said that he identified his life as having been crucified with Christ...the life he lived in the flesh is by faith in the Son of God (See Galatians 2:20). There should be an understanding that once one is baptized, after repentance, he or she does not spontaneously become sinless, but he or she should sin less. Righteousness before God is only through the blood of Jesus. We all sin, none are righteous by his or her own works (Romans 3:22-25 ESV the righteousness of God through faith in Jesus Christ for all who believe. For there is no distinction: for all have sinned and fall short of the glory of God, and are justified by his grace as a gift, through the redemption that is in Christ Jesus, whom God put forward as a propitiation by his blood, to be received by faith. This was to show God's righteousness because in his divine forbearance he had passed over former sins).

Abandoning the intimate true knowledge of God's Word and not adhering to the Word for fleshly reasons and creating some modification (Leap of Faith) to justify sinful actions is dissimulated in the mind and heart to make it seem to be in obedience to God. God allows this sinful behavioral manner of conducting oneself as a form of judgment against these individuals. These individuals will not grow spiritually in Christ unless they repent and pray for the guidance of the Holy Spirit to distance themselves from the love of the world (Refer to I Corinthians 3:1-4).

Ministers frequently ask repentant individuals to kneel on knees, showing respect and respect for God. Jesus demonstrated the correct way to pray in Luke 22:41, where He kneeled down and prayed to the Father. This does not limit prayer to just one particular environment, pray without ceasing anywhere, God is omnipresent. Don't pray in the place of worship like Jesus said the hypocrites prayed in the synagogue and on the streets to be seen by others. Don't try to impress with long winded empty phrases (Refer to Mathew 6:5-7). Genuflection is used in Catholicism where one lowers the body briefly, bending one knee to the ground in reverence to the Blessed Sacrament. There are many body positions that are used to show reverence to the Lord. The Lord loves communing with you more than with what position your hands and body are in. Crucifixion was considered a most shameful and disgraceful way to die, yet Jesus communed with the Father while nailed on the Cross.

Pray to the Comforter to increase obedience to God's will. In our attempt to live in a democratic society, we vote into law practices that are totally against the will of God. God never intended for two people of the same sex to bond in marriage. The description in Genesis 19:1-11 of two male angels invited by Lot (nephew of Abraham) to spend the night at his house. After they were fed and before they could lie down, young and old men of the city of Sodom surrounded Lot's house and called to Lot to send the two male angels out so they could have homosexual relations with them. Lot went outside closing the door behind him pleading to the gang of men not to harm the two male angels. Lot offered his two engaged to be married virgin daughters to them in place of the two male angels (See Genesis 19:14). They disregarded Lot's offer and charged the house to break the door down. The two male angels pulled Lot inside the house and afflicted the men with blindness so they could not find the door to the house.

When the morning came the angels told Lot to take his wife and two daughters and leave because the city would be destroyed because of the wickedness of the people there. When Lot left, God rained down sulfur and fire from Heaven destroying Sodom and Gomorra. The question raised by some is the fact that the young and old men that came surrounding Lot's house said in Genesis 19:5 ESV, "Bring them out to us, that we may know them." (A similar incident occurs in Judges 19:22)

Most scholars, from various sources, concur that homosexual rape is meant here by, "we may know them." There are others say that this story is not about homosexuality at all, rather, the lesson of Sodom is about pride and hospitality. Others say that it is more about Lot, his wife, and daughters who were admonished by the angels to comply and not to look back as they departed Sodom for the town of Zoar (Zoar defined – small or insignificant.

By Jewish tradition, it is said Lot's wife's name was "Ado" or "Edith" (The Bible does not mention her name). They fled to a small town named Zoar and she looked back with a longing and regretful heart and was transformed into a pillar of salt. Some scholars are more focused on the punishment for disobedience and loving the world more than loving God in this story.

One should look ahead and not look back at a past carnal life for deliverance by God). There are variations of commentaries which are at odds concerning the biblical interpretation of homosexuality between liberal and conservative scholars (This variation of opinions is because there is no word in the Bible explicitly termed homosexual. The first known publication using the term "homosexual" was found in a printed pamphlet in 1869 by a Hungarian journalist named Karl-Maria Kertbeny who used a pseudonym. Homosexual translates as "same-sex" with the Greek prefix meaning "same" and the Latin root "sex").

They feel this account of Sodom and Gomorra is used erroneously to victimize homosexuality is absurd and unfair. What is explicitly stated about homosexual acts as being sinful can be found in Leviticus 18:22, 20-13, Romans 1:26-28, Mark 10:6-10 (God's purpose for man and woman), I Corinthians 6:9-11, This is a bleak story in the Bible, but is necessary to show how much God hates sin. Before we vote against God's principles to make them righteous according to man's law, let us remember the Bible teaches us of the destruction God has already sent forth because of disobedience. God is almighty and reigns forever whereas man is here today and gone tomorrow like a puff of air. The Psalmists King David realizes this as he wrote in Psalms 144: 3-4 ESV I wonder why you care, GOD — why do you bother with us at all? All we are is a puff of air; we're like shadows in a campfire.

Under the Law of Moses in the Old Testament of the Bible men that had impairment of their sexual organs were excluded from attending the worship assembly (Deuteronomy 23:1). The males in the bible that had been castrated were called "eunuchs". The term eunuch also was used for men who had not been castrated but were officials assigned to duties of a kingdom.

In the New Testament in the book Acts eighth chapter, the Lord sends Philip from the church at Jerusalem to go out and evangelize a Gentile Ethiopian eunuch who was in charge of the treasury for Candace, the traditional name of the queen of the Ethiopians. The eunuch had been in Jerusalem to worship and was returning home. As the eunuch was riding along in his chariot, he was reading scripture from the book of Isaiah. Prompted by the Holy Spirit, Philip joined him in the chariot and interpreted the scripture for him which was the good news concerning Jesus.

The two came upon a stream of water and the eunuch requested to be baptized by Philip. Scripture says that Philip was then carried away by the Holy Spirit after the baptism (Acts 8:26-40). This illustrates that God accepts all believers who request to be accepted. (See Mathew 19:10-12 Jesus gives three examples of who is meant or not meant for marriage)

# CHAPTER 37

# Men Try to Explain Creation and Legalities other than the "Word" of the Omnipotent God

GOD TOLERATES US BECAUSE OF His Love and He made man for His own pleasure. God is patient with us; it would be justifiable for Him to just abandon this whole thing about our existence. God provided a way to tolerate and forgive our inherited sinful Adamic nature by allowing His Son, Jesus, to die on the Cross for the redemption of our sins. It is because of our faith in Jesus; He forgives us of our iniquities and cleanses us of our sins (Refer to1 John1:9).

Men have tried to formulate their own beliefs concerning how the universe was formed and how humans came into existence in this world such as Charles Darwin's theory of evolution. Creationists and evolutionists have debated over how humans were first formed since Charles Darwin's theory of evolution. Creationists are those who believe that the universe and all living organisms were created by the divine work of God as described in the Biblical account in Genesis 1:1-31.

Evolutionists are those who believe that organisms, including humans, inherently improved themselves through progressive inherited changes over time, and increase in complexity through evolution from a biological perspective.

Christian adherents believe in the Young Earth creationism (YEC) and advocate the literal interpretation as described by Moses in the first two chapters of Genesis in the Holy Bible. The Harris Interactive poll, in 2009, found that 39% of Americans agreed with the statement that "God created the universe, the earth, the sun, moon, stars, plants, animals, and the first two people within the past 10,000 years" (Psalms 33:6-7, John 1:3, and Isaiah 45:8 &12). Successive Gallup surveys conducted between 1982 and 2014 asked about views on the origin and development of human beings and found that between 40% and 47% of adults in the United States were inclined to the view that "God created humans in their present form at one time within the last 10,000 years". A 2011 Gallup survey reports that 30% of U.S. adults say they interpret the Bible literally. ("Evolution, Creationism, Intelligent Design" Gallup 2015 Retrieved 2015-06-13).

The Big Bang Paradigm is said to be the leading explanation of how the universe was formed, which means there are many who don't believe the Bible's infallible truth. The Big Bang Paradigm is a scientific theory explaining how scientists think the universe came into existence as a singularity thirteen million years ago. A layperson explanation of this process is that a small, dense, very hot mass was compressed and had a complete lack of any form of existence. This non-existence entity started inflating rapidly causing a big bang sending out the universe(s) with stars, galaxies, and our earth. This is the universe formation according to some scientists.

Scientists also have a theory concerning the evolution of humans occurring over millions of years from a single cell to what humans are today. There were evolution theorists before, during, and after the English naturalist Charles Darwin (1809–1882) whose theories of biological evolution are similar to his. Comparative anatomy was a course that I had to take while in college because it was one of the required subjects for biology majors at the college. Comparative anatomy is the study of similarities and differences in the anatomy of different species. It is closely related to evolutionary biology. I took the course for the credits and it wasn't easy. These types of courses were divided into two parts: the lecture portion in a large classroom and the laboratory portion. I can remember dissecting various dead animals such as sharks, frogs, etc. and comparing similarities of various organs in the laboratory.

There was an English biologist named Thomas Henry Huxley (05/04/1825 – 06/29/1895) who specialized in comparative anatomy. Huxley is credited with coining the term called Darwinism because he staunchly advocated Darwin's theory of the evolution of species by natural selection. There were some theories much earlier than Darwin's, such as the ancient Greeks who believed man developed from air and water.

Satan is the enemy and has planted deceit and doubt in the heart of some men and women against God. "It is God that made us, we did not make ourselves." The sea is his, for he made it, and his hands formed the dry land. (Refer to Psalms 100:3, 95:5). People have no excuse for being as ignorant of God today as they were in Noah's day. Nevertheless, historically and to the present day, as the human population increases, wickedness increases proportionately.

Biblical scholars are not in total agreement concerning who wrote the book of Ecclesiastes. Many biblical scholars' commentaries indicate that one needs to go no farther than Ecclesiastes 1:1 (The words of the Preacher, the son of David, king in Jerusalem) to identify King Solomon as the author. King Solomon was given great wisdom by God that excelled the wisdom of all the children of the east country, and all the wisdom of Egypt (I Kings 4:29-34). Ecclesiastes was placed in the canonical wisdom books of the Old Testament Christian Bibles. I will assume that King Solomon is the author of the Book of Ecclesiastes.

King Solomon wrote that man lives in sameness and repetitiveness throughout the ages (Refer to Ecclesiastes 1:9-11). God saw the wickedness of the people during the time of Noah and became sorrowful that he had made a man on the earth. Because of the wickedness and evilness of man, God decided to also include all the animals of the world under man's rule to the same fate as that of Noah's contemporaries. Only Noah's righteous standing with God allowed him, his single family, and two of every living thing with flesh to be spared from the water deluge of the whole earth (Refer to Genesis 6). Jesus, speaking of His second coming in Luke 17:26-30, said that just like in the days of Noah and Lot, people were eating, drinking, marrying, buying, selling, planting and building with no reverence for God and they were all destroyed. Jesus will be visible to all in His second coming. This repetitious nature of mankind of showing irreverence to God will not cease until the time of eternal Judgment spoken of in both the Old and New Testaments. The Christians are no longer under the law and will not face the condemnation of God (Romans 8:1). Whoever does not believe in Jesus is already condemned (John 3:18)

Laws have been implemented so that man can have a feeling of legality in his own mind. Many rights that are against the scripture are now being applied to civil rights. Civil rights include the ensuring of peoples' physical and mental integrity, life, and safety; protection from discrimination on grounds such as race, gender, national origin, Color, sexual orientation, ethnicity, religion, or disability.

Contemporaneous sins of this day and time cannot be justified as being accepted by God because of the lack of specificity in the Holy Bible. The world has changed considerably since the time that Jesus walked the earth. Scholars suggest that the 19th century profoundly changed daily lives with the invention of the steam engine and electricity. The twentieth century is said to be a century of revolutions which there were very many.

Briefly, but not inclusively, there was the women's liberation revolution, sexual-revolution, big government, and etc... As the population of the world increased there was also a proportionately increase in sin and evilness. The Bible's forty inspired writers do not specifically speak of the sins of today. By studying the Bible, many comparisons can be extracted or gleaned to be applicable to modern day sins such as prostitution.

Rudyard Kipling (December 30, 1865 –January 18, 1936) was an English journalist, short-story writer, poet, and novelist was the author of the phrase "the world's oldest profession" pertaining to a story he wrote in 1888 about a courtesan (a prostitute, especially one with wealthy or upper-class clients) named Lalun in the short story "On the City Wall".

The events in the book of Joshua Chapter 2 occurred by estimation, around 1250 B.C. approximately 3,138 years before Kipling described prostitution as "the world's oldest profession". The Israelites sent out two men on a reconnaissance mission and were aided there by a local named Rahab, a prostitute of the Canaanite city of Jericho who allowed two men from the Israelite camp to use her residence as a hiding place. The king of Jericho received information that two spies were hiding there so she had to use farther deception to avoid their being captured (Joshua 2:1-7). Because of her aid, her family was spared when the Israelites invaded Jericho and burnt it to the ground.

She committed her life to the God of Israel (See Joshua 6:22-25). She was a famous and highly honored woman among the Hebrews. Although Rahab's profession is identified as being a prostitute, there are other unnamed prostitutes and suggestive behaviors that suggest prostitution, immoral behavior and/or being unfaithful to God. Every Word of the canonical Bible is by the mouth of God which was done by a mysterious process (Holy Spirit) to the thirty- nine or forty inspired writers over a period of fifteen hundred years. There are some biblical scholars that say there were twenty-three writers of the Old Testament and eight writers of the New Testament while other scholars say there thirty writers of the OT and ten of the NT (The Apostle Paul validates God's Word written by men in II Timothy 3:16-17).

There are many versions of the Holy Scripture in print and media. Some have been edited to provide private interpretation(For example refer to the Jefferson Bible constructed by Thomas Jefferson, 3rd president of the United States, who cut and pasted sections of the four synoptic Gospels in the New Testament Bible excluding the miracles, supernatural acts, and the Resurrection of Jesus. Cutting and pasting used here by Jefferson is not the same as the modern day computer definition which is used to move files, folders and selected text to another location. Cut removes the item from its current location and places it into the clipboard which is a temporary memory location that works behind the scene. Paste removes the item from the temporary location and inserts the current clipboard contents into the new location.

The literal construction of Jefferson's bible was done by using a razor and glue to arrange and remove biblical content that he did not believe in such as the virgin birth, walking on water, and the divinity of Jesus, etc.). The Bible admonishes against contributing private or independent interpretations of the Holy Scripture (II Peter 1:20-21). Jefferson was not considered to be an atheist, but some modern Christians might be outraged by his eccentricities concerning the Holy Bible. He has been labeled as being a deist; a person who believes God exists but is not directly involved in the world affairs, and a heretic; a person at odds with what is generally accepted. Jefferson believed religion should be used in conjunction with governing a nation, Christianity specifically.

There were many false prophets in the first century modifying scripture to fit their own mind which caused the apostles to provide warnings to the early Church in Jerusalem. Beware of such practices of personal modifications to the Holy Scripture by some today.

When Apostle Paul wrote his good friend and fellow preacher at the Ephesian church, he warned him that there was heretical and ascetical teaching going on concerning the Old Testament Law (Mosaic Law). However, they confidently added to the law for financial gain. This led the apostle to write I Timothy 1:8-11 that laws were not written for the righteous and in good standing with God. He said that the Law is good if used lawfully for the motive they were designed for. The lawless sinful, ungodly, unruly, and anyone else opposed to the wholesome teaching and sound doctrine need the Law that the blessed God has provided in the superb Gospels.

Topics that were once prohibited to the public have recently come to the forefront, especially in the U.S. of America as the world watches to see what direction we are headed. From recent reports up to three-quarters of Americans support gay rights and civil unions, but half do not support gay marriage. Even the country leaders have spoken in favor of gay rights. Reuters news agency reported in 2013 that: "All legally same-sex married couples are entitled to approximately one thousand federal benefits as heterosexual married couples no matter which state they live in. This legality took place On June 26, 2013, when the U.S. Supreme Court issued its decision in the United States v. Windsor and struck down the section of the Defense of Marriage Act (DOMA) that defined marriage as a "union between a man and a woman." The United States Census Bureau as of September 15, 2016, says there are some 56 million opposite-sex married couple households and around 400,000 same-sex married couple households. The Pew Research Center says in 2015, the U.S. Supreme Court ruled (5 to 4) all state bans on same-sex marriage unconstitutional, allowing gay and lesbian couples to marry nationwide.

One of the most common sayings of homosexuals is that "it is not their fault because they were born this way", thus placing the blame on God. Research for this book could not find any information on genetics that causes homosexuality in individuals. If there is such information available, it has been elusive to scientifically prove that it exists. Even if it is counted as a hereditary "tendency" even this cannot be proven. Therefore the contention of this book is that the Bible says that when one gives his or her self to this practice it is against God's will and, thus, it falls in the same category as all other sins. Homosexual sinners deserve prayer, love should be in the heart of Christians to have a love for all sinners and pray for them, but we must hate the sin as God does. Jesus wants us to love as He loves us.

Americans should not condone what was common practice by Biblical Old Testament tribes such as the Canaanites. This practice of men lusting for men was a common degenerate and corrupt act done by them. When God gave the 2$^{nd}$ law to Moses and the Israelites, included was how He wanted to conduct warfare against several nations that practiced idolatry. God had given the Israelites the Promised Land that was inhabited by the Canaanites. God told the Israelites to completely wipe out every living Canaanite. The reason is that they worshiped idol gods called El and Baal. The worshipping of these gods was sexual in nature. After the Israelites had captured Canaan, God wanted the Canaanites completely wiped out so that the Israelites would not become emulators of idolatry (Refer to Deuteronomy 20:16-18). God detested the profound engrossment of the Canaanites to sexual divinity and sexual rituals. Their chief God El and his son Baal were completely morally nefarious.

There were some valuable texts discovered in 1929 by excavation on the Coast of Syria called the Ugaritic texts. These texts have provided enlightening parallels to the Hebrew Bible concerning the culture and various languages of the region. The Ugaritic texts show Baal as a weather god with powers over atmospheric conditions that affect the earth especially lightning, wind, rain, and fertility. Canaanites were dependent upon rainfall for their agriculture to grow. When Moses sent out twelve spies, each representing the tribes of the Israelites, to the "Promised land", the first part of the report concerning the impressive favorability of the land for agriculture was as God had promised. But the Canaanites attributed their god, Baal, for the rain and fertile land there. This is why God wanted all of the Canaanites there destroyed so that the Israelites would not assimilate Baal into their worship practice. They had shown that they could easily revert to their idolatrous ways as they had in the wilderness journey creating a "golden calf" to worship when Moses went up on Mount Sinai for forty days. Polytheism was customary while they were bondage in Egypt for 400 years (Genesis 15:13, Acts 7:6) or 430 years (Exodus 12:40-41).

Under Joshua's leadership, the Israelites captured the 'Promise Land" and settled into the land, they did not kill all of the Canaanites as God had instructed them to do. Again, their disobedience to God was shown by their picking up the habits of pagan worship from the idolatrous environment of the people they encountered.

All twelve tribes of the Israelites had received their own share of land in Canaan. The territory of Benjamin included a town named Gibeah. Gibeah, a Hebrew word meaning hill, was located in, Judges 19, approximately 3-4 miles north of Jebus (Jerusalem). The first Israelite king, King Saul had a house in Gibeah (1 Samuel 10:26).

There were four towns in different locations referred to as Gibeah in the Old Testament Bible. A bloody fierce war broke out between the tribe of Benjamin and the other Israelite tribes when the immoral men of Gibeah raped a concubine (concubine-generally is a female slave whose purpose was to serve as a secondary wife and surrogate mother) belonging to a Levite man (Judges 19:22-30). He had taken the concubine from Bethlehem in Judah. She became unfaithful to him and escaped back to her father's house in Bethlehem in Juda.

After four months had passed, the Levite went with his servant and donkeys to Bethlehem to bring her back. When they arrived at Bethlehem, the girl's father, his father-in-law, made merriment with the Levite and persuaded him to stay with him for four days as they ate and drank wine. On the fifth day, the father-in-law tried to persuade him to spend another night but he refused and left with his concubine. On the way back to the hill country, they by-passed Jebus (Jerusalem) and stopped in the town square of Gibeah. None of the people in the town square offered a place for them to stay until an old man came along. The old man was from the hill country of Ephraim also but did not know the Levite. The old man had a temporary residence in Gibeah and offered them to spend the night at his place. They went to his place and this is where the book of Judges describes the morally depraved men of Gibeah who attempted first to perform a homosexual sex act.

The men of Sodom, young and old, attempted a nearly identical homosexual rape of two male angels who were invited guests of Abraham's nephew, Lot. This similar incident is described in the book of Genesis 19:4-11.

In the book Of Judges, there were some good for nothing men of the city of Gibeah that came to the old man's house, beat on his door, demanding that the male guest (the Levite) be brought outside of the house so that they could have a homosexual relationship with him. The old man went outside of the house and pleaded with them not to do this immoral thing to his guest. He offered his virgin daughter and the Levite's concubine to them. The men didn't want the females for their immoral, detestable relationship. The concubine was sent out anyway and the men had intercourse with her all night and did not let her go until almost sunrise.

When daybreak came, the raped, abused concubine came to lie at the door of the house. Her master came out the house that morning saw her and said let's go but she was dead. The master took her body and cut it up into twelve pieces and sent the pieces throughout the territory of Israel. This was very strange and different, nothing like this was ever seen before by the Israelites who received the individual pieces of the concubine's body. The Levite owner of the concubine wanted the other eleven tribes of Israel to know what the Benjaminite men of Gibeah had done.

After receiving the dismembered parts of the murdered concubine and the explanation by the Levite, all of the other tribes of Israel were infuriated by the immoral act committed against her at Gibeah. The Israelites of the other eleven tribes upon hearing this explanation declared to avenge this atrocity with the exception of the people of Jabesh Gilead (Judges 21:8-9). They assembled before the Lord to seek His Divine guidance on what should be done to the Benjamites of Gibeah because of the immoral act. Eleven nations of Israel gathered four hundred thousand foot soldiers and went to war against the tribe of Benjamin setting fires to the cities and slaughtering the people (Judges 20).

There were six hundred Benjamite men that had escaped being killed by the Israelites and they had compassion for these men and did not kill them because they did not want to see this tribe become extinct. The remaining Benjaminite males were allowed to marry into the other tribes except the one mentioned above that did not join in the attack of Gibeah. The tribes of Israel decided to go and kill all of the men and women of Jabesh Gilead except for the virgin women. The Israelites did not want to abolish the Benjaminite tribe since they were Israelite brethren. They decided to spare six hundred of the men. The Israelites found 400 young virgins of the city of Jabesh-Gilead. They gave them to four hundred of the surviving male Benjamites. There were two hundred Benjaminite men left without wives so they went into a town named Shiloh and took wives there (Judges 21).

# CHAPTER 38

# It is Difficult to Deceive a Christian that is Imbued in God's "Word"

BECAUSE CHRISTIANS STRIVE TO HAVE compassion, righteousness, kindness, sympathy, empathy, and love in their hearts by the power of the indwelling Holy Spirit, they are sometimes not aware of the deception. Most of the time it is by someone who claims to be a Christian. The Christians that are deceived is because they attempt to do something good or give something of themselves, believing this will make them closer or in better standing with God. In just about every case, Christians are deceived out of money. But they can be emotionally and mentally deceived which places them on a guilt trip.

There was a case where an atheist homosexual professed on national television that Christians use their religion to bash lesbians and gay men. Should a Christians respond to these kinds of allegations? Well, they did respond trying to convince this person that all Christians are not like that. The response from many Christians to this person's allegation indicates they, indeed, felt guilty for what some other Christians had said.

It was also reported that homosexual children were being harassed and bullied. Naturally, it should not be condoned to bully and harass anyone for any reason if this is true. Anytime children have reported they have been abused, this will, naturally, bring about the greatest sentiment. Yes, Christians should be sympathetic toward someone who is harassed. It was said early on that Christians should always conduct themselves in a way that anyone observing will see love and kindness manifested in their actions. Christians should not compromise the will of God given by the empowerment of the Holy Scripture regardless how someone tries to play on their sympathy.

An appropriate acronym: ACATHS – All Christians Adhere to Holy Scripture. Satan is the great deceiver. He builds up this stronghold that leads to the belief that there are meanings that are hidden concerning God's "Word". It is not uncommon that verses have been used that are not in context with the full meaning of a passage. God's Word is sometimes edited or manipulated to appropriate and fit personal benefit. These individuals are people of flesh. If it is only flesh we are dealing with, then we may be able to deal with this warfare. But we are dealing with Satan so we need a higher power to enable us to deal with this deception. The Apostle Paul was well aware of this as he wrote to the church at Corinth: II Corinthians 10:2-6 ESV I beg of you that when I am present I may not have to show boldness with such confidence as I count on showing against some who suspect us of walking according to the flesh. For though we walk in the flesh, we are not waging war according to the flesh. For the weapons of our warfare are not of the flesh but have divine power to destroy strongholds. We destroy arguments and every lofty opinion rose against the knowledge of God, and takes every thought captive to obey Christ, being ready to punish every disobedience, when your obedience is complete. There were individuals in Corinth that slandered the apostle Paul and tried to discredit his apostolic authority because he was not a part of the original twelve disciples that walked with Jesus before the Crucifixion. The worldly outlook on life is a stronghold that Christians need divine help in overcoming.

It is difficult to deceive a Christian who studies God's Word with prayer and is generously given wisdom by the Spirit (James 1: 5-7). Many of the prosperity ministers, not all, speak of how you can be prosperous by sowing seeds to their ministry. Media networks are paid to allow "sowing seed" telethons for these ministries. The prosperity some are speaking of is their own.

235

The gospel Gentile writer, Luke, wrote in the Book of Acts 8:9-24 of an individual whose name was Simon the Sorcerer or Simon the Magician, in Latin Simon Magus in Greek who was a Samaritan Zoroaster (Magician). Simon tried to purchase power given by the Holy Spirit for financial gain. Philip, a disciple of Christ, had gone to neophyte Christian believers in the city of Samaria and preached concerning the Kingdom of God, the name of Jesus and baptized many of the men and women there including Simon the magician. Simon followed Philip around the city and was amazed at all miracles and signs performed by the disciple. All along, he was wondering how he could incorporate the miracles he saw performed by Philip to his array of sorcery and bewitchery to increase his financial status.

The Apostles, Peter, and John, were sent to Samaria to inspect what they heard about the people there who had received the Word of God so that they could also pray for new believers so that they may receive the Holy Spirit. These neophytes had received water baptism but had not been bathed in the Holy Spirit. There are two types of baptisms, done first the baptism by water and then the baptism by the Holy Spirit (Acts 11:17). Simon received the water baptism but had not been baptized by the Holy Spirit.

The Apostle Paul's epistle to the Roman church asked a question to those baptized concerning whether they knew that all being baptized into Christ Jesus were baptized into his death (Romans 6:3-4 ESV Do you not know that all of us who have been baptized into Christ Jesus were baptized into his death? We were buried therefore with him by baptism into death, in order that, just as Christ was raised from the dead by the glory of the Father, we too might walk in newness of life).

Water baptism symbolizes the death and burial of carnality and rising of a new life in us by faith. John the Baptist preached repentance and then baptized those that repented. Repentance from a biblical perspective means turning away from evil or Satan and turning to good or God. The Holy Spirit baptism unites a believer with other believers in a permanent union in the body of Christ (I Corinthians 12:13).

The Holy Spirit was received by those who were touched by the hands of Peter and John. Simon the Sorcerer observed that the Spirit was given to those who were touched by the apostles, so he offered money to obtain the power to provide the Spirit by the laying of his hands. The Apostle Peter was upset with the magician for thinking he could buy this gift from God with money. The Apostle rebuked Simon by saying to him "the money that he had should vanish for thinking this gift of God was something that could be purchased." Peter told him to repent and pray to the Lord that this thought would leave his heart if there was to be any possibility of hope left for him. Peter said these things because he saw Simon as being imprisoned by sin. Simon believed what Peter said and asked him to pray for him so that what he said about him would not come true.

Using the Holy Spirit for self-aggrandizement along with pursuing wealth by use of the ministry of religion was a topic that the Apostle Paul warned about in his epistle to the young pastor, Timothy at Ephesus. The apostle warned that godliness should not be used as a means of financial gain. God said, by means of the apostle, that the love of money is the source of all kinds of evils. The Apostle also said the person that experiences contentment received from "True Godliness" receives a great gain as opposed to those with depraved minds that think financial wealth can be gained from spirituality (I Timothy 6:5-6).

This is not contrary to what was said earlier concerning bad mouthing men of God in the ministry that use the power of the Holy Spirit to do the will of God. These individuals that become vainglorious are tempted by Satan and are called "false teachers". It is not uncommon for Christians to continue to make donations, besides tithing, to these false teachers. Their belief is even though they know that person is doing wrong, his or her position is, supposedly, an anointment from God and final judgment is God's alone.

The church should not be thought of as a financial institution where you deposit money, set up an account, and interest is added to the deposit based on the interest rate and length of time the initial deposit remains in the account. The thought I have heard implied by proponents concerning "sowing seeds" is that if you invest (sow) money to the affiliated church your investment will increase (reap) based on the amount you invest. All the offers of financial gain, healing, becoming debt free, etc., provided by "sowing" to these individuals are freely given by the faithful empowered by the Holy Spirit.

The use of agricultural terminology in the bible was because there was a limited amount of different occupations and farming the land was the primary occupation of most of the people. The Israelites, in the vicinity of the Sea of Galilee's occupation were fishmongers. When Jesus started his ministry, he taught parables related to agriculture which was easy for listeners to identify with.

The Gospel of Luke 12:13-21 is about a person called "A Rich Fool" whose land produced an overabundance of crops. He surmised that the barns that he used for storage of crops were too small, so he decided to tear them down and build bigger barns. He thought that by doing this he would have crops for many years and that he could relax, eat, drink, and be merry for many years. God spoke to this rich fool and told him all these abundances that he is accumulating on earth will mean nothing to him after he is dead. His earthly riches will become useless when he enters into the kingdom of Satan or the kingdom of God.

God's message is to store up treasures in your heart pertinent to Heavenly living because one day we will have to present ourselves as suitable to His will and not our own. Acquire the wisdom provided by the Holy Spirit to discern heretical religious opinions that are contrary to Christian doctrines. Tithing and donations should be given to churches and organizations that are about God's work and His Word. The ministry, utilities, landscaping, mission trips, donations to the poor, etc. have to be funded. The essential part of making donations to church is that it is from the heart.

The amount of your donation or non-donation has no implication for a better or less standing with God. God cares about the less fortunate, so when you help them by your donations to the churches or charitable organizations, this pleases God. You should not hoard what God has provided for you like the "Rich Fool" was trying to do in Jesus's parable of the "Rich Fool' earlier discussed. If you are specifically expecting that your donation to the church will guarantee a return, you are in the wrong place physically and spiritually. You need to consult a financial institution.

Christians need to know whether the televangelists that propose the benefits of sowing and reaping are not being deceitful. As said earlier, the Holy Bible has many scriptures related to cultivation which are used in a positive and negative sense such as Galatians 6:7-8 ESV: Do not be deceived: God is not mocked, for whatever one sows, that will he also reap. For the one who sows to his own flesh will from the flesh reap corruption, but the one who sows to the Spirit will from the Spirit reap eternal life (Also See Proverbs 22:8).

The prophet Samuel was the last judge in ancient Israel, best I can tell from internet research is that the date was around the 11th century B.C. When Samuel became old, he appointed his two corrupt sons, Joel and Abijah as judges in Beersheba, which is 70 kilometers or forty-four miles southwest of Jerusalem (bird fly). The bible does not go into much detail describing what corruption the two sons were involved in, but his sons did not walk in Samuel's ways; they turned aside after dishonest gain, took bribes, and perverted justice. This complaint led to the Lord allowing Samuel to anoint the first king of ancient Israel, King Saul a Benjaminite (I Samuel 8:1-22).

The term "lucre" is used concerning the behavior of Samuel's sons. The English word, lucrative, is an adjective for the noun, lucre, which means "gain". (I Samuel 8:3 ESV Yet his sons did not walk in his ways but turned aside after gain. They took bribes and perverted justice).

The Bible says that someone seeking to become a deacon in the church should not be greedy of filthy lucre to mean covetousness in obtaining financial gain (I Timothy 3:8 KJV).

In order for Christians to be effective workers for the Lord, learn, then display the learning obtained from the "Word". Your walk in the spirit should be apprehended by all and in particular, a neophyte. If a person unfamiliar with Christian doctrine asks a believer why their religion of choice is Christianity, there should be an accurate expeditious response that can be confirmed by Biblical scripture. Unfortunately, some Christians seem to be ashamed or afraid in many cases. The first Christians, especially the disciples and apostles, who boldly professed publically that Jesus was raised from the dead for the salvation of all faithful believers, were severely punished or martyred for preaching this gospel. The Apostle Paul was neither afraid nor ashamed to preach this gospel to the Jews and the Gentiles (Roman 1:16-17).

There are some countries where a person could be martyred for professing to be a Christian believer in this present-day. In North Korea the leader of the country must be worshipped literally, any other worship makes one an enemy of the state. In Somalia, Islam is the religion of the state, any other religion is illegal. In Iraq and Syria, there have been public executions of Christians by The Islamic State of Iraq and Syria (ISIS). There are other countries in the world, in the twenty-first century, where Christians are rejected or killed such as Afghanistan, Sudan, Iran, Pakistan, Burma, Djibouti, Egypt, Ethiopia, India, Turkmenistan, Kenya, Qatar, Central African Republic, Vietnam, etc. All of the countries that oppose Christianity in some form of aggression or rebuttal are not listed here, but this is an indication that the freedom of religion is something that is to be greatly appreciated in the United States.

The United States is characterized by immigrants having a diverse nature along with a diversity of religions. Christianity is the religion of choice of the United States populace. The first amendment of the U.S. Constitution guarantees the freedom of religion to all or non-religion in the U.S.

God expects everyone that are believers, not only preachers, teachers, and ministers, to spread the gospel, the good news about Jesus Christ our Savior. Before Jesus ascended into Heaven, He requested of the Father to provide the Holy Spirit for all of our needs according to His will.

# CHAPTER 39

# We Shall All Stand Before the Judgement Seat of God

THE FOCUS FOR EVERY BELIEVER in Christ Jesus is not to please self but to please the Lord. We must give an account of what we have done while we're alive to the end of pleasing Him. "For we must all appear before the judgment seat of Christ, so that each one may receive what is due for what he has done in the body, whether good or evil" (II Corinthians 5:10 ESV).

All believers have a mission that is to implore others to be reconciled to God. Christ reconciled us to himself and gave us the ministry of reconciliation (II Corinthians 5:18-20). When mature believers minister to neophytes they should emphasize that salvation does not come from their own intellect but is provided by the free grace of God. The power of the Holy Spirit sometimes reveals new wisdom to mature Christians concerning scripture they have studied for years.

It is God that judges. The Apostle Paul's epistle to the church in Rome, Chapter 14, is his concern about the Christians passing judgment on each other. They were passing judgment concerning the dietary choices of some members there. The spiritually mature Christians knew that what a person eats has no bearing one way or the other concerning their spirituality or salvation. Some did not want to give up certain requirements of the laws such as prohibiting the eating of certain foods. Apostle Paul stated that whether one abstained from

241

eating certain things or not, both sides motivation is to the serve the Lord and to give thanks to whatever is provided (Romans 14:1-6).

If you know that a fellow Christian doesn't eat pork, you should stay in the *Spirit* and the *Spirit* within will never allow offensive food preparation to be served at such a gathering. Christians do not have to agree on matters concerning their life in Christ but they shouldn't try to force it on someone else. God's servants should not be criticized, even when they fall short. Leave judgment to God as it is written, not to judge one another, seek self-moral correction. It is better to bite your lip and filter your thoughts before speaking. Whatever you say leaves your mouth it is gone like an irretrievable e-mail when the "send button" is pressed.

The Word admonishes us that if one of us fall short God will lift us up. The Word makes it plain that we do not live or die for ourselves. Living or dying is for the Lord. One should not think more highly of himself or herself by placing themselves on a pedestal (vertical communication) in their own minds looking down, and not being at eye level (horizontal communication) with others. This person places himself or herself on the "Bench" (bench –location in a courtroom where a judge sits) in their own minds judging and critiquing others. Romans 14:10-12 AMP Why do you criticize and pass judgment on your brother? Or you, why do you look down upon or despise your brother? For we shall all stand before the judgment seat of God. For it is written, As I live, says the Lord, every knee shall bow to me, and every tongue shall confess to God [acknowledge Him to His honor and to His praise] and so each of us shall give an account of himself [give an answer in reference to judgment] to God.

This scripture tells us that we all will stand before God to be judged, then we will have to answer to Him. Discussing other's inadequacies in a negative way instead of offering up prayer is not using the provisions of wisdom provided by the Holy Spirit. This is long overdue for many, but not too late.

In the book of Matthews, Jesus gave a parable about the graciousness of God given to the outcasts and latecomers into the kingdom of God. Many interpretations by various scholars try to analyze this parable.

The parable is sort of like a bunch of day workers hanging around the vicinity of Home Depot looking to be hired. In this parable, the hirer is God and the workers are those that come into God's kingdom late and they, Christians who have been in the faith a long time are disgruntled because the latecomers are offered the same heavenly benefits as them.

This parable only occurs in the gospel of Matthew (Matthew 20:1-16) Jesus allegorically uses vineyard workers and the owner of the vineyard to describe the generosity of God to those who are late in becoming believers. The owner of the vineyard hires workers at various times of the day who are contracted to be paid a certain fixed wage rather than an hourly rate. The vineyard worker who was hired first earlier in the day finds out that the workers that were hired later at various times of the day are paid the same wage as he. He expresses his discontentment because he had worked more hours yet the other workers were paid the same salary as he. The vineyard owner informs him that he was paid justly because this is the wage that was agreed upon before he started work.

This allegory is about a gracious God who accepts those who come late into faith and is afforded the same generosity as those who has had a long experience in faith. Some have used this to demonstrate the fairness of being paid wages for work. There was no wrong done by the owner of the vineyard because he paid what was agreed upon. The master of the vineyard could have paid whatever he wanted which could have been accepted or refused. He actually paid the same salary that was being paid to the Roman soldiers at that period of time which was described as one denarius a day. So he was a fair man and was not paying anyone below the minimum wage for this work.

Right now is the time to repent and ask God into our hearts and lives. We don't want to be left outside the vineyard and lost to the kingdom. None of us are finished works. But as Christians, we can lean on one another and help each other.

# Each Should Give Unto the Lord According to their Abilities and Talents

WE SHOULDN'T TRY TO MEASURE our works based on the works and deeds of someone else. If your tithes are not as large as someone who has donated more, don't fret. God looks at what you give from the heart and not for show. Churches of today offer several choices to donate and some have moved away from the weaved baskets or metal pan receptacles passed around for collecting offerings. Some churches use envelopes to place donations in, which are dropped in a collection box strategically set up in various places in the church offering privacy for the donator. Some churches have set up online interface websites for donating and tithing to an account set up at a financial institution. Others have set up "Giving kiosk" in various places in the church where donors can swipe their credit or debit cards to make donations. The seller of these collection devices reports that donations received by churches have increased because of the convenience.

Jesus observed people in the Jerusalem temple making offerings. In the temple, there were thirteen offering containers shaped like the part of a trumpet called the bell. Some of these offering receptacles were in the part of the temple that was as far as women were allowed to enter. "Court of Women", as it was called, was a large square courtyard with four tall lampstands in each corner. This is the place where the eighty-four year old prophetess, Anna, worshipped and prayed daily. (Luke 2:36-38). Luke 2:22 is about Jesus being brought to the temple at Jerusalem by His parents, Joseph and Mary for His dedication which had to be at least forty days after His birth.

Mary, in obedience to the Mosaic Law given to the Israelites in Leviticus 12, a woman who gives birth to a son is ceremonially unclean for seven days after the birth, which is the same way she is considered unclean during her monthly menstrual cycle. She has to wait an additional thirty- three days to be purified from her bleeding after giving birth. She is not allowed to touch anything sacred or go to the sanctuary until her days of purification have ended. The length of time for the purification process after the birth of a daughter is doubled (Leviticus 12:5). Mary has completed the requirements of the purification law so she brings a year-old lamb for a burnt offering and a young pigeon or a dove for a sin offering to the priest at the entrance to the tent of meeting (Leviticus 12:6-7).

Anna, the prophetess, mentioned earlier was a widow who never left the temple and prayed and fasted there night and day. The day that Mary had completed the purification process, she and Joseph brought the baby, Jesus, to the sanctuary for His dedication. The Gospel of Luke 2:25–35, relates that also at the temple with Anna was a devout man named Simeon who met Mary, Joseph, and Jesus as they entered the Temple to fulfill the requirements of the Law.

Jesus had been circumcised at eight days old in accordance with the Law (God's Covenant with Abraham – Genesis 17:9-14). Anna was there for the dedication and was grateful to have seen the baby knowing that He was the Messiah spoken of in prophecy. She treasured this for the remainder of her life (Luke 2:36-38).

Even the adult Jesus had not been inside the temple itself because the same Jewish laws concerning entering the temple from the Old Testament tabernacle were still in place. Only selected priests (in the OT tabernacle, it was Moses's brother Aaron and his sons) were allowed into the Temple sanctuary. The High Priest of the Jerusalem Temple (18-37 A.D.), who would have been Caiaphas at the time of

Jesus' adult life, was allowed to go into the Holy of Holies in the back of the temple once a year on the Day of Atonement.

The only mention of a priest going into the temple in the New Testament was when Zachariah, a priest, however, he was not the high priest, experienced a once in a life time opportunity, by the drawing of lots, to burn incense at the golden altar in the temple (Luke 1:9). A priest was allowed to perform this service only once in his lifetime, so to be chosen by lot, as was Zachariah or any priest being chosen, it was a very high honor. Zachariah and his wife, Elizabeth, were the parents of John the Baptist (Luke 1:57-66).

There were twenty-four priests that rotated service in the temple at Jerusalem on a weekly basis, they were chosen by lots. This was carried over from the OT procedure implemented by Aaron, the first High Priest and forefather of Israelite priesthood. This tradition of rotation of priestly service carried over into the New Testament era which is why Zachariah was performing this ancient Israelite priestly duty.

In the book of Luke, the now grown man, Jesus, first observes the rich making their offerings in the temple treasury. Then the scripture says He observed a poor widow woman drop two copper coins into the collection box. Either He could tell by the sound the coins made when they dropped into the offering container or He knew the amount supernaturally (Luke 21:1-4).

(In reference to the coins, some other Biblical translations or versions call the two coins mites. The Greek version of the Bible in Mark 12:42 say that she dropped in "two lepta, which is a kodrantes." Other biblical versions listed says: KJV: two mites, which make a farthing, RSV: two copper coins, which make a penny, NASB: two small copper coins, which amount to a cent NIV: two very small copper coins, worth only a fraction of a penny, ESV: two small copper coins, which make a penny HCSB: two tiny coins worth very little, and NLT: two small coins).

Translations vary but most Biblical scholars probably except the fact that the coins were worth a fraction of a penny something like 1/64 of a penny. Jesus is impressed more with the quantitative comparison of what she gave, because, even though it was a small amount, it was one hundred percent of all the money that she had.

The various Biblical versions may differ on the wording concerning the coins but just as the penny is the smallest denomination in circulation in the United States, the coins that she deposited were the smallest in circulation in the Holy Land at that time. Even though the rich threw large sums of money in the offering boxes, it was not all that they had in comparison to the poor widow woman. We don't have to give all we have but the minimal tithing should be one-tenth of our wages at least.

This precedence of charitable giving of ten percent was started by Abraham described in Genesis 14:17-20. After Abraham and his army had defeated and slew a king named Chedorlaomer and three other armies of kings that were allied with him, Melchizedek king of Salem and priest of God Most High, brought bread and wine to Abraham and his army and blessed them. Abraham gave Melchizedek a tenth of all the spoils taken during the battle.

It was not uncommon for priests and kings to have combined dual duties of a territory during the life of Melchizedek. Even though there is not much about Melchizedek in the bible, there are indications from the book of Psalms 110:4 that portray the high priest as a prototype of Jesus. Scholars have stated in biblical commentary concerning the book of Hebrews 7:1-11, that the meeting of Melchizedek and Abraham, Melchizedek was an embodiment of Jesus. Verse 11, this verse can be interpreted that Jesus did not come from a line of high priests that were imperfect, such as the first Israelite high priest, Aaron, but rather, from the line of a perfect high priest, Melchizedek.

According to I Samuel 8:15, one-tenth is the amount of the people's worth given to the king of the land. Abraham recognized the blessing that he received from Melchizedek as an invocation of blessing from the Lord. Likewise, Abraham wanted this king and all other kings to know, that his tithe was for the Lord and that he would not be indebted to any king for this tithing.

We can't all give the same monetarily. We might not be talented enough to sing in the choir or to preach to a congregation, God gave each of us different talents and abilities. But we must give according to our talents and not try to measure ourselves by someone else.

# CHAPTER 41

## *Focus on Following Jesus*

OVER AND OVER IN THE Bible, it can be seen where God uses situations that initially seems dire, in the end, it turns out that no situation is too big for Him to turn around for the good. Remember earlier Joseph's brothers sold him as a slave to the Egyptians. With the power that he obtained as second in command to the pharaoh of the entire Egyptian empire, he could have sent soldiers to kill his brothers for what they did to him (selling him to slave traders). Instead, he rationalized that God had a plan for him to be where he was so that he could rescue his family from the famine that happened in all the lands which included Canaan where his father, Jacob and eleven sons lived. Benjamin, the youngest of the brothers, was the full brother of Joseph and the other ten brothers were half-brothers. (See Genesis 41and 42)

A hateful mindset, attitude, or disposition can be changed by God at His will. Goes does not want us to worry about the affairs of someone else, but to stay focused on Him. This is illustrated in the scripture after Jesus was resurrected and appeared to seven of His disciples who were fishing on a boat in Lake Tiberias (also known as The Sea of Galilee, Kinneret, or Lake of Gennesaret). The seven disciples were Simon Peter, Thomas (called the Twin), Nathanael of Cana in Galilee, the sons of Zebedee, and two others of his disciples who names were not given (John 21:2, Matthew 4:21 names the sons of Zebedee – John and James.

This episode happened after the Resurrection during the time

Jesus spent forty days on earth before the Ascension (John 21). The seven had fished all night without catching a single fish. That morning at daybreak, from the shore, Jesus asked them had they caught any fish. He then told them to cast their nets on the right side of the boat which they did and miraculously caught one hundred and fifty-three large fish. The net was so heavy that they could not haul the fish unto the boat but had to drag the heavy net one hundred yards to the shore. At this particular time, Simon Peter did not recognize that it was Jesus on the shore that told them to cast the net on the right side of the boat. John, the disciple that Jesus loved, identified and told Simon Peter that the man on the shore was the Lord Jesus (The Gospel of John refers to an unnamed disciple whom Jesus loved that was accepted in the latter part of the first century AD as John the evangelist).

After they were gathered on the shore, they had breakfast. It was at this seashore breakfast that Jesus reversed the denials made by Peter prior to His Crucifixion with three affirmations of His love for him. This is called by scholars, The Restoration of Peter and also, The Re-commissioning of Peter. Jesus lifted Peter's guilt for the denials and restored him to the fellowship. The Apostle Peter made many blunders; he was impulsive, not well educated, and spoke before understanding the situation. Yet later, after the ascension of Jesus, the Holy Spirit's metamorphosis of the Apostle Peter led him to become the leader of Christian believers.

The Apostle's preaching to a group of one hundred and twenty of the brethren in an upper room on the day of the Jewish Feast of Weeks named the Pentecost (The 50th day after the Sabbath of Passover Week- see Leviticus 23-15-16) was a supernatural event where the Holy Spirit, sent from heaven, filled the room where they were sitting with a noise described as being like a violent rushing wind, filling the whole house where they were gathered.

One of Jesus's prophecies at the renowned "Last Supper" concerns the denial of Peter three times when he was questioned about whether he knew Jesus. This event is the reason Peter had to be restored to the fellowship at the seashore. Jesus had been arrested by the Temple guards of the Sanhedrin at the Garden of Gethsemane for heresy and blasphemy leading up to six trials and eventually crucifixion. These events were recorded in all four of the Canonical Biblical Gospels (Matthew 26:69–74, Mark 14:66–72, Luke 22:54–62, and John 18:15–18, 25–27). The events concerning the Last Supper, the Crucifixion, and the Resurrection of Jesus is referred to as "The Passion."

Jesus prophesied that a rooster, somewhere in the earshot of the courtyard of the Jewish temple at Jerusalem would not crow until Peter had denied Him three times. Peter made these denials after a servant girl of the high priest (Joseph Caiaphas), who was in the courtyard of the temple, saw Peter standing by a fire to keep warm and inconspicuously attempting to get first-hand information about the trial proceedings concerning Jesus. She identified and questioned him about being acquainted with Jesus which was heard by bystanders there.

There was something said by Peter in his denials which was a telltale sign to the bystanders that Peter spoke with a Galilean dialect and was a disciple of Jesus, the Nazarene. Peter swore and cursed that he did not know Jesus. At that moment a rooster was heard crowing a second time which reminded Peter of the prophecy Jesus had spoken about him at the "Last Supper". Jesus had said that before the rooster crows twice, you will deny me three times. Peter knew that his three denials of knowing the Messiah had fulfilled the prophecy, and he wept.

Jesus made three validations of Peter's continuance in discipleship with forgiveness for the transgressional denials after they had finished the seashore breakfast. The three questions asked by Jesus to Peter affirmed Peter's love for Jesus (John 21:15-17).

Peter and Jesus were walking along and Peter turned and saw John, the disciple whom Jesus loved, following them. Peter expressed concern to Jesus about what were the plans were for this disciple. The question Peter asked of Jesus about his fellow disciple, John, could be interpreted that he was concerned about John's future or it was just his impetuous nature to ask such a question. Some scholarly comments suggest that Peter might have been jealous of the disciple that Jesus loved. Regardless of the reason he asked, he was mildly rebuked for his impetuousness. He was showing too much concern for someone else's affairs commonly called being nosy or informal language "off into someone else's business." (John 21:20-23) Jesus said to Peter twice, "Follow Me" (v.19 and v.22) which has a fuller meaning than to just walk along with him but to follow Him in suffering and death. (Matthew 10:38 and 16:24).

God desires that we keep our mind stayed on Him, trust in Him so that we can become more efficient at doing His will (Isaiah 26:3).

Ballast is a term used in the simplest form of human air flight which is ballooning by hot air or gas balloons. Ballast is a means of controlling stability and control, for example, the draft of a ship or the buoyancy of a balloon or submarine. The gas balloons use sandbags that are placed somewhere on or in the basket or gondola. The gondola is attached by cords to the balloon technically called the envelope. When the pilot wants to ascend higher, sandbag(s) are dropped off of the balloon. Sin is the sandbag(s) for believers that need to be removed to achieve the height of spiritual maturity and enhanced revelation of God's word. If one wants to move higher and become closer to God, the sandbags of sin must be dropped off. Believers can use spiritual ballast when instability and heavy burdens are encountered in their lives caused by the perpetrator, Satan. God provides the stability, calmness and lifts heavy burdens.

Jesus calmed down a storm on the Sea of Galilee by the word of His mouth as He and His disciples left Capernaum and headed to the country of Gadarenes. The region is also called the country of Gerasenes, or Girgesenes (Matthew 8:23-27, Mark 4:35-41). Jesus rebuked the wind and raging waves by saying, "Peace! Be still." What spiritual ballast. God has control of all His creations.

If you are a strong and mature Christian reach out and help to strengthen someone else who hasn't quite made it there. This a moral burden that we must carry for someone who is weak or who has been weakened to fulfill the Law of Christ. Never think we are too good to reach down and lift a brother or sister up (Galatians 6:1-10) There is no time in this life for anger, bitterness, hatred, prejudice, or any other unworthy thing displeasing to God.

It is not always necessary to divulge sensitive information directly to someone or about someone else. If the situation can be corrected privately without disclosing your thoughts or feelings, then that is what should be done in certain situations.

In Genesis chapter nine, there are several things revealed with the main emphasis on the Noahic Covenant that applies to all of humanity and living creatures on earth after the world was flooded by God because of the nimiety of sin by man. God's promises never again to destroy all life on Earth by flood and created the rainbow as the sign of this "everlasting covenant between God and every living creature of all flesh that is on the earth".

After the great flood, God blessed Noah and his sons and told them to be fruitful, multiply and fill the earth. This is more than just a story about a father and his three sons leaving the ark. We know that when Noah and his sons left the ark, these would be the people who would become representative of many nations on earth, which had become depopulated by the great flood. Ham, the youngest son of Noah, ancestor to Canaanite and Egyptian tribes, Shem the Semites or Hebrew tribes of Israel, and Japheth represented the northern Hellenistic tribes or Greek tribes.

Nakedness occurs early in the Bible in Genesis when Adam and Eve sinned they realized they were naked and tried to cover themselves. Thus nakedness was a thing of shame for the fallen man. Nakedness in the Old Testament scripture, due to the falling of Adam and Eve, represents the loss of human dignity.

After the worldwide flood during the life of Noah had subsided, nakedness again plays a part in the lack of dignity. Noah began to farm the land just as his father, Lamech, had done after the flood. He planted a vineyard and made wine from the grapes. He got drunk and laid in his tent naked. His son, Ham, came into the tent and saw his father naked. Instead of covering his father he went out and made it known to his brothers Shem and Japheth of their father's nakedness. Shem and Japheth went into the tent walking backward to avoid seeing the nakedness and covered their father.

Researching this passage only reveals that what Ham did was

perplexing to understand his sin and also Noah's drunkenness as well. There is controversy concerning why the transgression of Ham caused Noah to place a curse on his son Canaan. However, the context that we are speaking of here is about the mocking and ridiculing by Ham to his brothers by their father's nakedness. Both Noah and Ham's sins were wrong, but Ham did not just snicker about his father's nakedness, he tried to get his brothers to join in on his mockery.

(Nowhere in Genesis 9 does it say that Ham was black. However, Genesis 9:25-26 was once used during the historical era of slavery in America; Southern American Christians readers were encouraged by the commentary of this scripture as justification to biblically sanction slavery of black people. Noah cursed Ham's son, Canaan, and prophesied that he would be a servant to Japheth and Shem. Canaan It was also used to validate slavery inclusive to all color of people groups).

One lesson from Ham is that he did not show respect and reverence for his father. Japheth and Shem did not dishonor their father (Genesis 9:24). This scripture said that when he awoke he found out what Ham had done and inexplicably, placed a curse on Ham's son and his grandson, Canaan. Noah was aware of Ham's disrespect when he became awoke, but the bible does not say whether Japheth and Shem related Ham's mockery to their father.

The interpretations and comments about this particular scripture of the Holy Bible have received many varying clarifications by biblical scholars. Some comments seem inappropriate and will not be discussed here. The lesson mentioned here is one of many. The first thought should be to try and support, honor, respect, and strengthen family members and fellow brethren. Galatians 6:10 ESV So then, as we have opportunity, let us do good to everyone, and especially to those who are of the household of faith.

# The Righteous Shall be Separated from the Wicked

MEN AND WOMEN OF GOD are who Satan goes after to devour, which is the reason we should be in constant prayer for one another. There is no reason for Satan to utilize time pursuing those who are already spiritually ruined. We know that Jesus revealed to His disciples at the Last Supper that Satan would be coming after them to "sift them out". Jesus was speaking directly to Peter when He said that Satan would "sift him out", this was meant to inform all of the disciples that Satan would try to bring them to spiritual ruination.

Jesus often used the art of cultivation in His parables. In the Gospel of Luke 22: 31-34 as He admonishes Peter (Simon) that Satan had demanded from God to allow him to be sifted as wheat is sifted. This was a most inspiring revelation that the Apostle Peter received when Jesus informed him that He had prayerfully interceded for him. By the power of the Holy Spirit, we can obtain this same intercession against Satan who is perpetually trying to sift believers.

Two of Jesus' twelve disciples failed him prior to the crucifixion, Judas Iscariot's (betrayal) and Simon Peter's (denial). It is a great blessing that Jesus Christ, the Messiah, would single out Peter and pray for Him. Even though Peter would fail miserably by his denial, he did not lose his salvation.

Christians may falter and experience the pitfalls of this world but must continue in the faith of God's covenants and promises. The only way we can curtail failing is to lean on the Triune God for the direction of our paths. Jesus had prayed for Peter's path although He knew Peter would falter. Peter had been converted from the time that Jesus passed by his family's fishing business and told him to follow me and be fishermen of men, and he did. V.31, Jesus called Peter's first name twice (*Simon, Simon*) to ensure He had his attention.

It should be noted that Jesus said that He had prayed for Peter, who He called Simon in this instance. This eventually saved Peter's faith. Jesus prayed for all believers not just His disciples because He knew that His Gospel would spread from that day on and into the future (Jesus' long prayer for believers was that they may receive eternal life by His sacrifice of death. John 17:1-26).

There is not one reason for our faith to fail unless we turn away from the Word; we need to turn away from the world. Jesus' prayer in the Gospel of John 17 v.15, "I do not ask that you take them out of the world (believers), but that you keep them from the evil one." We must have faith, belief, reverence, and be spiritually minded to receive God's revelations. If we stay busy doing the worldly things, arguing and fighting with each other, we're not being spiritually minded. Be slow to speak, weigh carefully what we say. Pray to the Holy Spirit for guidance to avoid that which does not please the Lord and causes us to sin.

If someone thinks of themselves as being God- fearing but does not control what comes out of their mouth, they have deceived themselves and are not earnestly God-fearing (See James 1:26). The author of the Book of James in the NT was James, the brother of Jesus, addressed the Jewish Christians about how they should conduct themselves. This is applicable and edifying for us today. The book of James devotes the first chapter admonishing us on the Believer's walk and differentiating between those who are doing it according to the Word and those who are not (James 1: 19-21).

Satan, In this case, would be trying to perform the same process on the disciples as he had done to Job by God's permission. The process of sifting the chaff from the wheat indicated that Satan would be at work to prove that the disciples were "worthless" and their righteousness was only about their own worldly personal gain.

In the book of Ruth 1:22, it states that Naomi and her Moabite daughter-in-law returned from the country of Moab to Jerusalem at the beginning of the barley harvest season. This process is often used metaphorically in the Bible as an illustration of God separating the sinful from the righteous and the byproduct, chaff, which is worthless for human consumption, which would be burned in an unquenchable fire. The grain (righteous) would be separated from the chaff (wicked) by a process called winnowing. It is basically done by throwing the grain in the air with a pitchfork and letting the wind separate grain from the chaff. In the case of a grain such as wheat, the crop turns from green to brown when ready to harvest and the stalk bends over from a vertical position to an angle to release its seeds. The ripe seed of the wheat is surrounded by thin, dry, leaf-like scaly bracts (called glumes, Lemmas, and paleas), forming a dry husk (or hull) around the grain. Once it is removed it is often referred to as chaff. This chaff could be used to feed livestock.

The harvesting that took place in the book of Ruth took was in Bethlehem of Judea in the months of April and May. The bible says that Ruth gleaned in the fields of Boaz. Boaz was a relative of Ruth's deceased husband Elimelech. Boaz was wealthy and owned land in Bethlehem in Judea. This land is where Ruth was encouraged by her mother-in-law, Naomi to glean in the fields of Boaz. Boaz appears in the genealogies of Jesus in the New Testament in Matthew 1:5 and Luke 3:32. The gospel of Matthew traces the genealogy of Jesus starting with Abraham whereas the gospel of Luke traces the genealogy reversely from the time that Jesus started His ministry. Matthew1:5 states that Salmon and Rahab were the parents of Boaz and Boaz and Ruth were the parents of Obed who was the father of Jesse who was King David's father.

Gleaning, in the book of Ruth, is the process of gathering stalks of barley or wheat left behind by the men who had cut the grain and had not collected all of it from the ground. Gleaning seems to be something done by women in this event. The process of sifting was done after the grain had been winnowed and threshed. Sifting done by the winnower was the process of removing any residual matter. The barley grain spoken of in the bible was used by poor people to make bread and feed for horses and asses. Jesus fed five thousand with five loaves of barley bread and two fish (John 6:9). The prophet Elisha also had the experience of the provision made by God when he fed a hundred men with only twenty loaves of barley bread and fresh ears of corn II Kings 4:42-44)

In Matthew 3, John the Baptist uses the process of winnowing metaphorically concerning separation of the evil from the good. He was purposely directing his preaching at the Pharisees and Sadducees (Matthews 3:12). John the Baptist spoke of the eschatological judgment occurring at the second coming of Jesus when the righteous will be separated from the wicked and the wicked will suffer an unquenchable fire prepared for Satan and his followers. The Bible figuratively uses "chaff", the unusable, or poor quality of grain as being wicked and separated (sifted) from the righteous (good element). All of us are either righteous (wheat) or unrighteous (Chaff) (See Psalms 1:3-4, Amos 9:9-10).

# The Desires of the Flesh are Antithetical to the Walk in the "Spirit"

WALK AS WE ARE INSTRUCTED by God to walk. Walk in the Spirit and be led by the spirit. If we walk by the Spirit we will be able to not accommodate trying to satisfy fleshly desires. Fleshly desires and the desires of the Spirit are opposed (antithetical) to each other.

The Apostle Paul is reasserted as an apostle in Galatia. The Judaizers in Galatia accused Paul of not being a true apostle because he was not teaching certain requirements of the Judaic law to Gentiles there to make his teaching more appealing. He taught justification was by faith and not by works of the law. The theme of his epistle is that if you walk by the spirit then you are not under the law.

The empowerment received from the Holy Spirit allows for the controlling of desires of the flesh and allows for walking in the Spirit to inherit the kingdom of God (Galatians 5:16-21). Satan will continue trying to implant sinful desires in us. By the prompting and power of the Holy Spirit, we are able to conquer these desires. Galatians 5:25 ESV If we live by the Spirit, let us also walk by the Spirit. It is always amazing how intelligent we can be by studying, but we let our actions, words, thoughts, and those around us (environment) cause us to act differently from the inner knowledge that we possess. We may study the "Word" and memorize verses, but to always walk and talk in the Spirit of the "Word" is a daunting task (James 1:22-24).

There are times when we are not in control of the negative conversation that we find ourselves confronted by even in the church. What we are in control of is how we want to be influenced or not be influenced by negative thoughts out of the mouth of these individuals. We can politely say stop or remove ourselves from the situation. There have been individuals throughout the history of the church similar to today, concerning disruptive, uncooperative people who try to upset the church.

This same disruptive behavior occurred in the churches established by the Apostle Paul which is addressed in the letter that he wrote to his young pastor, Titus. These individuals were just like the "holier than thou" people we see in modern day churches. Paul refers to them as the circumcised group. These were the people hanging on to the old Mosaic laws of circumcision so as to uphold the Jewish laws (Titus 1:10-11). There are people who talk and dwell on worthless things and refuse to cooperate. They've led others to be like them, gossipers, haters, backbiters, and etc. It is a church phenomenon how these kinds of people can change churches and are immediately connected with people of the same disruptive interests at that other church. They will not lean on the understanding provided by God but prefer to lean on their own understanding and befriend each other in chaos.

The epistle to Titus written by the apostle Paul expressed his concerns about the reaction of the believers at the church at Corinth because of the severe letter he had sent there. It was the third letter to Corinth that was severe. This letter is not in the Canonical Bible. Scholars' comments indicate there were four letters written to the church at Corinth by the apostle but only two are in the bible, I and II Corinthians. In II Corinthians 2:4 ESV Paul writes: For I wrote to you out of much affliction and anguish of heart and with many tears, not to cause you pain but to let you know the abundant love that I have for you.

Apostle Paul spent approximately a year and a half organizing the Church in Corinth. After he left the church false teachers took over the church and questioned Paul's apostleship. Biblical scholars suggest that Titus might have brought the severe letter to the church. Paul had gone to Corinth and had a painful experience there with the false teachers.

Paul sent the epistle known as Titus to the island of Crete where Titus was organizing the Christians there. This epistle was written to give Titus guidelines for the opposition that he might face, instructions for faith and conduct, qualifications for elders, and deceptive teachers especially of the circumcised group. This letter spoke of certain Cretans who profess to be believers who are full of sin who hear the Word and reject the truth. Nothing is pure in them. Their minds and consciences have been corrupted and ruined. They pretend they know God but their actions belie the fact that they truly accept Him. To those who are pure all things are pure. They look at bad situations and look for the good that can come out of bad situations.

A pure in heart person does not allow corrupted things to steal their mind. They look to God for peace that surpasses all understanding of man which keeps their hearts and minds focused on Christ. As a result of God's peace answered unto them, they think about things that are good and worthy of praise. The fruits of these thoughts are honorable righteousness, pure and beautiful thoughts, and respectful things. In order to be able to accomplish these kinds of thoughts, one must focus on growth into Christian maturity which allows for inner peace the world cannot give, only God. This is the peace that Jesus left for us.

Jesus didn't leave and abandon us when He ascended and went to sit at the right hand of the Father. However, on the day that Jesus ascended into Heaven, He instructed the disciples to remain in the city limits of Jerusalem despite the danger there. He informed His disciples to wait for the gift His Father would send to them, the "Comforter" (The Paraclete) before leaving for other districts to profess and bear witness about this great news.

The gift of the Holy Spirit provided empowerment for them to go boldly out and bear witness as far as they could technically travel. Those who had received water baptism were baptized with the Holy Spirit (Acts 1:4-9). Jesus brought this message to the disciples because He knew they were weak and afraid to bear witness publicly concerning His life, Death, burial, and resurrection.

Jesus brought this message to the disciples because of the possibility of being martyred was greater in Jerusalem at that particular time because of the religious rulers. The Pharisees and Sadducees were headquartered there and also the Romans governed there. These religious leaders were afforded privileges from the Roman government and were concerned about their reaction, concerning any upheaval among Jewish subjects that might cause them to rescind these privileges. The religious leaders in Jerusalem had a passionate dislike for Jesus because He spoke against their religious system and their hypocrisy before He was crucified.

There are two occasions in the Holy Bible which indicate that the religious leaders of the temple in Jerusalem allowed the use of the "Court of the Gentiles" as a retail outlet. Jesus saw this and ran them out of the court. Allowing the retailers, to sell in the Temple court suggests that high priests were receiving payment for the use of the court and became angry, wanting to kill Jesus for interfering with this arrangement. There was a court for Gentiles in the Jerusalem Temple which was the outermost court. Gentiles could go no further than this court into the temple areas. This is the court that Jesus entered and saw the retailers there selling oxen, sheep and pigeons, and the money-changers that were sitting there. Jesus overturned the tables of the money changers and threw them out.

Jesus quoted from the Old Testament book of Jeremiah 7:11 ESV as He threw them out, "Has this house, which is called by my name, become a den of robbers in your eyes? Behold, I myself have seen it, declares the Lord. The time frame differs in the Gospel of John from the synoptic Gospels which causes speculation by biblical scholars if there were one or two events. The Gospel of John has it occurring at the beginning of Jesus' ministry and the three synoptic Gospels have this event occurring near the end of Jesus ministry (Matthew 21:12-17, Mark 11:15-18, Luke 19:45-48).

The Sanhedrin thought that by murdering Jesus, they would be relieved of His interference. The Sadducees did not believe that someone could be resurrected from the dead. When Jesus was killed, nailed to the wooden Roman cross, He was taken down and moved to a tomb donated by a man named Joseph of Arimathea. Joseph had the tomb constructed for his own burial with the entrance covered by a huge stone. Joseph of Arimathea(Arimathea was probably a city of Judea near Jerusalem since Joseph's tomb was just outside of Jerusalem) was described as a righteous man who sought after the Kingdom of God even though he was a member of the Jewish Sanhedrin council; he was not in agreement with the council for crucifying Jesus. He took it upon himself to provide his own tomb for the burial of Jesus (Matthew 27:57-60, Mark 15:43-46, Luke 23:50-53, and John 19:38-42).

The Gospel of John also relates that Joseph of Arimathea was joined by Nicodemus in the burial of Jesus. The Roman seal was placed on the stone rolled over to cover the entrance to the tomb. The seal was placed on the stone authenticating that Jesus was in the tomb. Roman soldiers were ordered to guard the tomb, because religious leaders, the Sanhedrin, scribes, and elders, thought that someone would remove His body and falsely claim that He had been resurrected. The Pharisees and the chief priests came before Pilate and told him that the Messianic impostor, Jesus, had said before His death, He would arise from the dead in three days after His burial. This is the reason they took these precautions (Matthew 27:62-66).

Anyone caught tampering with the Roman seal placed on the huge Stone covering the tomb would receive punishment. The seal on stone signified that the tomb was under power and authority of the Roman Empire. ` Moving the stone would break the Roman seal. Anyone caught breaking the seal would receive severe punishment and possibly put to death.

Regardless of the precautions taken, the huge stone had been rolled away from the entrance of the tomb on the third day and Jesus' body was gone. The Romans guards were there when the earth quaked and an angel of the Lord rolled back the stone and sat on it. The Roman guards were so terrified of the appearance of the angel they became like dead men.

The word spread concerning the Resurrection of the Lord Jesus.

This caused the religious leaders to become especially perturbed and attempted to subdue and punish anyone spreading this news. The Roman guards were paid money by the chief priests and elders to say that they fell asleep and the disciples came and stole Jesus's body (Matthew 28:11-15).

The responsibility and commitment of all Christians are to continuously spread the news that Jesus died and was resurrected by the Father for the expiation of our sins. The Disciples were not able to travel the world as we know it today and we may not be able to travel the world to spread the word concerning the Resurrection.

According to polls at the time of this writing, there is approximately 29.4% of the populace in the United States who are not Christians according to polls such as the "Pew", so there is some Jesus witnessing that can be done here. Jesus fulfilled prophecies introduced in the OT and revealed to all in the NT Gospels by letting us know that we can now have fellowship with God because of the redemptive acts of the blood-shedding Crucifixion and the Resurrection.

Jesus left peace for us and not the kind of peace offered by the world (John 14:27-31). Satan had no claim on Jesus while he was here on earth or ever because, unlike us, He was sinless. Jesus admonishes us to help those who have fallen away and never knew that He loves them also. If they have a preconceived notion that they need money or something else, to come and let them know otherwise, that there is nothing to pay because the debt has been paid in full.

# CHAPTER 44

# Whosoever Believes In Their Heart Will Be Filled With Living Water

JESUS REMINDED US OF THE spiritual water without cost from the prophet, Isaiah (Isaiah 55:1-3). In the Gospel of John, on the last day of the Feast of the Tabernacles (Feast of the Tabernacles or Feast of Booths and Sukkot is the last of seven feasts and one of the three feasts to be observed each year that the Lord commanded the Israelites to observe in Deuteronomy 16:16).

Jesus stood up and said, "If anyone thirsts, let him come to me and drink. Whoever believes in Me, as the Scripture has said, 'Out of his heart will flow rivers of living water." (John 7:37-38). It is generally accepted that living water means the Holy Spirit in the Bible. In the OT the prophet, Jeremiah, uses living water as being Yahweh (See Jeremiah 2:13) Some scholars contend that Jesus is the living water, but it is believed here that he was referring to the Holy Spirit that dwells in us as illustrated by the Word of God in the epistle to the Ephesians written by the Apostle Paul. The Apostle denotes blessings received through the Father, the Son, and the Holy Spirit or the Trinity blessings (Ephesians 1:3-14).

"Living Water Discourse" - Jesus confounded a Samaritan woman at Jacob's well, located approximately one half-mile away from a town named Sychar in Samaria, when he told her of the "Living Water" that would cause her to thirst no more. She had come to the well at an odd time of day most likely to avoid the other women of the town. Biblical commentators describe her as an immoral, unmarried woman living with the sixth in a series of men. The women of the town gathered at a certain time of day to draw water from Jacob's well making it a social event. This woman was not socially accepted by the other women of Sychar so she came at a certain time of day to avoid them and to prevent being shunned.

The Jews would avoid going through Samaria when traveling because they looked down on the Samaritan people. The Samaritans were a mixed race of Israelites caused by the intermarriage with Assyrians. The Samaritans were said to have descended from people deported by the Assyrians, from other parts of the empire, during the 8th B.C.E and resettled in Samaria. They were hated by the Jews because of this cultural mixing, and because they had their own version of the religion, Judaism mixed with idolatry, and they had their own Holy temple on Mount Gerizim instead of in Jerusalem.

Jesus did not avoid the Samarian town because of the universal message that He had for the world. Water was a commodity to be appreciated in the desert regions of Israel. Based on the conservation she engaged in with Jesus, she initially misinterpreted the message that Jesus presented to her. Jesus told her that whoever drank the water she was about to draw from the well would eventually become thirsty again and have to draw more water. Then He said that whoever drinks the water that He provided would not thirst again. The Samaritan woman most likely thought that she wouldn't have to go to the well again to draw water, based on how she interpreted what Jesus had said. She might have displayed some sarcasm toward this statement until Jesus revealed to her that He was the Messiah. He told her things that a stranger passing through this town would not have known. She might have thought that even the folks of Sychar had no knowledge of all the things that Jesus revealed about her lifestyle.

Jesus set up His ministry headquarters in Capernaum in Galilee because His own people in Judea did not recognize Him as the

Messiah and rejected Him. He traveled to Bethany at night from His headquarters. The shortest route from Galilee to Judea was through Samaria in which the religious Jews chose to detour by going eastward to Perea in Transjordan then headed southward to Jerusalem. Their great dislike, distrust, and animosity of the Samaritans, especially by the Pharisees, caused them to take this circuitous route. The distance of this route was obviously greater than the seventy-five miles from Nazareth to Jerusalem by going through Samaria. The land on the eastern side of the Jordan River that they used to bypass Samaria not only was an extra distance to travel but also was barren.

Jesus had a mission to accomplish which is why He chose the shorter route through Samaria. The Pharisees would have never chosen this route and if they did, they certainly would have stayed a distance away from the Samaritans. Only Jesus could have revealed Himself as being the "living water" or the Messiah to these people. On this journey, He encountered the Samaritan woman around the sixth hour at Jacob's well. The sixth hour is around 12 noon our time according to most Bible scholars. (The following biblical times are generally accepted: The third hour would correspond to our 9 a.m., the sixth hour 12 noon, the seventh hour 1 p.m., the ninth hour 3 p.m., the tenth hour 4 p.m., and the eleventh hour 5 p.m.)

Jesus displayed the human trait of being tired and weary, so He stopped at Jacob's well to rest and get a drink of water. Even though His disciples traveled with Him, He sent them into town to buy food. The Apostle John recorded this event in John 4:1-42.

The historical origin of Samaria from biblical writings informs us that the kingdom of Israel became divided into northern and southern territories after the death of King Solomon. It is difficult to discern whether the Samaritans were named after the region of Samaria or the region was named after the Samaritan people. It also tells why the Samaritans were so disliked by the southern Jews. Discussed earlier, the northern portion was still called Israel and the southern section became known as Judah. Samaria became the Capital of the northern kingdom of Israel. Jesus and his disciples had to walk about 35 to 42 miles from the southern town of Jerusalem to reach Samaria north of it.

The sixth King of Israel, Omri meaning "pilgrim" or "life" who ruled for 11 years (885-874 B.C. bought the hill of Samaria (named in honor of its former owner Shemer). He made it the capital of Israel and built his palace there. Omri's son and successor to the throne, Ahab, may not be as familiar as was his wife Jezebel who had her husband build an altar to Baal, a pagan god, for idol worship. The palace that he built was made of ivory as an indication of the economic prosperity of Samaria during his reign (I Kings 22:39). Ahab was a wimpy king who was dominated by his wife Jezebel.

Around 722 B.C., The Assyrians attacked Samaria. The nation that conquered another nation, in those days, would deport or kill most of the people of the nation captured and bring other captives into that nation so as to weaken them to avoid rebellion. The Assyrians deported many of the Israelites but left behind those that were distraught and posed no threat to rise up later in rebellion. The people that were imported to Israel (non-Jews) eventually intermarried with the Jews that had not been imported. This mixed race of people became known as Samaritans. In 332 B.C. Alexander the Great captured Samaria during his conquest of Palestine. During the reign of Herod the Great, the city was rebuilt and renamed Sebaste. It was destroyed in A.D. 66 by the Romans but eventually rebuilt.

According to Greek tradition, Photiona was the Samaritan woman with whom Jesus spoke to at the well as was recounted in the Gospel of St. John, chapter four. Deeply moved by the experience, she took to preaching the Gospel, received imprisonment, and was finally martyred at Carthage. Another tradition states that Photina was put to death in Rome after converting the daughter of Emperor Nero and one hundred of her servants. She, supposedly, died in Rome with her sons Joseph and Victor, along with several other Christians, including Sebastian, Photius, Parasceve, Photis, Cyriaca, and Victor. They were perhaps included in the Roman Martyrology by Cardinal Cesare Baronius holding to the widely held view that the head of Photina was preserved in the church of St. Paul's Outside the Walls. Wikipedia.

Tradition relates that the Apostles baptized her with the name "Photine" meaning "enlightened one." Her feast days are celebrated on February 26 with those who suffered with her (Greek tradition), March 20 (Slavic tradition), and the Sunday of the Samaritan Woman.

## LIFE OF THE SAMARITAN WOMAN

The Gospel of John (4:5-42) relates the encounter of Photine (traditional name), the Samaritan woman, with Christ at Jacob's well. She repented after a very gentle and wise conversation with Christ and went and told her townspeople that she had met the Christ. For this, she is sometimes claimed as the first to proclaim the Gospel of Christ. She converted her five sisters (Ss. Anatole, Photo, Photis, Paraskeve, and Kyriake) and her two sons (St. Photinos, formerly known as Victor, and St. Joses). They all became tireless evangelists for Christ.

After the Apostles Paul and Peter were martyred, St. Photine and her family left their homeland of Sychar, in Samaria, to travel to Carthage to proclaim the Gospel of Christ there. In 66 AD, under the persecutions of Emperor Nero, they all achieved the crown of martyrdom, along with the Duke St. Sebastianos, the close friend of St. Photinos.

The "Water of Life Discourse" John 4:10–26, "The Bread of Life Discourse" John 6:22-59, and "Light of the World" title in John 8:12 are all similar and builds on the Christological theme that Jesus possesses the same life as the Father: John 5:26-27 ESV 26 For as the Father has life in himself, so he has granted the Son also to have life in himself. 27 And he has given him authority to execute judgment because he is the Son of Man.

# CHAPTER 45

# The Savior's Salvation is Accessible to Anyone Who Comes to Him in Faith Seeking Mercy

As CHRISTIANS, WE MUST FOLLOW the example of Jesus by helping the lost sheep, that is, those individuals that have fallen away. In the Gospel of Matthew, He shows the gradual transformation of Jesus who first instructed His disciples to minister only to the Jews, and then, later on, included the Gentiles. Earlier in this text, it was explained why the Jews had a dislike for the Samaritans and all other uncircumcised Gentiles. In Matthew 10:5-6 ESV, the apostle's records first instruction regarding these Samaritans and Gentiles: 5 these twelve Jesus sent out, instructing them, "Go nowhere among the Gentiles and enter no town of the Samaritans, 6 but go rather to the lost sheep of the house of Israel.

This did not mean that Jesus did not help those needy Gentiles who sought Him in the name of God. When people all over the region heard of Jesus' miracles and healing powers, He would often have to go into seclusion in order to pray, especially in desolate areas called the wilderness, desert, or up into the mountain. Jesus began his ministry in Capernaum a city on the northern shore of the Sea of Galilee thus fulfilled the prophecy of Isaiah (Isaiah 9:1-2).

The word about Jesus spread past the boundaries of Capernaum by those who had heard him teach and witnessed Him cure a variety of ailments supernaturally, and perform exorcisms while He visited or passed through districts. When Jesus and His disciples traveled around to various districts, people recognized Him and brought those who needed relief for their condition or ailment. Some followed by foot from towns because they were fascinated by His sermons (See Matthew 14:13). He and His disciples went about 35-50 miles from Capernaum to the district of Tyre and Sidon respectively.

In the Gospel of Matthew, chapter fifteen, there is an occurrence concerning a woman of faith that sought help from Jesus when she heard He was in the district. The way she initially requested Jesus' help, it seemed as if she was requesting help for an ailment that she had when she said, "have mercy on me, O Lord, Son of David; but she then said that it was her daughter that needed His help because she was subjugated by a demon (Matthew 15:22). Her daughter was described as being afflicted with an evil spirit. There are at least thirty two episodes in the New Testament alone related to demon possession.

The Gospel of Matthew says that this woman in faith was a Canaanite woman that came to Jesus asking for help for her daughter, whereas in the Gospel of Mark describes the same woman as being a Gentile, a Syrophoenician woman, a Syrian woman born in Phoenicia (Mark 7:26).

Phoenicia at that time was governed by Syria. Gnaeus Pompeius Magnus, known in English as Pompey, a military and political leader of the late Roman Republic, annexed Syria as an early Roman province in 64 BC. The name for this territory called Canaan was the land promised to Abraham in the OT and given to his Israelite descendants. There is no contradiction or conflict between the Gospels because the term "Canaanite" as used in the Gospel of Matthew serves as an ethnic catch-all term covering various indigenous populations and not a geographical area.

This woman, a descendant of the ancient Canaanites, came to the outlying district where Jesus and His disciples were. On this particular visit to this district, Jesus did not want anyone to know that He had come there. Apparently, some saw and recognized that He had come.

Jesus had a spiritual tradition where he sought solitude to be alone and pray and meditate on God. Wherever He went when the people realized He was there, multitudes sought Him usually for conditions or ailments that were beyond the scope of normal remedies.

According to what the disciples said to Jesus when he did not answer the woman, after she had made her desperate plea, was that this woman had been annoying them for some time about seeking an audience with Him. They refused her request up until this time. When they saw that she was with Jesus, they requested of Him to send her away. Somehow, she was able to have an audience with Jesus without their help. She spoke as if she knew His lineage when she referred to Jesus as O Lord, Son of David (Genealogy of Jesus -Matthew 1:1-17, Luke 3:23-38) which can be referenced to Old Testament Scripture fulfillment (II Samuel 7:15-16 God promises an everlasting kingdom for Israel with a Messiah from the royal line of David. The text II Samuel 23:5, King David expresses this promise to be an everlasting covenant with God for his descendants).

When Jesus spoke to her, He informed her that He was the Messiah that she spoke of, but His personal earthly mission was to preach specifically to the people of Israel. She knelt before Him anyway pleading for help. What Jesus said next has been commented on many times by ministers, biblical scholars and, students, etc., (Matthew 15:26): And he answered, "It is not right to take the children's bread and throw it to the dogs."

Even though this sounds like Jesus is being unbelievingly rude toward her, most scholars agree that He is testing her faith. She didn't reply as if she was offended by what Jesus said when she replied in agreement: She said, "Yes, Lord, yet even the dogs eat the crumbs that fall from their masters' table." By her reply, Jesus knew that this woman was a woman of faith and her daughter was instantly healed (Matthew 15:21-28 ESV).

Remember earlier, His ministry was first for the Jews. The woman did not display any anger over being called a little dog. It can be said because of her honest and sincere belief that Jesus was the Jewish Messiah, He could cure her daughter. It was her faith. So Jesus put aside

His theology and let His love in His heart take over for this woman and healed her daughter. In the latter part of chapter 15 of Matthew, Jesus went about healing many people that included Gentiles (Matthew 15:29-31).

There were other Gentiles that Jesus helped and performed many miracles that the Apostle John said were too numerous to write (John 21:25 NIV Jesus did many other things as well. If every one of them were written down, I suppose that even the whole world would not have room for the books that would be written).

# PERSONAL DIRECTIVE FROM JESUS TO HIS DISCIPLES AND ALL FOLLOWERS OF CHRIST TODAY

Later on, in contrast to the previous commandment given in Matthew 10:5, Jesus issues the Great Commission to the disciples after His crucifixion and resurrection concerning ministering to all people that had formed a union and commitment to Him: Matthew 28:19-20 ESV Go therefore and make disciples of all nations, baptizing them in the name of the Father and of the Son and of the Holy Spirit, teaching them to observe all that I have commanded you. And behold, I am with you always, to the end of the age."

So what are we to do? Help them that have fallen away and counsel those that never knew of Christ the savior. Tell them of Jesus love for us and the grace and redemption we received because of the ultimate sacrifice on the cross, it was the blood. The Lord is not willing that any should perish for all souls belongs to him (Ezekiel 18:4) He wants everyone to come to Him and repent their sins (II Peter 3:9 ESV The Lord is not slow to fulfill his promise as some count slowness but is patient toward you, not wishing that any should perish, but that all should repent).

# CHAPTER 46

## *Focus on Carnality Causes the Loss of Godly Birth Right and Blessings*

THERE ARE MANY INCIDENTS IN the bible that we should use as examples in our daily living. We must not turn away from the blessings that are given to us. Such an example is the story of the twin brothers, Esau and Jacob in the book of Genesis. These twin brothers were born from their parents, Isaac and Rebekah. Esau was his father's favorite of the two because he grew up to be a skilled hunter. But he was easily manipulated by his shrewd bother, Jacob.

Old Testament scripture (Genesis 25) reveals that Esau had been out hunting one day and came home famished. His twin brother, Jacob, had cooked some lentil stew. Jacob, conniving, traded a bowl of the lentil stew to Esau to obtain his birthright. Esau was the oldest of the twins. What the birthright meant in biblical times is that the firstborn had privileges inherited to him that had great importance and was considered sacred. This spiritual position entitled the oldest son to share part of the inheritance and carry the title of the family name forward for future generations.

This is not an ordinary inheritance though. If we look back at the biblical scriptures found in Genesis 12:1-3 and Genesis 15: 18-21, God made an unconventional covenant with the Jewish patriarch Abraham known as the Abrahamic Covenant. This covenant did not require Abraham to do anything. This covenant involved the possession of land for the descendants of Abraham, bestowing the blessing on the nation of Israelites, God called out the Israelites as a special people for himself that eventually included all people (Galatians 3:7-9, 14).

The disagreement between two future nations begins with Isaac's wife, Rebekah, difficult pregnancy with the non-identical twins struggling within her. Instead of asking God to relieve this difficulty, she asked God why this was so. God revealed to her that the two struggling sons in her womb would be the progenitors of two nations (Jacob/Israelites and Esau/Edomites) that would be in disagreement with each other for many generations. God revealed that the older of the non-identical twins, Esau, would serve the younger twin, Jacob.

After the twins were born, Rebekah favored Jacob, and Isaac favored Esau (See Genesis 25-19-28). When Isaac had grown old and his sight had failed him, he decided to bless his eldest son, Esau. He thought that it was getting close to his death. He started making preparations for the blessing that was traditionally bestowed on the eldest son. The first son born who was Esau so he was going to be anointed with benefits and greater responsibilities than his sibling, Jacob. Isaac would have still been living at the time in which he was going to bless Esau. Esau would have been second in command to his father. This ancient birthright law stated that upon the death of the father (Isaac), Esau, being the older of the non-identical twins was entitled to the birthright, which was a double portion of Isaac's estate and would become the leader of the family. He would become responsible for the care of Rebekah.

In preparation for the ceremonial blessing, Isaac told Esau to go out and hunt some venison, cook it for him, and he would eat and then bless him afterward. The blessing bestowed upon Esau is similar to a will. Rebekah overheard the conversation and started plotting to steal the blessing for Jacob. She knew that Isaac's sight was such that he had to rely on smell and touch to identify things. Rebekah then quickly devised a plan so that Jacob would receive the blessing that was Esau's. She and Jacob manipulated Isaac's intended will and testament so that Jacob would receive the birthright blessing instead of Esau (Genesis 27:1-41).

The last part of this episode (Genesis 27:41-46), Rebekah found out that Esau was angry enough to kill his brother Jacob over losing his birthright. She ordered Jacob to leave and go to her brother Laban's house in Haran, just south of Canaan. She thought that Esau's anger about what she and Jacob had done would decrease over a period of time. Esau didn't know that his mother was a co-conspirator in the plot. She convinced Isaac to send Jacob away by telling him that she didn't want Jacob to marry Canaanite women who worshipped idols as Esau had done. After Isaac sent Jacob away to find a wife, Esau realized his own Canaanite wives were evil in his father's eyes and so he took a daughter of Isaac's half-brother, Ishmael, as his wife beside the wives that he already had. After knowing that his father was bound by the decision of the birthright issue, he was still trying to find favor with him (Genesis 28:6-9).

This is a biblical story whereby we can have pity for an individual such as Esau who was not the protagonist of these events. Esau was completely faithful to his father and did everything Isaac requested to the very end with the exception of marrying idolatrous women. Isaac, the second of the patriarchs, can also be pitied. It appears that his wife was the dominant matriarch of the family who used her guiles to deceive her husband. It seems that she should have told Isaac about the revelation she had received from the Lord when she inquired about her difficult pregnancy (Genesis 25:22-24). Jacob would become the father of the Israelite nation (Jacob's name was changed to Israel when he wrestled with God and God recognized Jacob as His servant by changing his name in Genesis 32:22- 28). Esau's descendants were the Edomites (Edom/Idumea). This is why Edom is referred to in biblical passages as a "brother" of Israel. The Ammonites and the Moabites were excluded from worshipping with the Israelites in the temple but not the Edomites (Deuteronomy 23:3-8).

Esau and Jacob were the grandsons of Abraham. God had made a covenant with Abraham which would later produce the bloodline of our savior Jesus Christ. Abraham had great faith in God. So great was his faith that God called him "friend" (II Chronicles 20:7, Isaiah 41:8, James 2:23). Esau was forty years old when he farther detached himself permanently from being the patriarch of the Israelite Nation by marrying two Hittite women who made life bitter for his father and mother, Isaac and Rebekah.

The commandment not to marry Canaanites or any idolatrous people came much later than the time of Abraham. Although he lived among the Canaanites, he made his servant, who was in charge of his household, swear by the Lord that he would not get a wife for his son, Isaac, from among the Canaanite women. He told the servant to go back to his country and choose a wife for his son from among his relatives. (According to Stephen's speech in Acts 7:2 Abraham lived in Mesopotamia before he lived in Haran: And Stephen said: "Brothers and fathers, hear me. The God of glory appeared to our father Abraham when he was in Mesopotamia before he lived in Haran,)

The woman chosen to be Isaac's wife was to be brought to Canaan (Genesis 24:1-4). The servant made a supposition that the woman might not want to leave her land and come to Canaan. He suggested that Isaac is to be brought to her land. Abraham emphasized that without exception, the woman would have to be brought to Canaan because of the covenant God had made concerning Abraham's descendants who were to inherit this land (later called "The Promised Land"). Isaac's wife would have to be suitable and an appropriate mother for the descendants of the Abrahamic line (Genesis 24:7). If the woman refused to come to Canaan then the servant would be released from the oath.

The genealogy of the Messiah traces from the lineage of King David, Jacob, and Abraham (Two accounts of the genealogy of Jesus can be found in the Gospels of Matthew and Luke). Esau failed to see the value and importance of his sacred position that he gave away for a bowl of soup. Esau despised his birthright. He came home from hunting and told Jacob he was famished (NIV version). Esau probably had not gone more than twenty-four hours without eating.

An article by Alan Lieberson in Scientific American states "The duration of survival without food is greatly influenced by factors such as body weight, genetic variation, other health considerations and, most importantly, the presence or absence of dehydration." Generally, it appears as though humans can survive without any food for 30-40 days, as long as they are properly hydrated.

When Esau came home from hunting, his sensories of sight and smell (of the food) at that particular time caused him to forfeit his firstborn birthright privilege. He allowed his cunning brother, Jacob, to make the proposition of selling the highly valued birthright that his father, Isaac, was going to bless him with (Genesis 25:19-34). Jacob and his mother, Rebekah, manipulated the aged and blind Isaac, to give the blessing of the birthright to Jacob (Genesis 27)

We can't take a chance on doing what we want for our own personal satisfaction and gain, with the thought that we will repent at the last minute, because of God's mercy we will be forgiven and allowed entrance into the kingdom (Philippians 3:18-19 ESV 18 For many, of whom I have often told you and now tell you even with tears, walk as enemies of the cross of Christ. 19 Their end is destruction, their god is their belly, and they glory in their shame, with minds set on earthly things.

# CHAPTER 47

# Be Warned of Written or Spoken Personal Presuppositions of Biblical Text (Eisigesis)

MANY BIBLICAL SCHOLARS HAVE SPECULATED and written articles concerning Esau which shouldn't be believed to be true by Christians. Some teachings in time past up until today are eisegesis in nature which means a person used the process of interpreting a text or portion of text in such a way that it introduces one's own presuppositions, agendas, or biases into and onto the text. This is commonly referred to as "reading into the text". The act is often used to "prove" a pre-held point of concern to the reader and to provide him or her with confirmation bias in accordance with his or her pre-held agenda. Eisegesis is best understood when contrasted with exegesis. This process can possibly cause a person who relies only on the spoken word of a teacher or minister to be misled.

Exegesis is a critical explanation or interpretation of a text, especially a religious text. Traditionally the term was used primarily for exegesis of the Bible; however, in contemporary usage, it has broadened to mean a critical explanation of any text, and the term "biblical exegesis" is used for greater specificity. Exegesis includes a wide <u>range</u> of critical disciplines: textual criticism is the investigation into the history and origins of the text, but exegesis may include the study of the historical and cultural backgrounds of the author, the text, and the original audience. Other analysis includes classification of the type of literary genres present in the text and an analysis of grammatical and syntactical features in the text itself.

The terms exegesis and hermeneutics have been used interchangeably. However, hermeneutics is a more widely defined discipline of interpretation theory: hermeneutics includes the entire framework of the interpretive process, encompassing all forms of communication: written, verbal and nonverbal, while exegesis focuses primarily on the written text.

The Bible warns against using eisegesis for biblical interpretation. II Peter 1:20-21 ESV 20 knowing this first of all that no prophecy of Scripture comes from someone's own interpretation. 21 For no prophecy was ever produced by the will of man, but men spoke from God as they were carried along by the Holy Spirit.

Earlier in this book, taken from the scripture, is an excerpt where the Apostle Paul and Silas had to escape Thessalonica and travel to Berea, a city in Macedonia, because of the rioting Jews there in Thessalonica. At Berea, we are told that the Jews there were nobler than most that the Apostle had encountered because they went and studied what had been preached to them to ensure that it was correct. That is exactly what we need to do today instead of being spoon fed on Sundays and at mid-week bible studies. Pray for understanding while we are alone with our bibles.

There are interpretations of the scripture that are non-canonical which can be perceived as satanical. One such interpretation is that of the theory of the "Serpent's Seed". Theories such as this one are so farfetched that no other details about the theory will be presented here. It is amazing how certain eisegesis can be espoused by people that profess to receive biblical inspiration as a revelation for such an interpretation.

Christians must not cease to pray for understanding of the Holy Scripture to avoid being ill-advised and manipulated by those who have transformed biblical scripture into their own understanding. Instead of accepting what is right and wrong according to the Word of God, they use scripture to create their own worldly interpretation(s). There was a pastor who created what can be considered a cult following that led to the death of many ill-advised members including him.

The "Jonestown Massacre," that happened in Jonestown, Guyana on November 18, 1978, when Jim Jones, the leader of an American Cult called the Peoples Temple, caused over 900 members, under his direction, to commit suicidal-murder by drinking cyanide-laced grape-flavored Flavor Aid. Jones brainwashed people who were seeking a new way of living by preaching racial equality, helping the poor, healing, and other good sounding promises. Large portions of his members were African Americans, middle class, poor, and those of different racial backgrounds. Jones offered a new way out for people who were disappointed about the present condition of America.

If this sounds familiar, it is because, during campaigning, politicians promise to create an ideal society, on a larger scale, for all Americans if and when elected. Jones offered a Utopia Socialism which would move followers into an ideal society within a small community that was of like minds. Jones had convinced some members that he was from a higher power, even that he was God. He would profess to heal the sick during his services by using staged healing practices to receive devotion from his followers.

His followers thought that he taught and practiced the concepts of unity found in the Bible. He was able to manipulate those that had come from a world of discrimination and sought equality in their lives. By establishing a cult-like community in a remote settlement Jonestown, Guyana, he could prevent the members from being influenced by outside sources.

The Peoples Temple was created in Indianapolis, Indiana in 1955 before moving the congregation to California in 1965. The Peoples Temple members were harassed because of the Jones's religious-political ideology so he re-located over a third of the 3000 members to an agricultural site in South America which was then called the "Peoples Temple Agricultural Project. The common name for this community is better known as Jonestown named after Jim Jones.

What Jones did was similar in nature to Cenobitic (or coenobitic) monasticism in the sense only of stressing community life and isolation. This monasticism is monkhood where one gives up worldly pursuits and devotes oneself fully to spiritual work. The only similarity or comparison between Jonestown and monasticism mentioned here are the isolation and the stressing of community way of life. In Jim Jones communal setup, none of the members could leave the camp without his approval. Also, there are recordings where Jones urged the members to commit revolutionary suicide.

Jones instructed the adults at Jonestown to give the poison to the children before taking their dose and some 304 children died of cyanide poisoning on that day in 1978. This was murder by the parents because the infants and children did not choose to commit suicide.

Jim Jones was ordained as Disciples of Christ pastor. The Disciples of Christ or the Christian Church is a Protestant Christian denomination in the United States. Jones was a communist and cult leader that determined the best way to promote his religious and political beliefs was by infiltrating the church. There have been six or more documentaries, dramas, songs, etc., concerning this event. This horrific tragedy is about the gullibility of Christians that turn to the word of man instead of God.

The pastor or minister should be a godly person but never to be considered as God incarnate. Only the New York Trade Center Towers destruction by the hijacked aircrafts used by suicidal pilots on September 11, 2001, caused more loss of American lives. Jones did not die by taking the cyanide-laced punch that he urged others to drink, but is believed to have committed suicide by a shot to the head, or had someone else do it for him.

The Apostle John warns that words found in the book of Revelation should not be altered by adding or taking away from its contents. Biblical scripture should not be transposed to promote hatred of a people, group or race which was practiced by those wishing to use religion for justification of slavery in America. Most Christians today believe slavery is contrary to the will of God. That is why when eisegesis is used, biblical scripture becomes adulterated. We are not to add or subtract any meaning of the Lord's word which is stated early in the Old Testament scripture in Deuteronomy 4:2 ESV You shall not add to the word that I command you, nor take from it, that you may keep the commandments of the LORD your God that I command you. (See also -Deuteronomy 12:32, Proverbs 30:5-6, Galatians 3:15, Revelation 22:18-19) Revelation 22:18-19- the Apostle John recorded the instructions by Jesus concerning the Book of Revelation specifically.

I say to you that many people have been accused wrongly because of misunderstanding and failure to seek correct knowledge from the word of God. That is why the "Word" tells us to lean not on our own understanding. Motives and attitudes play a great part in our actions. One may speak well or do well and still have a wrong motive or attitude in their heart. Those who are in authority (elected governmental officials) have the greatest opportunity to dispense mendacities to the uninformed and gullible. That in itself is sinful.

The bible tells us to keep our own hearts with all vigilance for out of it are the issues of life (Proverbs 4:23). If we keep good things stored up in our hearts, our words and actions will be a reflection of this or the fruit of the Spirit we display. To receive the vigilance that we need for storing things in our hearts we must allow the Holy Spirit to dwell in us which will allow the right understanding of the intent of the word of God. With this achieved, the storms of life are less turbulent. Then we will understand more and more how to be careful about forming our own opinions, decisions, and judgments about others that we have no actual knowledge of.

For instance, a judge asked a witness why he had sunglasses on in her courtroom. This individual had an eye infection that caused his eyes to be sensitive to lighting. The judge probably initially thought this individual was being disrespectful until the ailment was revealed. We have to be careful about rushing to judgment when we see only the outward appearance.

Only God knows the true heart of a person. Just as Cain refused to listen to God, his satanic mindset caused him to commit the first murder ever by killing his brother Abel (Genesis 4:8). Today we may not be physically murdering our brothers and sisters in Christ but we kill and assassinate their character with the idle gossip that comes out of our mouths. We are not only talking about non-Christians here; it is the church folks that let their own carnal opinions out against other church members. Don't you know Satan grins from ear to ear while causing disruption in the church? Satan causes such blindness that when the "Word" is being preached some do not listen because they think it is not applicable to their standing with God. Do not miss the point; the "Word" is speaking to all of us so that we will have unflappable instructions for daily living.

The Apostle Paul said that some have a form of godlessness that they are forever learning and never come into the knowledge of the truth (See II Timothy 3:1-9). In this epistle to the young pastor, Timothy was in the city of Ephesus, and Paul was in prison in a cold dungeon in Rome and would be martyred shortly after this writing. The Apostle's letter was concerning the arrogance and godlessness of the people of the day and the main topic described the commencement of "End Times" or the beginning of the church age when Jesus comes back a second time.

The Apostle could have been ministering to any Christian modern church and the message would be applicable. The people have heard the gospel many times, but have they learned to apply it to their lives? In this age of technology, there are so many resources to obtain biblical precepts and commentaries that it is almost limitless. There are many that can be obtained complimentary or can be purchased on the internet.

Many people have gone out to find the truth that suits their opinions instead of the eternal truth of God. They read and research and never learn how to apply God's eternal instructions to their lives. There are many who have memorized many biblical scriptures, which are a very good thing, if not used to exalt themselves. Since all blessings come from God, one should not think more highly of themselves and develop a superior attitude of self-righteousness.

Use the blessing you received to think things through using sensible judgment. Faith can be considered the whole entity that God has in His possession and He does not give the whole portion to any one individual but each receives a fractional part according to His will.

The portions given by God to each individual are distinct. Since all portions are given by God to fulfill His purpose, there is no reason for self-exaltation (Romans 12:3).

All the knowledge obtained by a person is from God. The Word of God has been read by some and based on their own knowledge, have turned away from the faith (apostasy). Faith in God is the key to all blessings and covenant promises. The Apostle Paul understood that some will depart from being faithful by a revelation he received from the Holy Spirit (I Timothy 4:1 ESV Now the Spirit expressly says that in later times some will depart from the faith by devoting themselves to deceitful spirits and teachings of demons,).

The Apostle Paul emphasizes that unless a believer receives the Holy Spirit (the Paraclete) he or she will not know the deep things of God. It does not matter how prepared a preacher may be with his sermon or how eloquently he or she presents it; the unbeliever will be at a loss to understanding it. Things of God are hidden from the unbeliever that is freely given to the believer. Wisdom is received from the Holy Spirit (I Corinthians 2:10-13).

# CHAPTER 48

# The Mind of Christ in Us

WHEN SOMEONE HAS THE MIND of Christ they send forth love and not hate. Kindness, instead of bitterness will be on that person's lips. When someone doesn't mind speaking in a boastful manner about disliking or hating someone they are to be pitied and need prayer. People cannot see your faith because it is a mental state. When they see your actions, they form a good or bad opinion about you.

Some Bible readers wrongly think there is a conflict between what James, Jesus' brother, and the Apostle Paul says on receiving justification by works and/or faith (The Apostle Paul on Justification by faith: Galatians 2:16 KJV Knowing that a man is not justified by the works of the law, but by the faith of Jesus Christ, even we have believed in Jesus Christ, that we might be justified by the faith of Christ, and not by the works of the law: for by the works of the law shall no flesh be justified.

The Book of James speaks of being justified by works. James states in James 2:21 KJV Was not Abraham our father justified by works, when he had offered Isaac his son upon the altar? What he meant is that the righteous action of Abraham exemplified his genuine faith in God... There is no conflict because James knew it was impossible to receive justification by works of the law although many of his contemporaries thought they could receive salvation by their good works (See James 2:14-26). Only faith in Christ brings salvation. If one has faith in Jesus then good works will follow.

Some readers called Humanists who, have apparently read the Bible, reject the fact that it is the word of God. They believe that the writers of the bible were ignorant superstitious humans who created a book full of errors and fallacies. Some scriptural materials in the bible have scholars scratching their heads. Especially, the New Testament Gospels that have different writers relating the life of Jesus from their perspective. On the other hand, some readers believe the bible is the word of God but some facts were lost in translation from Biblical Hebrew and Biblical Aramaic to the first translation of the Greek language. The Septuagint 200-300 BCE is a Koine Greek translation of the Hebraic text also called the Greek Old Testament which was later included in the canonical Hebrew Bible.

The narrative behind the story of how the Torah (God revealing of His Law to Moses in the first five books of Hebrew Scripture or the Pentateuch) was translated from Biblical Hebrew to Greek is found in the pseudepigraphic Letter of Aristeas or Letter to Philocrates (his brother).

The narrative relates that seventy-two Jewish scholars or elders were placed in seventy-two different chambers by the order of King Ptolemy of Egypt. They were not told why they had been called and placed in these chambers. The king went into each chamber and requested each to translate the Biblical Hebrew Torah (Pentateuch) by their teacher Moses into the Greek language. By the works of God, they all translated identically.

John Wycliffe's Bible Middle English translation appeared 1382-1395. The King James Version of the Bible began translation in 1604 and was completed in 1611 because King James wanted an accurate as possible English translation of the bible. This is probably why some readers think that some original meanings of the Hebrew scripture might have deficiencies despite measures taken to provide the best possible accurate translation.

Those that have the attitude that good works are sufficient for salvation may not know it but are of Satan and not Christ. It may be difficult to approach an individual on what the Bible says about bitterness and hatred. Again, this demonstrates that these individuals are living by their own self-righteousness and opinions. You cannot correct these individuals using conversation that is spiced with "salt or sugar" because their ignorance is unapproachable. Some people want only "sugar" critique concerning themselves. These are individuals that will church hop looking for sugar-coated sermons and avoid sermons that are in conflict with what they want to hear and do (salt).

God's instructions are not complicated; they are a matter of do's and don'ts. God left the bible which allows for resolving any situation that might confront a believer. A believer has to go that extra mile not only lifting himself or herself up but to reach out to others and raise them up. Keep negative thoughts to yourself, avoid degrading speech, and pray to rid yourself of this malignant spirit (See Ephesians 4:29-30). So, not only should believers avoid being a sensational news spreader and finding faults with others, falling into the trap of Satan, but must diligently always seek to edify others. No corrupt communication should proceed out of your mouths but minister the good grace and the good news about the Savior (gospel). Controlling or taming the tongue is such an important command for Christians that the Apostle James spends the first twelve verses of the third chapter of his book on the subject.

It is a small portion compared to the whole body; it poses a difficult task that if one can control the tongue, then many other facets of life can also be controlled. According to the apostle, a Christian is considered a Mature Christian and perfect person if he or she can control the words that come out of the mouth (James 3:2).

The tongue never tires if it does not have any disorders. Some words can be spoken without the tongue, but the tongue is needed for most words. The tongue is used because of the fact that it produces the sound for most of the spoken word. Many have falsely thought that the tongue is the strongest muscle in the body. The sounds that come from the tongue that is orchestrated by the brain can be filtered and controlled (James 3:1-12). The tongue can sin, it can blaspheme, and it can repent and praise God.

Proverbs speaks of the tongue as having the power of life or death:

Proverbs 18:21 ESV Death and life are in the power of the tongue, and those who love it will eat its fruits.

Christians should not speak things that are not edifying. Hurtful and hateful things out of the mouth may not cause physical damage but it certainly can cause mental hurt. Sometimes it best not to make a comment if it is not pertinent for encouragement and reproofing should be a blessing to the listener such as the reproofing in Proverbs 9:8 ESV Do not reprove a scoffer, or he will hate you; reprove a wise man, and he will love you. The scoffer from a biblical perspective will not accept anything that critiques their belief. This person stands against God and tries to get others to be in agreement. This could be the same person mentioned earlier that causes conflict in the church.

In the epistle to the church at Ephesus, the Apostle Paul's exhortation concerned lifting up the listener by your conversation and to avoid saying unwholesome and profane things. He says your conversation intent should be to cause a paradigm shift of spiritual enlightenment to the listener(s). When someone speaks or does something that is known to be wrong it grieves the Holy Spirit. Forgive one another as God in Christ forgives (Ephesians 4:29-32). We must strive to live a life that measures up to the standards of God.

# CHAPTER 49

# Unimaginable Sacrifice and Suffering for the Salvation of Mankind

How many will give their lives away to death or the life of a child away to death for even one other person for whatever reason? The answer is an overwhelming, none. God did not only give his only begotten Son away for our sins, but Jesus suffered unimaginable physical pain from the Roman soldiers that flogged and scourged Him for all to see.

God had already set forth the crucifixion:

Acts 2:23 NKJV Him, being delivered by the determined purpose and foreknowledge of God, you have taken by lawless hands, have crucified, and put to death.

I Peter 1: 20-21 NKJV 20 He indeed was foreordained before the foundation of the world but was manifest in these last times for you 21 who through Him believe in God, who raised Him from the dead and gave Him glory, so that your faith and hope are in God.

In the Romans' mind, crucifixion was reserved for rebellious slaves, mutinous troops, vile criminals, and insurrectionists against the state. Roman citizens, especially the upper class, were normally exempt from such an ignominious death no matter what their crime. The reason for this was that crucifixion was viewed not just as a means of death, but also as a means of portraying shame. Therefore only the most despicable was crucified. To be hung on a cross meant more than that a crime worthy of death had been committed. It meant that the accused was considered to be a lowly, vile, reprehensible person, in addition to being a criminal.

That is the same idea behind the Jewish practice of hanging a criminal's body on a tree. It was for this reason that Joshua hung the body of the king of Ai on a tree (Joshua 8:29) and the bodies of the five kings of the southern confederacy on five trees (Joshua 10:26-27). He was interested in more than their execution. Exposing them to public shame and ridicule was the primary motive for this practice.

# CHAPTER 50

# Call on the Lord Jesus Regardless the Circumstances

PHILIPPIANS 4:4-7 NIV84 4 REJOICE in the Lord always. I will say it again: Rejoice! 5 Let your gentleness be evident to all. The Lord is near. 6 Do not be anxious about anything, but in every situation, by prayer and petition, with thanksgiving, present your requests to God. 7 And the peace of God, which transcends all understanding, will guard your hearts and your minds in Christ Jesus.

The Holy Spirit is our indwelling advocate and helper and we should appeal to the Spirit in Jesus' name in times of trouble and in good times with faith. The book of Hebrews is chocked full of exhortations. Our daily exhortation is to bless and praise the Lord at all times. We tend to lean toward calling on the Lord in times of trouble more so; He wants to be in fellowship with us and He wants us to fellowship with other believers (I John 1:3-7).

A true Christian is always in contact with the sovereign God by prayer. When we come to the Lord in times of trouble, it could be something dire, a terminally ill loved one, problems on the job, lack of a job, marital problems, disobedient child, etc., or any trouble or problem that confront us, we must come in faith. All of the healings or demonic removal from individuals that sought out Jesus in the four Gospels indicated that the recipients displayed faith.

Jesus also approached and healed some who had no idea who He was. One such case is that of a lame man in the Gospel of John chapter five who had been lame for 38 years hoping for a cure by dipping in a pool at a certain time when it was thought to be stirred by an angel from Heaven. This Pool of Bethesda was in Jerusalem near a place called Sheep Gate where people went for physical ailments. (John 5:1-16). The Pool of Bethesda is in the Muslim quarter of old city Jerusalem on the premises of St Anne's Church.

John 5:14 implies the man sins might have been the cause of his affliction. After the man is healed by Jesus, there is not any indication that he had faith or that he repented. It appears likely that this man betrayed Jesus because he went directly to the Jewish leaders and told them that Jesus had healed him. Jesus had healed this man on the Sabbath and the Jewish religious leaders were more interested in persecuting Jesus rather than the man carrying his mat on the Sabbath. Under the many Mosaic Laws, working on the Sabbath was forbidden; carrying the mat and healing were considered work.

They completely ignored the fact of the miracle healing of a man that had been paralytic for 38 years. After healing the man at the pool, Jesus slipped away into the crowd without the man ever knowing He was the Messiah. Later when Jesus saw the man in the temple and told him to sin no more or else his malady would be worse than the one that he had for 38 years. When Jesus and the man met in the temple, at this time, he knew who Jesus was so he went to the Jewish authorities with this information. The Jewish leader's hostility toward Jesus increased because of His supernatural acts and teaching challenged the Sanhedrin. They relied heavily on trying to convince the Jewish people that He was disobeying the Mosaic Covenant which had a penalty of death. From this time on the Pharisees sought ways to kill the Lord accusing Him of blasphemy and many other charges.

The temple priests, the Pharisees, and Sadducees were allowing merchants to operate on the temple courtyard which produced wealth for the temple and them. Jesus disrupted the merchandising when He and His disciples traveled to Jerusalem for Passover (Synoptic Gospels of Matthew 21:12-17, Mark 11:15-19, and Luke 19:45-48). Scholars believe that John 2:13-16 indicates that there may have been two separate incidents of Jesus disrupting the temple merchandisers.

The woman with the issue of blood for twelve years had spent all that she had searching for a cure to no avail with all the available physicians. Her illness, which is described in the KJV as "the woman with the issue of blood" also referred to by the original New Testament Greek term as the haemorrhoissa. She was beyond the scope of human healing. Because of her illness, she should have been quarantined because she was ceremonially unclean. This is probably why she wanted to go unnoticed and received healing without being recognized. She probably felt ashamed. She was there to touch the fringe of Jesus's garment because she had heard that people had been cured by such a touch (Matthew 14:34-36, Mark 5:28).

She knew because of her ailment, which caused her to be ceremonially unclean, she wasn't supposed to be there in the crowd but she had become desperate and destitute of money. This was one of the laws given to Moses for any of the Jews who were classified as being ceremonially unclean during their wilderness journey. Quarantine orders were used to prevent the spread of disease to the healthy Jews (Leviticus 15:25-31)

In the Gospel of Matthew chapter 9, Jesus crossed over the Sea of Galilee to His own city of dwelling which was Capernaum. A paralytic man was brought to Him and healed. It is in this chapter, Matthew, the tax collector, was chosen as a disciple of Jesus. A synagogue ruler named Jairus came to Jesus and knelt before Him and informed Him that his twelve-year-old daughter was terminally ill. Jesus and His disciples were in the process of following Jairus to his place where the terminally ill daughter was when the woman with the issue of blood came up behind Him and touched the fringes of His garment. This woman's desperation caused her to ignore the Judaic sanitation and purification laws. The woman's faith was immediately recognized by Jesus and He healed her instantaneously.

THE WOMAN WITH THE ISSUE OF BLOOD- Legend was not long in providing the woman of the Gospel with a name. In the West she was identified with Martha of Bethany; in the East, she was called

293

Berenike, or Beronike, the name appearing in as early a work as the "Acta Pilati", the most ancient form of which goes back to the fourth century. The fanciful derivation of the name Veronica from the words Vera Icon (eikon) "true image" dates back to the "Otia Imperialia" of Gervase of Tilbury, who says: "Est ergo Veronica pictura Domini vera" (translated: "The Veronica is, therefore, a true picture of the Lord.") an issue of blood (Matthew 9:20-22). Legends- There is no reference to the story of St Veronica and her veil in the canonical Gospels. She is known as the woman who wiped Jesus's face with her veil. Then the image of Jesus's face appeared on it. The closest is the miracle of the woman who was healed by touching the hem of Jesus's garment (Luke 8:43–48); her name is later identified as Veronica by the apocryphal "Acts of Pilate". Source Wikipedia.

After the woman's blood issue ailment was healed, some came from Jairus's house and told him that there was no need to inconvenience Jesus by requesting Him to come to the house because the twelve-year-old daughter had died. Jesus, overhearing the conversation told Jairus not to fear, that the little girl would be restored to a healthy condition. When Jesus came to the house of Jairus, He only allowed His disciples Peter, John, James, Jairus and his wife to enter with Him.

The events concerning Jesus healing a man with demons, the woman with the issue of blood, and raising Jairus's daughter from being dead, are recorded in the synoptic Gospels (Matthew 9:18-26, Mark 5:21-43, Luke 8:40-56), only Mark uses the Aramaic language to describe the little girl being raised from the dead: Mark 5: 41 ESV Taking her by the hand he said to her, "Talitha cumi, "which means, "Little girl, I say to you, arise."

There were many recordings of the miraculous healings performed by Jesus in the New Testament of the Bible. Earlier in this book, it was mentioned that the Apostle John in his gospel wrote that Jesus had done so many miraculous things that were too innumerable to be written into text (John 21:25). There are many verses of scripture in the New Testament of people bringing their troubles to Jesus. He healed those that he came in contact with while teaching. He fed the hungry miraculously.

When His mother came to Him at a wedding because the wine had run out, Jesus performed His first recorded miracle by turning water into wine. His mother wouldn't have asked Him if she didn't have faith that He could perform this provision. Perhaps she had seen him perform other miracles prior to this that was not written in the canonical manuscripts.

You must come to the Savior with faith. Whenever Jesus brought a person or persons back to normality from an illness, deformity, death, or to salvation, He would say," your faith has made you well," or "your faith has saved you."

Jesus marveled at the faith of a Roman Centurion (a Gentile) whose servant He made well from a distance (Matthew 8:5-13). He healed a Canaanite woman's daughter from a distance (Matthew 15:28).

During the time of Jesus, a Centurion was a high ranking Roman officer who had to perform twenty years of service in this position. Marriage was not allowed. The Centurion was a commander over one hundred Roman soldiers. An ordinary Roman foot soldier would not have a servant. The servant living with this Centurion was most likely the only adopted family that he had. He was fond of this servant as if he was a family member that was gravely ill and near death. The Centurion had heard that Jesus had the ability to heal so he summoned him by requesting that the Jewish elders and friends would bring him to his house. The Centurion had more recognition of Jesus' power and status as being the Son of God than the Jewish religious leaders. After contemplating Jesus' status as being the Jewish Messiah, he felt unworthy to have Jesus come to his home.

The disciple, Peter, displayed this attitude of unworthiness when he witnessed the manifestation of the incarnate Jesus while fishing described in Luke 5:7-9. When Jesus began choosing disciples at the beginning of His ministry, He was standing on the shore of Lake of Gennesaret, known as The Sea of Galilee in the other three gospels. Other names for the Sea of Galilee in the Bible are Kinneret or Lake Tiberias.

Jesus saw two empty boats and fishermen near them washing their fishing nets. Jesus got into the boat owned by Simon Peter and asked him to pull away from the shore a small distance. There were other people near the shore together with the fishermen and Jesus taught them from Simon's boat. When He had finished teaching, He told Simon Peter to take his boat out to deeper water so they could fish. Simon Peter respectfully told Jesus that he and other fishermen had toiled all night long and didn't catch any fish but we will do what you say. When the fishermen let down the fishing nets, so many fish were caught in the nets that the nets started to break. They filled the boats with so many fish that they were about to sink. Simon Peter then realized that this was no ordinary man, from His teaching and the orchestration of this miraculous catch of fish, this man was the Messiah. Simon Peter fell down on His knees confessing that he was a sinful man and was not worthy of being in His divine presence. He not only astonished Simon Peter but all that witnessed the miraculous catch of fish were equally filled with astonishment.

The miracles performed by Jesus marveled all witnesses. Jesus displayed His humanity by also marveling. This is indicated by the gospel writers twice that said Jesus was filled with wonder, specifically, He marveled. "Marvel" The Greek translation is thaumazo (pronounced thou-mad'-zo) definition is to wonder, wonder at, marvel, to be wondered at, to be had in admiration. He marveled at the Centurion's faith that he knew that Jesus could heal his servant from a distance without coming to his home. (Matthew 8:10)

The second occasion that Jesus marveled was for the lack of faith by the Jews in His own hometown of Nazareth. The unbelief of the people there, including family, was such that Jesus did not perform any great miracles there with the exception of laying His hands on a few sick people and healing them. The people of Nazareth remembered that He had worked as a carpenter with His stepfather, Joseph, so they felt He didn't have the proper credentials to be ministering in the synagogue.

In the Gospel of Mark 3:20-21, after Jesus had completed selecting His twelve disciples, He and the disciples came down from the mountainside by Galilee and went into the home of Simon and Andrew to eat. The crowd outside was riotous over the fact that Jesus healed on the Sabbath and taught in the synagogue without the usual credentials of the Pharisees. His family came and carried Him away and said He was out of His mind. They knew his mother, Mary, and His siblings, James, Joses (Joseph), Judas (Jude), and Simon. They mentioned his sisters whose names are not given in the New Testament Bible. There is much.

Information concerning whether these were Jesus' biological brothers and sisters. Because of their remembrance of Jesus as a carpenter, they took offense to His teaching in the synagogue (Mark 6:1-6).

# CHAPTER 51

# Generational Apostatizing

CHRISTIANS EASILY APPREHEND THE NECESSITY for the Holy Spirit to provide help in understanding the wisdom of the Word of God. The rich and famous who consider acquiring a certain status and wealth places them in a situation where there is no destitution and thus no need to repent and seek salvation. It is most likely that when someone is destitute they will seek God's help and they might not seek Him any other time until their situation becomes calamitous.

Earlier in this book, Jesus asked a rich young ruler to give up all his wealth to become a disciple. The bible doesn't say whether he conformed to giving up his worldly possession but he went away sorrowful. The believers of the 1st -century church gave all of the worldly possessions to the church and everything was common among them (See Acts 2:44). The Lord does not want anyone who boasts of anything about themselves but boasts in the reliance on Lord and the totality of His provisions. An example of this is found in the epistle that the Apostle Paul wrote to those who were believers in Jesus in the church at Corinth. God provides wisdom, righteousness, sanctification, and redemption which is hidden from the wise because of their foolishness (see 1 Corinthians 1:26-31).

This foolishly is the increasing apostasy of the current living generations. Wikipedia defines the "word generation as a cohort in social science which signifies the entire body of individuals born and living at about the same time, most of who are approximately the same age and have similar ideas, problems, and attitudes." This discussion is about the generations of people, that a considerable number are still living today. There are still people living from the generation called the GI generation which includes veterans that fought in World War II that were born from 1901-1924 and also lived during the Great Depression. Just in case someone reading this is not familiar with the Great Depression, in 1929 the United States Wall Street (stock market) crashed sending the economy into a deep recession causing high unemployment, poverty, low profits, deflation, plunging farm incomes, and lost opportunities for economic growth and personal advancement. The Depression also resulted in an increase of emigration of people to other countries for the first time in American history. For example, some immigrants went back to their native countries, and some native US citizens went to Canada, Australia, and South Africa. The depression spread worldwide.

The next generation after the GI generation was called the Silent Generation, also known as the Lucky Few, was born from approximately 1925 to 1945. The next generation after the "Lucky Few" is called the Baby Boomers born 1945 to 1964. This is the generation that believed that families that prayed together stayed together. Most attended the church of their faith. Many of this generation are retired and many are deceased. Generation Xs were born from 1965 to 1980. The next generation called the Millennials or generation Ys were born from 1977 to 1995.

The dates of these generations sometimes overlap as far as dates of births are concerned on websites. For instance, US News has categories of millennials called "older millennials (born 1981-1989) and younger millennials (born 1990-1996). The millennial generation, for the purpose here, is important concerning religion in American. Polls indicate that as many as one-third of millennials do not have any religious affiliation and many don't attend any church services on a routine basis. For those that attend, it is once or twice per year. Some of the major hotel chains are catering to the non-religious needs of the millennials by removing Bibles from their night- stands.

According to a survey by STR, a hospitality analysis company, in

2016 found that the percentage of hotels that offer religious materials has dropped significantly over the last decade from 96 percent of hotels in 2006 to 48 percent (excerpt from an article By Hugo Martin- Los Angeles Times "Bibles find less room at the inn"). Luke 2:7 scripture is about Mary giving birth to Jesus in a stable in the city of David called Bethlehem because she and her husband Joseph could not find any unoccupied rooms at the inn there. (And she brought forth her firstborn son, and wrapped him in swaddling clothes, and laid him in a manger; because there was no room for them in the inn KJV).

Businesses cater to the needs of people who use their services. To be fair to the millennials, the removal of religious material can also be attributed to the diversity of the clientele who use their services. The hotels that removed the Bibles are trying to be cautious and sensitive to their clients. To be fair to the hotels, some that removed religious material from the nightstands have Bibles or other religious material at the front desk which can be dispensed to whoever needs it.

I hope that generation IGen, Z or the Centennials, born 1996 and later, that have been raised by the remaining Christian parent(s) will reach out to their contemporaries concerning the salvation found only in Jesus. I pray that the Paraclete will open the eyes of the babes (spiritual) that they not be deceived by false prophets and politicians who strive to use Christian evangelicals for monetary and political gains respectively.

As Christians see this apostasy and atheism unfolding and increasing in the United States and the world, the Gospel of Jesus (His death, burial, and resurrection for our sins) needs to be evangelized more and more. Jesus intended for all believers to become evangelists of His unadulterated gospel without the infusion of politics that has caused division even among Christians. The first and greatest commandment is that we love God with all of our hearts, souls, and minds. The second greatest commandment is similar in that we are to love one another as we do ourselves. He is coming back to claim His sheep (faithful believers) and to pass judgment on the world. When He returns, there will be one hundred percent bowing down on knees confessing that Jesus is Lord. The work of the Holy Spirit by Jesus- John 16:5-15.

The Old Testament Bible was described earlier as a shadow or umbra of the coming of Jesus Christ. There has to be a light source to create a shadow. In the Old Testament Jesus is the light that creates the shadow. Simply speaking, two things must be present to create a shadow, light, and someone or something to block the light. Technically, there are three terms in physics that pertain to the parts of a shadow which are usually associated with celestial bodies. The distinct parts of a shadow pertaining to these bodies are named the umbra, penumbra, and antumbra. The umbra used here is about a heavenly person who is the (point) source that blocks the source of light revealing the shadow of the coming Messiah. The heavenly body that is the point source of the shadow in the Old Testament is Jesus.

In the New Testament Jesus is revealed as the Messiah and brought to public attention by his cousin, John the Baptist, who preached repentance and made preparation for His arrival (Luke 3:1-9). John the Baptist was so Christ-like that many thought that he was the Messiah (See Luke 3:15-17). After Jesus was baptized by His cousin, the light that the prophets, psalmists, king, etc., of the Old Testament, spoke about is revealed as the Holy Spirit descends upon Him in the form of a dove (Luke 3:21-22). It is not necessarily paramount that one reads and understands all of the Old Testament but it is deemed a prerequisite by most ministers and biblical scholars.

The Spirit of God or the Holy Spirit is first spoken of in the Old Testament beginning in the book of Genesis Chapter 1 verse 2. There are many verses of scripture related to the Holy Spirit in the OT. If someone chooses to rely only on the New Testament of the Bible for spiritual edification, it is possible to assume that the commencement of the provisions and instructions of the Holy Spirit occurs in the book of Acts 1:1-8 and Acts 2:1-13. Strong's Exhaustive Concordance will benefit in researching the works of the Holy Spirit in both biblical testaments. There are many websites on the internet where verses concerning the Holy Spirit can be found throughout the Holy Bible.

The permanency of the indwelling of the Holy Spirit in individuals who have placed their faith in the Lord Jesus is more defined in the New Testament than the Old Testament. New Testament scripture about the indwelling Holy Spirit provides consolation in our earthly lives by the realization that the Spirit has complete control over sin and death (see Romans 8:2 and Romans 8:9-11). The Apostle Paul speaking of future glory said that the suffering in this earthly life does not compare to the future glory of being with the Lord (Romans 8:18-25).

Old Testament scripture describes the empowerment of prophets, such as Isaiah. The psalmists, kings, and etc., also were empowered by God's Spirit in the Old Testament era. It also describes the Holy Spirit leaving an individual because of disobedience such as the first Israelite King, Saul (See I Samuel 16:14). The Holy Spirit left King Saul and went into David, the second king of Israel. King David was aware that the Holy Spirit had left Saul and prayed that he would not suffer the same consequence (Psalm 51:10-11).

Christians need not worry about the indwelling Holy Spirit departing. Mature Christians realize that the love of this world and the lust of the flesh are in opposition and are hostile toward God (Romans 8:7). Even though the indwelling Holy Spirit is permanent in Christians, the residency of this life on earth is only temporary. The Bible makes it clear that a Christian's life on earth has a short endurance according to God's standard. King David, the Psalmist, wrote in Psalm 39:4-5 ESV: 4 "O LORD, make me know my end and what is the measure of my days; let me know how fleeting I am! 5 Behold, you have made my days a few handbreadths (A Hebrew linear measure containing 4 fingers, or digits, and equal to about 3 inches), and my lifetime is as nothing before you. Surely all mankind stands as a mere breath! Selah. The Holy Spirit leads us to be good ambassadors for Jesus while in this land that is not our home. (

The inheritance received by being adopted children of God is only by the redemptive work of Jesus dying on the cross and being resurrected for the salvation of believers. God has an everlasting love for us and wants to be in communication with us. We communicate with the Lord by means of prayer. Satan tries to disrupt this communication even in seasoned prayer warriors. When believers have moments of weakness and feel their prayers are inadequate, the Holy Spirit intercedes with groaning, according to the will of God, with words too deep for human interpretation (Romans 8:26-27). The indwelling Holy Spirit intercession for believers is, indeed, consoling and comforting. To God Be the Glory Forever! Amen.

# ABOUT THE AUTHOR

LONNIE D. MILLS IS FROM Houston, Texas, and he received a Bachelor of Science degree in biology and respiratory therapy from Texas Southern University. After traveling a circuitous wilderness journey, he worked in supervisory positions in the tool and die-making industries for 19 years and 20 years in the chemical industry that specialized in producing polysilicon for computer wafers and solar panels. Today he is retired and has been led by the Spirit to share God's Biblical Truths. Lonnie and his wife, Lois, are members of Sagemont Baptist Church in Houston Texas pastored by Dr. John D. Morgan, where they serve as greeters.

Printed in the United States
By Bookmasters